HENRY VIII

HENRY VIII
A HISTORY OF HIS MOST IMPORTANT PLACES AND EVENTS

Andrew Beattie

AN IMPRINT OF PEN & SWORD BOOKS LTD.
YORKSHIRE – PHILADELPHIA

First published in Great Britain in 2023 by
PEN AND SWORD HISTORY
An imprint of
Pen & Sword Books Ltd
Yorkshire – Philadelphia

Copyright © Andrew Beattie, 2023

ISBN 978 1 39900 778 8

The right of Andrew Beattie to be identified as Author of this work has been asserted by him in accordance with the Copyright, Designs and Patents Act 1988.

A CIP catalogue record for this book is available from the British Library.

All rights reserved. No part of this book may be reproduced or transmitted in any form or by any means, electronic or mechanical including photocopying, recording or by any information storage and retrieval system, without permission from the Publisher in writing.

Typeset in Ehrhardt MT Std 11.5/14 by
SJmagic DESIGN SERVICES, India.
Printed and bound in the UK by CPI Group (UK) Ltd.

Pen & Sword Books Limited incorporates the imprints of Atlas, Archaeology, Aviation, Discovery, Family History, Fiction, History, Maritime, Military, Military Classics, Politics, Select, Transport, True Crime, Air World, Frontline Publishing, Leo Cooper, Remember When, Seaforth Publishing, The Praetorian Press, Wharncliffe Local History, Wharncliffe Transport, Wharncliffe True Crime and White Owl.

For a complete list of Pen & Sword titles please contact
PEN & SWORD BOOKS LIMITED
George House, Units 12 & 13, Beevor Street, Off Pontefract Road,
Barnsley, South Yorkshire, S71 1HN, England
E-mail: enquiries@pen-and-sword.co.uk
Website: www.pen-and-sword.co.uk

or
PEN AND SWORD BOOKS
1950 Lawrence Rd, Havertown, PA 19083, USA
E-mail: uspen-and-sword@casematepublishers.com
Website: www.penandswordbooks.com

Contents

Introduction   vi

**Part I: From Greenwich to Hampton Court:
Henry's Palaces Along the River Thames**

Chapter 1	Introduction	2
Chapter 2	Greenwich Palace	4
Chapter 3	Between Greenwich and Westminster	28
Chapter 4	The Palace of Whitehall and St James's Palace	47
Chapter 5	Westminster	67
Chapter 6	Chelsea and Richmond	82
Chapter 7	Hampton Court	98

**Part II: Henry VIII in Provincial England and
Northern France**

Chapter 8	Introduction	120
Chapter 9	Windsor Castle	123
Chapter 10	Eltham Palace	137
Chapter 11	Nonsuch Palace	146
Chapter 12	Kent	156
Chapter 13	Surrey and Hampshire	177
Chapter 14	Oxfordshire and Buckinghamshire	186
Chapter 15	Hertfordshire, Essex and Middlesex	193
Chapter 16	The West Country, The Midlands, Northern England and East Anglia	200
Chapter 17	Across the Channel	207

Bibliography and Further Reading	223
Acknowledgements	226
Index	227

Introduction

'He excels all who ever wore a crown'

The words are those of the Papal Nuncio Francesco Chieregato, who in 1517 visited London and was stunned by the magnificence of the court of King Henry VIII, England's 26-year-old monarch. 'The wealth and civilization of the world are here,' the Nuncio gushed – and dominating everything he saw was 'this invincible king, whose acquirements and qualities are so many and excellent that I consider him to excel all who ever wore a crown.' Yet thirty years later, when Henry died, his reputation was vastly different to the Renaissance prince that Francesco Chieregato had so admired. By then Henry had acquired the dubious distinction of being a tyrant whose hands were soaked in the blood of those he had executed, including two of his six wives, and whose body, bloated from years of over-indulgence, was ravaged by illness that left him in constant pain. This is the Henry that everyone seems to recognize: the larger-than-life monarch who presided over an England wholly refashioned after the catastrophe of the Wars of the Roses and the dour rule of his father, whose hallmark in everything was excess, and who was portrayed in all his majesty in a painting by Hans Holbein. It is the Henry that Charles Laughton caricatured the 1930s film *The Private Life of Henry VIII*, lusting over wenches and throwing chicken bones over his shoulder as he presided over yet another feast in yet another palatial great hall, an almost comic glutton whose reputation was ripe for parody in a much later film from the 1960s, *Carry On Henry*.

No other English monarch was ever parodied in the famously bawdy and irreverent *Carry On* films. But that's the point: Henry is by some considerable distance England's most famous monarch, and the subject

Introduction

of countless other films, as well as novels, plays and TV series. He is the subject of Shakespeare's last play, *Henry VIII* (which was probably written with the collaboration of another dramatist, John Fletcher), while in more recent times his discarded wives (particularly Anne Boleyn) have had their lives dissected by popular historical novelists, and his scheming minister Thomas Cromwell has been the subject of three historical novels of a more literary slant by Hilary Mantel. In the 1960s theatregoers (and later filmgoers) watched as Henry's Lord Chancellor, Sir Thomas More, refused to bend his conscience to Henry's formidable will in the play and film *A Man for All Seasons*: the Henry that Robert Bolt portrayed in his play and screenplay was the Renaissance Prince, '*not* the Holbein Henry', as Bolt writes in his description of the characters, which perhaps made the monarch's cold-blooded ruthlessness all the more shocking. None of these, however, top *The Autobiography of Henry VIII*, written by the American historical novelist Margaret George, published in 1986 and in print ever since: weighing in at over 900 pages, it's a fictionalized version of Henry's life, told by the man himself – 'with notes by his fool, Will Somers'. Henry even appears in children's fiction: he dies part way through Mark Twain's novel *The Prince and the Pauper*, though not before terrifying the unfortunate London pauper Tom Canty from the royal deathbed, while in 2011 the novelist H. M. Castor introduced her young adult readership to a more rarely seen and strangely vulnerable Prince Henry in her novel *VIII*. No other monarch has been the subject of so much fictional examination – all of which sits alongside the popular historical narratives and more academic biographies that have been published over the centuries.

For Henry has proved endlessly fascinating to historians. Most noted among them are Geoffrey Elton, who derided Henry as an 'egocentric monstrosity' whose reign 'owed its successes and virtues to better and greater men about him' with 'most of its horrors and failures' caused directly by the king himself. Lacey Baldwin Smith, ploughing a similar furrow, considered Henry to be an egotistical borderline neurotic who was prone to great fits of temper and deep and dangerous suspicions; his Henry, however, was characterized by a deeply held piety and limited intellect. Certainly he was an imposing man: Thomas More wrote that 'among a thousand noble companions, the king stands out the tallest, and his strength fits his majestic body,' and when his tomb at Windsor Castle was opened in 1813 and his skeleton measured, he was found to have stood

1 metre 88 centimetres (6 foot 2 inches) tall – though after his jousting accident his girth ballooned, as his remaining suits of armour attest, and he was so heavy that ramps were built at his palaces so he could get on his horse. All of this makes the task of teasing out the *real* Henry all the more difficult; he was, to be sure, arrogant, ruthless, overbearing, selfish, brutal and egotistical, with an unpredictable temper that led to often terrifying rages, but he was charismatic too, and a learned and scholarly appreciator of music, art and literature.

While it might be hard to pin down what Henry was like as a man – and his character seemed to undergo a sea-change after a jousting injury he sustained in 1536 – what is undisputed is that he presided over the most magnificent court in Europe. No English sovereign ever owned as many palaces and houses as he did, or spent so lavishly on a lifestyle that was calculated to enhance his own prestige. And this lavishness permeates this book; for its purpose is to examine the still-visible legacies of Henry's reign, and that legacy shines most intensely in the myriad palaces that he built, enriched and extended. Most famous of all are the great palaces of Greenwich, Whitehall and Hampton Court, all situated beside the Thames as it flows through London. But Henry adored hunting in the countryside around the capital, which is peppered with lavish houses that served as hunting lodges (or refuges from the plague) and were situated amidst what were then the forests of Surrey, Kent, Essex and Berkshire. And although there are other reminders of his reign – such as fortifications he built in Portsmouth on the south coast of England and Tournai in what is now Belgium, or the associations that can be found with him in Westminster Abbey and St Paul's Cathedral in London – it is the palaces that take centre stage in this book, just as they once took centre stage in Henry's reign.

Henry's Palaces and Castles

In the sixteenth century there were two types of royal residence. In the 'greater houses' the 'hall was kept' so that the whole court could be accommodated, with servants fed in the great hall; the 'lesser houses' were much smaller in capacity and were usually used by Henry while travelling or hunting. The greater houses numbered eight in all and included the Palace of Westminster, which burned down part way through Henry's reign

Introduction

and was replaced by the Palace of Whitehall, which was (confusingly) still sometimes known as the Palace of Westminster; the Tower of London, which was a royal palace as well as a prison; Greenwich Palace, where Henry was born; Richmond Palace, which had greater associations with Henry's father than Henry himself; Eltham Palace, where he spent his boyhood; Woodstock Palace, near Oxford; and Windsor Castle. Of his country residences, Henry acquired a great number of properties over the course of his life, many of which he never visited; others he extended, adding royal lodgings built to his own design.

Henry loved to carry out extensive and wholesale extension and rebuilding work on his properties. William Harrison, the Elizabethan-era clergyman who compiled and wrote his *Description of England* in 1577, considered Henry to be 'nothing inferior in this trade [the builder of palaces] to Hadrian the Emperor and Justinian the Lawgiver', and that such palaces 'as he erected excel all the rest that he found standing in this realm; they are a perpetual precedent unto those that come after. Certes [for certain], masonry did never better flourish in England than in his time'. In 1534, Thomas Cromwell, with his eyes on the royal purse, observed how extravagant Henry was in his love of building – the 'great charge it is to the king to complete his buildings in so many places at once … if the king would spare for one year, how profitable it would be for him'.

Yet in Henry's day, there were no architects. Instead, most wealthy men who wished to build their own property sought assistance from surveyors and craftsmen such as master masons, though Henry himself was able to draw up competent building plans, which he kept in his closet (meaning his private offices) in his great palace at Greenwich, along with drawing instruments such as scissors, compasses, drawing irons and a steel pen. At Greenwich, and at his other great palaces at Whitehall and Hampton Court, there were drawing offices which were kept busy designing the extensions and alterations that Henry demanded for his grandiose homes. The king would often ask for reports on any building work that was taking place, and he would also make inspection visits. Any workman could be 'impressed' – that is, forced – to work for him at any time, even if the workman was engaged on another project. And what work it was; not surprisingly, Henry was a demanding employer, often insisting that men worked through the night by candle light to meet the punishing schedule he set. When the weather was poor, canvas tents would be hung over scaffolding so that work could continue, though on one occasion at midnight the king provided a snack of bread and cheese washed down with beer to labourers standing knee-deep in mud, digging foundations for a new wing to one of his palaces. A number of workmen were killed or injured in the haste to get places finished.

Our knowledge of Henry's palaces comes from several sources, including his household and government accounts (which specify which building materials he ordered to be used, for example) but also the sketches of the Flemish topographical artist Anton van den Wyngaerde, who made a number of important drawings of Henry's palaces in the 1540s that contain a wealth of detail (Wyngaerde also made similar sketches of Spanish palaces for the king of Spain). Henry's preferred style was English late perpendicular, characterized by low, wide 'Tudor' arches with pointed apexes, large windows with thin mullions and transoms (dividing bars), and doorways enclosed by a square head above the arch, leaving spaces (spandrels) that could be filled with decorative elements such as carved quatrefoils (which comprise four conjoined semicircles or arcs). However, a number of Burgundian and Italian influences were also visible in Henry's new palaces, and master craftsmen from Europe also worked on them, ensuring the spread of architectural fashions from the continent. One distinguishing feature of many palaces was the grand, multi-storey gatehouse with crenellated turrets, bay windows and tall chimney pots (the best example of these is Anne Boleyn's Gateway at Hampton Court). The palaces beyond them were constructed around single or multiple courtyard(s), with many exterior adornments including royal coats of arms, heraldic badges, initials, mottoes and other emblems, executed in stone, terracotta, glass, paint and decorated glass.

Inside and Outside the Palaces

The arrangements of public and private rooms in most of Henry's palaces were the same. The first of the state rooms was designated a 'watching chamber' where the Yeomen of the Guard stood on duty – though the room, which was often hung with tapestries, would also serve as a dining room for senior administrators or members of the nobility who were visiting the palace on official business. Next door was a room used by page boys where courtiers could dress in their robes of state (at night the pages would sleep on the floor of the watching chamber on straw pallets). The watching chamber also served as a place where groups of visitors would gather before being ushered into the next room, which was the presence chamber or throne room. This room was dominated by a chair of estate placed on a dais and surrounded by a rich canopy, and it was where Henry held court, received ambassadors and dined in state. This was the most formal and richly decorated room, and courtiers had to doff their caps whenever they passed the throne (even if it was empty).

Beyond the presence chamber were Henry's private rooms, separated from the public rooms by a short passageway. Here the king conducted his private life. This was where he slept, took his meals, worked on state business, and relaxed with his books or his musical instruments. The complex of rooms included a bedchamber, a garderobe (where clothes were kept), a robing chamber for dressing, a study, a library and a bathroom. Only a few of Henry's most favoured and intimate courtiers were allowed here. They included the Groom of the Stool, who was the head of the Privy Chamber, and attended to Henry's most intimate bathroom needs. In some palaces there were two bedchambers, and at Greenwich and Hampton Court Henry maintained a third, on the queen's side. Also within this complex of rooms were closets fitted out with altarpieces for private worship. Throughout, these rooms were crammed with cupboards, tables, boxes, chests, clocks, and curios and objets d'art that took Henry's fancy and were displayed in glass cabinets.

As Henry's character changed through the course of his reign, so did his living arrangements. Before 1530 it was common for the king's private rooms to be stacked on top of one another in a building called a 'donjon' (a throwback to the 'keep' of medieval castles) that was situated on the south side of the palace, to make best use of the daylight. Later, however, the king's lessening mobility meant that his public and private rooms were all likely to be on one floor (usually the first floor), with the queen's rooms on the same level. (The queen's rooms also consisted of a presence chamber and private living quarters beyond.) It was for this reason that Eltham and Richmond palaces, with their 'stacked' lodgings, began to fall out of favour in the second part of his reign. Another architectural feature that fell out of favour during Henry's reign was the great hall. Henry grew up with a close knowledge of one of England's most magnificent medieval great halls, at Eltham Palace, but the one he built at Hampton Court was the last ever built in the country. Here and in other palaces the hall served as a dining hall for household servants as well as a venue for feasts and banquets. And while the great hall was consigned to the past, other architectural features became newly fashionable, especially covered long galleries, where the king and his associates could walk in the dry and talk over affairs while admiring the palace gardens. These galleries were also a place where tapestries, pictures, mirrors and maps could be hung and admired – and they were private, too, as Henry was usually the only keyholder.

Most palaces were surrounded by gardens. Roses were a particular favourite of Henry's (his physician Thomas Linacre introduced the damask rose into England). Other flowers that were planted in Henry's gardens include lilies, violets and primroses. Palace gardens were formal in design and comprised laid paths and lawns dotted with features such as sundials, fountains, statues, columns, urns and topiary trees. Such a garden can be seen in the background of the famous painting *The Family of Henry VIII* that was painted and initially hung at the Palace of Whitehall (and which is now at Hampton Court). In some palaces there was a knot garden, which comprised square flowerbeds edged with bricks and tiles that contained shrubs and flowers shaped into interwoven geometrical patterns; Henry also added pavilions that served as summer banqueting houses. Gardeners were recruited from France to care for these gardens, where Henry would often transact business with courtiers, officials and diplomats on fine days.

Part I

FROM GREENWICH TO HAMPTON COURT
Henry's Palaces Along the River Thames

Chapter 1

Introduction

On 29 May 1533 the River Thames in London provided the stage for an extraordinary and extravagant festival of pomp and pageantry. In the morning fifty barges, hired or belonging to the twelve London livery companies, each one draped in flags and bunting and packed with musicians and cannons, set off against the tide from Billingsgate to Greenwich. The Lord Mayor of London's barge was the most striking. It was hung with cloth of gold and silver and displayed thirty-six shields displaying the coats of arms of two families, the Boleyns and the Tudors – for it was on this early summer's day that Anne Boleyn was making a grand procession along the river prior to her Coronation three days later. Accompanying the procession was a wherry with mechanical monsters, including dragons that could 'breathe' fire, and on another wherry was Anne Boleyn's principal badge, which depicted a crowned white falcon perched on red and white roses that grew from a golden tree stump on a hill, all of it surrounded by singing virgins. When the flotilla reached Greenwich Palace, Anne, dressed in cloth of gold, boarded her barge with her ladies, while her husband the king boarded another; with other barges carrying guards, trumpeters and minstrels, the armada that sailed up the Thames that afternoon, into the summer sun, numbered 300 vessels, large and small. Helped by the tide they managed to reach a speed of seven knots. As they passed the Tower its guns fired a salute – as did cannons on many of the ships moored to the bank that the flotilla swept past. It was a day of spectacle and theatre, and it demonstrated to Londoners Henry's defiance – that he could marry and crown whom he wanted, whatever the Pope in Rome said. And the fact that this display played out on the Thames was appropriate: for when he was wooing Anne Boleyn, Henry often had himself rowed in secret from Whitehall to Greenwich, where

Introduction

he had established her as his mistress (and Anne's notorious last journey, from Greenwich Palace to the Tower, was also, of course, to take place by river, though in rather less exalted circumstances).

These days it's tourist launches rather than Henry VIII's royal barge that ply the reach of the river between Hampton Court, Westminster and Greenwich (though a suitably costumed 'Henry VIII' was rowed through London from the Tower to Hampton Court in June 2009, to commemorate the 500th anniversary of his succession). The route plied by tourist launches upstream from East to West London provides the narrative thread for this chapter – beginning in Greenwich, where Henry was born and which throughout his life was one of his principal palaces, then passing the Tower of London and the site of Bridewell Palace before reaching Westminster where the Palace of Westminster, Whitehall and St James's Palace stood near the river and to each other. Further upstream, in what is now London's fashionable western suburbs, is Hampton Court, Cardinal Wolsey's grandiose show of pomposity that came into Henry's hands after the churchman's fall from grace. In Henry's time these palaces had jetties where his state barges could pull up, ready to transport him and his court along London's great watery artery to the next palace where his ever-itinerant court would establish itself. The vessels were looked after by the Master of the King's Barge and his team of Royal Watermen, and were lavishly decorated – in 1530 the court painter Vincenzo Volpe was paid the considerable sum of £15 (now £4,500) for decorating a new one. Henry's own barge was called the *Lion*. However, even the emblem of England could make no headway when the Thames was frozen – as it was during the Christmas of 1536, when the chronicler Edward Hall recorded how Henry and Jane Seymour galloped back to Greenwich along the iced-over river after attending the service at St Paul's Cathedral.

Chapter 2

Greenwich Palace

Greenwich pier – 'for the *Cutty Sark* and Historic Greenwich' – is now one of the most easterly termini of London's riverboat services (clippers continue east to Woolwich and Barking). Adjacent to the pier, in its own dry dock, is the *Cutty Sark*, once the fastest 'clipper' afloat, and beyond it are a myriad of attractions that make this one of the busiest areas for London's tourists outside the centre of the city – including a bustling market and town centre, the maritime museum, and on the hill overlooking it all, the Observatory

The view from the Greenwich Observatory over the Baroque buildings that occupy the former site of Greenwich Palace, with the skyscrapers of London's Docklands beyond.

with its opportunity for visitors to 'straddle' the line marking the prime (or Greenwich) meridian. Fronting the river, just downstream of the pier, is a glorious array of early-eighteenth-century buildings that are the work of Sir Christopher Wren and his associate, Nicholas Hawksmoor. Built to house the Royal Hospital for Seamen at Greenwich, and latterly occupied by the Royal Naval College, some of the buildings now house departments of the University of Greenwich while the most splendid are open to visitors, including the Old Royal Naval College Chapel and the so-called 'Painted Hall'. All these buildings, of course, came after Henry, but they mark the exact site of Greenwich Palace, Henry's favourite royal palace and the place where he was born – indeed they were constructed on the site after it had been neglected during the Civil War and Cromwell's time. However, Wren and Hawksmoor's project redeveloped the area so comprehensively that virtually nothing of the Tudor palace – the 'Palace of Placentia' – remains, bar a few archaeological remnants which poke up here and there among the extravaganza of Baroque architecture that today's visitors (and students) can enjoy.

The Palace's Origins and Appearance

The Tudor palace at Greenwich had its origins in Bella Court, a riverside property constructed in the 1430s by Humphrey, Duke of Gloucester, the brother of King Henry V. After 1447 the palace was remodelled for the queen of Henry VI, Margaret of Anjou, who renamed it 'Placentia' (or Pleasaunce), and stocked the surrounding park with deer. At the turn of the sixteenth century Henry VII rebuilt the palace in red brick around three great courtyards, taking inspiration from the Prinsenhof, the grand palace of the Dukes of Burgundy in Ghent, where the Emperor Charles V was born (nowadays only one part of this building survives, the the so-called Donkere Poort, or Dark Gate). Just as now, the most striking aspect of the location was the river frontage: the royal apartments overlooked the river, with the bay windows reflected picturesquely in the water. On the landward side of the palace were glorious gardens replete with fountains, lawns, flowers and orchards. Although the royal apartments were stacked on top of each other in a 'donjon', in other respects the design of the palace was revolutionary. There was no moat and the building was essentially a domestic residence rather than a fortified castle, just like Burgundian palaces; the palace, renamed Greenwich Palace by Henry VII, thus set

Henry VIII: A History of his Most Important Places and Events

Detail from a sketch made by Anthon van den Wyngaerde in the 1550s, showing Greenwich Palace and the Thames. (*Wikimedia Commons*)

the fashion for palaces and manor houses that was to be the hallmark of the Tudor era.

Only a few traces of the palace survive, and certainly not enough to suggest what the palace might have looked like. In the 1550s Anton van den Wyngaerde made a sketch of its exterior, which showed that the donjon was situated between a chapel and the privy kitchen, but little is known of its interior. The donjon housed Henry's private and public rooms, which overlooked the Thames and were decorated with murals depicting the life of St John. His antiquary John Leland visited the palace and not surprisingly was rather overawed by its opulence. 'Lo! With what lustre shines this wished-for place,' Leland wrote in his *Survey of England* (completed in 1543), 'Which, star-like, might the heavenly mansions grace/What painted roofs! What windows charm the eye!/What turrets, rivals of the starry sky!' In an inventory of 'jewels, plate, stuff, ordnance, munitions, and other goods belonging to our great sovereign lord King Henry the Eighth' and made up after Henry's death, we learn that the privy chamber had 'a breakfast table of walnut tree, a round table covered with black velvet, a square table, a cupboard of wainscot, three joined forms with three stools, a table and a pair of trestles, a clock, a painted table, a standing glass of steel, a branch of flowers wrought upon wire, three comb cases of bone, four little coffers for jewels, a chair of joined work, one pair of regals (small pipe organs) with a case, one pair of tables of bone and wood (backgammon boards), a pair of gridirons, a fire shovel and a fire fork'.

Henry's Birth and Early Years

Henry was born in Greenwich Palace on 28 June 1491, the third child of King Henry VII and his wife Elizabeth of York – a union that was intended to bring together the warring factions of Lancaster and York after the Wars of the Roses. In those days the palace was something of a private riverside retreat for the queen, and when Henry was born, in high summer, the place was quiet as the plague was raging and had chased many courtiers to the country. Henry was also the 'spare' – his brother Arthur, the 'heir', was then 4 years old – and little is documented about Henry's birth and the months that followed. It seems likely that after his birth and christening he was handed over to be suckled by a wet-nurse by the name of Anne Uxbridge, and for the first two years of his life she was the person closest to him – a surrogate mother both emotionally and physically. Assisting her were two 'rockers' of the cradle, Margret Draughton and Frideswide Puttenham, both paid £3.6s.8d per year according to household accounts (Anne Uxbridge was paid £10). In the *Ryalle Book*, a manual and account of royal practices first issued by Edward IV and updated by subsequent monarchs, it is described that Henry and his older sister Margaret (whose later marriage to James IV of Scotland eventually led to the Stuarts succeeding the Tudors in 1603) shared a nursery apartment consisting of a sleeping chamber, a receiving chamber and smaller service rooms. Here also stood Henry's 'great' and 'little' cradles, the little one in the sleeping chamber made of gilded wood with silver-gilt pommels on the corners and covered by a rich counterpane of cloth of gold and ermine, with a 'sparver' or canopy above the cradle and a curtain that could be drawn round it. The larger cradle in the receiving room was covered in cloth of gold and had the royal coat of arms at its head. Gentlemen doffed their caps and bowed to the cradle, and ladies curtsied, even if it was empty. In the service rooms were 'two great basins of pewter for the laundry in the nursery,' a 'chafer' to heat water, a brass basin in which the child was washed, and a leather cushion on which Anne Uxbridge sat while breast-feeding Henry.

As we shall see later, Henry was principally brought up at Eltham Palace, some six kilometres southeast of Greenwich and, at the time, deep in the Kent countryside. When he was 10 years old, his older brother Arthur died, bringing Henry much more into the spotlight as the new Prince of Wales and heir to the throne. This was probably when he began spending more time at Greenwich and it was here that his earliest surviving letter was written. The recipient was Philip of Burgundy, the ruler of the Burgundian Netherlands, and the letter, written in French, is dated 9 April 1506 – when Henry was nearly fifteen. 'Vostre Humble cosyn, Henry Prynce de Galles' is how Henry signs himself – 'Your humble cousin, Henry Prince of Wales' – though the substance of the letter is fairly mundane, and asks that Philip shows his favour to Catherine of Aragon's Lord Chamberlain, who had cause to travel to Spain on official business.

Henry's presence at court began to become more prominent during 1508, when he turned 17 and his father's health began to deteriorate; this was not surprising, for England's future was vested in this virile, athletic young prince who was just coming of age and who must have seemed such a contrast to his dour father. Many of the events of that year played out at Greenwich. In February the ailing king moved here from his favourite palace of Richmond, as it was thought that the air was cleaner, and on the 15th of the following month Prince Henry stood in for his father for the first time, dining in the King's Chamber with some assembled lords. In May the royal historian, Bernard André, recorded that while the king was at Eltham recovering from a serious bout of illness, his son was busy honing his jousting skills at Greenwich – 'daily' he was running at the ring 'with his companions in arms'. Jousting was to become one of Henry's favourite past-times; it involved two mounted knights armed with lances thundering towards each other either side of a wooden palisade, with victory coming to those who were strongest, most courageous and had the most astute sense of timing. On 15 June, in the high summer of that year, 'the jousting at Greenwich in the presence of the nobility was very heavily attended on account of the excellence of the young armed prince, supported round about with nobles on all sides', while in December festivities took place at Greenwich to celebrate the marriage of Henry's sister Mary, then aged 12, to Charles, Archduke of Austria, the 9-year-old son of Philip of Burgundy (Henry's first known correspondent). According to the account printed by Richard Pynson, official printer to both King Henrys, this event was the 'most notable alliance and greatest marriage of Christendom'. When King Henry received the Burgundian ambassadors at Greenwich, under a cloth-of-gold canopy, his son and heir was stood beside him – learning statecraft from his father. The court then moved to Richmond, where the proxy wedding between the two children was staged – neatly summing up the peripatetic nature of Henry VII's court, which constantly switched between the two palaces (after the wedding everyone returned to Greenwich for Christmas).

Pomp and Pageantry at Greenwich Palace, 1509–16

King Henry VII died on 21 April 1509, leaving his kingdom to his son, who was then two months away from his eighteenth birthday, and therefore his majority. Soon after his father's burial on 10 May, Henry declared that he would marry Catherine of Aragon (in accordance with what he claimed was his father's dying wish). The marriage duly took place the following month in the Friar's Church at Greenwich (of which more later). In March the following year lavish preparations were made at Greenwich for the birth of Catherine's first child, but the pregnancy turned out to be false, and it is thought that the swelling in her belly might have been the result of an infection. By this time Henry was dividing his time between Greenwich and Richmond palaces (though in the end it was Greenwich that was to become his favourite palace for at least the first half of his reign). At Greenwich he enjoyed hunting and hawking in the vast park that surrounded the palace, he often rode to nearby Deptford and Woolwich to oversee naval ships being built in the dockyards, and London was easily accessible by barge.

So, it was at both Greenwich and Richmond that Henry revelled in his role as a high-spirited, energetic Renaissance prince; he gathered young aristocratic men around him of similar age and passions and indulged with them in his favourite obsessions of jousting, hunting, feasting and making merry. (Cardinal Wolsey thought such men were a poor influence on Henry and often tried through cunning to have them removed from the court and replaced with more 'suitable' companions.) The tone was set early on, when in the summer of 1510 the king devised a new game at Greenwich that involved fighting with battle axes in the presence of Catherine and her ladies. *The Great Chronicle of London*, probably written by Robert Fabyan, a sheriff and alderman, notes that Henry's first opponent in this dare-devil contest was 'one Guyot, a gentleman of Almain (Germany)'. The following year the king celebrated May Day at Greenwich in typically lavish style, with the chronicler Edward Hall describing how Henry 'held jousts against all comers' during which 'many a sore stripe was given and many a staff broke'. Three fellow-jousters joined him on this occasion: Charles Brandon, Duke of Suffolk, who might have been as young as 16 at the time, and who was probably Henry's closest friend – and certainly the only one who successfully retained the king's affection throughout his reign; Edward Neville, Henry's Esquire of the Body, at the time a trusted courtier, though later executed for treason; and Thomas Howard, the 3rd Duke of Norfolk, the uncle of both Anne Boleyn and Catherine Howard, who at the end of Henry's reign was to narrowly avoid the block simply because Henry died just before his execution was due to take place.

Christmas and New Year also proved to be a time of extravagant celebration. Hall noted that Henry celebrated the Christmas of 1510 at Greenwich 'with great and plentiful cheer in a most princely manner, where was such viands [tasty food dishes] served to all comers of honest behaviour as hath been few times seen'. On New Year's Night a spectacle entitled *The Fortress Dangerous* was staged in the palace's Great Hall, featuring a castle with towers and a dungeon, 'garnished with artillery and weapons, after the most warlike fashion', inside which were six ladies wearing gowns of russet satin 'laid all over with leaves of gold'. Somewhat inevitably the castle was 'assaulted' by the king and five other knights, the ladies seeing the assailants to be 'so lusty and courageous' that they readily yielded, came down from the battlements and danced with the men. As the new year got under way the composer, dramatist and actor William Cornish devised a novel entertainment for Twelfth Night. 'The king with eleven other were disguised in the manner of Italy, called a masque, a thing not aforeseen in England,' noted Edward Hall. 'They were apparelled in garments wrought with gold, with visors and caps of gold.' The entertainment Hall describes – the masque – was a form of drama in which plot took second place to a succession of disguises, poetry readings, music-making and dancing, often with an underlying allegorical or political theme. Henry liked masques, which allowed him to show off his talents as a performer, and over the course of his reign they gradually replaced the extravagant pageants that were more a feature of medieval courtly entertainments.

Different again was a mummery, a folk play or mime performed by masked performers. One was performed at Greenwich during the Christmas of 1513, when Hall notes that the Royal Wardrobe issued twelve yards of yellow sarcanet (a delicate silk) to Sir Henry Guildford and Nicholas Carew, for a mummery in which Charles Brandon and 'Mistress

Greenwich Palace

Carew' (Nicholas's wife Elizabeth) also took part. (Carew was the son of the Captain of Calais and had shared his upbringing and education with Henry; another of Henry's 'rakish' friends, he too fell out of favour and was eventually executed for conspiracy.) Soon afterwards Henry had a recreational complex built in the palace that consisted of two high brick octagonal towers overlooking a long gallery and tilt yard, which could be used for both jousting and performances such as masques, with seating space for a large audience. Edward Hall described how in May 1514 this was where the king and his friend the Duke of Suffolk appeared in disguise as hermits, Suffolk in black and Henry in a white velvet habit with a leather cloak thrown over it. In a theatrical flourish they cast off their disguises and threw them to the assembled watching ladies before beginning the jousts.

Elizabeth Carew also played a prominent role in a pageant staged at Greenwich in the Christmas of 1514. Along with the wives of Henry Guildford and the Spanish ambassador, the ladies, dressed in blue velvet gowns and doffed gold caps and masks, took part in a drama of derring-do in which they were rescued from danger by four gallant Portuguese knights, played by the king and Suffolk, along with Nicholas Carew and the Spanish ambassador. There was much laughter when the identities of the dancers were revealed, and at the dances that followed the king danced openly with his mistress Elizabeth Blount, despite his wife once again being pregnant (the infant prince was to die within a few days of his birth at Greenwich in February).

The following May one of the most celebrated and spectacular pageants of the reign was staged at Greenwich. In this one the Venetian ambassador Sebastian Giustinian was assigned an important role. The 'theme' of the pageant was Robin Hood and his Merry Men – though it was played out in the forests around Greenwich rather than in Sherwood Forest near Nottingham. Giustinian and his secretary Niccolo Sagudino both wrote detailed accounts of the pageant, describing how the ambassador and his entourage were conducted to Greenwich where they and the 'chief lords of the kingdom' mounted their horses to escort Catherine of Aragon three kilometres into the wooded countryside, where they met the king. Henry, dressed entirely in green, was mounted on his stallion *Governatore* and was accompanied by 200 archers 'in livery of green with bows in their hands'. One of the archers was dressed as Robin Hood and by his side was a certain Mr Villiers, who was dressed as Maid Marian, in a red kirtle. 'Directly we came in sight, the king commenced making his horse curvet,' one of the eyewitness accounts reads (that is, Henry made his horse do a series of low leaps where all its hoofs left the ground). The king went on to perform 'such feats that I fancied myself looking at Mars'. Then 'Robin Hood' asked the queen if she and her damsels 'would like to enter the good greenwood and see how outlaws lived' and the queen agreed, so long as the king accompanied her, which he did, and led her by the hand (and to the sound of trumpets) to some carefully constructed bowers decorated with flowers and birds where tables had been set for a 'proper good breakfast'. Venison was the main dish, accompanied by wine served by archers and eaten to the accompaniment of singers and musicians 'who played on organ, lute and flutes for a good while during the banquet'. A conversation then took place in which Henry asked the envoys how he compared in height and body to the king of France, before the party headed back to the palace, 'musicians sounding the whole way on trumpets, drums and other instruments, so that it was an extremely fine triumph and very pompous, and the king in person brought up the rear, in as great state as possible, followed by the queen, with such a crowd on foot to exceed, I think, 25,000 persons'. Sagudino thought the whole thing was designed to impress Piero Pasqualigo, another member of the party, who was returning to France and would no doubt tell King Francis, in awestruck tones, of the glorious spectacle he had witnessed in England.

Births and Weddings at Greenwich Palace, 1516–28

By the time of the Robin Hood pageant, Catherine had given birth to a healthy baby – a girl, though, not the longed-for prince. The labour during the previous February had been difficult, and the little girl, born at Greenwich like her father, was christened Mary. In October 1518, in the queen's great chamber at Greenwich, Princess Mary, then nearly 3 years old, was formally betrothed to Francois, the Dauphin of France, in the presence of the king and queen, Cardinal Wolsey, the Pope's representative Cardinal Lorenzo Campeggio, the Venetian ambassador Giustinian and assembled groups of lords and ladies. The splendidly named Guillaume Gouffier de Bonnivet, Lord High Admiral of France, stood proxy for the future bridegroom, who was just a few months old. When Wolsey lifted Mary up and placed a great diamond ring on her tiny finger, apparently the little girl asked Bonnivet 'Are you the Dauphin of France? If you are, I want to kiss you!' which must have gone some way to leavening the solemnity of the occasion. The two Cardinals then blessed her and celebrated Mass 'with every possible ceremony' before the inevitable banquet in the Palace's Great Hall. Four years later, however, alliances had shifted, and in 1522 Princess Mary was betrothed a second time, this time to Holy Roman Emperor Charles V, who was her cousin (her mother Catherine of Aragon was the sister of Charles's mother, Juana the Mad). A grandiose ceremony was again staged at Greenwich Palace in high summer, on 2 June; Charles's retinue numbered 2,000, some of whom were billeted in local houses.

Pageants staged at Christmas, New Year and Twelfth Night were still a feature of royal life at Greenwich at this time. One, entitled *The Garden of Esperance*, featured an entire artificial garden on a float. But *The Castle of Loyalty*, staged during the Christmas of 1524, was to be the last in which Henry participated. It featured a castle built in the palace tiltyard – the king had designed it specifically, but according to Edward Hall 'the carpenters were so dull they understood not his intent, and wrought all things contrary'. As a result much of the planned pageant had to be abandoned, though Catherine still seated herself in the castle and greeted two 'knights of old' who appeared from the age of chivalry; not surprisingly disguises were unveiled and the knights revealed themselves to be Henry and the Duke of Suffolk. And if traditional medieval pageants were now abandoned, the feasting certainly wasn't; early in January 1527 Cardinal Wolsey held a feast at Greenwich which was interrupted half-way through by cannon fire from outside – whereupon a party entered in disguise, and the Cardinal was challenged to guess which one was the king; he ended up identifying Henry's favoured courtier Sir Edward Neville as the sovereign, to everyone's amusement and Wolsey's embarrassment – which he tried to hide by calling for the next 200 dishes to be brought in. In the summer of that year, Henry and members of the court gathered to watch more jousting tournaments at Greenwich; in one of them Nicholas Carew entered the lists with his horse blindfolded so that the animal would not rear in fright at the sight of three men carried on a twelve-foot-long tree trunk that Carew then used instead of a lance 'to the extreme adulation and astonishment of everybody', according to the *Venetian Calendar of State Papers*.

It was also at Greenwich that Henry was introduced to Will Somers, his fool, in 1525. Somers had previously been in the employ of a rich

Northamptonshire merchant, Richard Fermer, and it was he who gave him to Henry – who was constantly delighted by Will's acrobatics and wicked sense of humour. No one was safe from Will's jokes or witticisms. Robert Armin, a member of Shakespeare's company of players and a comic author who might have helped the bard develop the 'fools' who populate his plays, wrote in his 1608 book *Nest of Ninnies* that Somers' 'melody was of a higher strain … Will Somers, born in Shropshire, as some say/was brought to Greenwich on a holy day … Lean as he was, hollow-eyed, as all report/and stoop he did too; yet in all the court/few men were more beloved than was this fool/whose merry prate [prattling] kept with the king much rule'.

In 1527 Henry embarked on some major rebuilding works at Greenwich that coincided with the signing of a peace treaty with France. These works comprised the construction of a grand Banqueting House and a theatre (or 'disguising house') at either end of the gallery that overlooked the tiltyard. These were deliberately plain structures that could be embellished with stage sets, hangings and other temporary decorations. 'The windows were all clerestories, with curious mullions strangely wrought,' Edward Hall wrote. 'At one side was a haut [high] place for heralds and minstrels.' It is thought that these structures survived for some eighty years and were opened on occasions to the public. They featured paintings and a triumphal arch by Hans Holbein, here completing his first royal commission (Henry was probably introduced to him by Thomas More). The glorious ensemble was unveiled on Saturday, 5 May when the French and English envoys arrived and were treated to a feast in the Banqueting House, in which there hung a large painting by Holbein (since lost) of Henry's victory over the French at Thérouanne (a somewhat tactless choice of decoration given the circumstances, as a Venetian observer commented). According to Hall, the French ambassadors were 'entertained after a more sumptuous manner than had ever been seen before'. The next day Henry watched some jousting, dressed in a costume of purple Florentine velvet trimmed with gold, though he couldn't take part himself, due to an injury sustained to his foot during a tennis match. Another lavish banquet followed and then the Chapel Royal choir performed under Holbein's ceiling, which depicted 'the whole earth envirned with [surrounded by] the sea, very like a map … a cunning thing and a pleasant sight to behold'. Then two masques were performed, in which Henry and his daughter Mary took part, and there was dancing until sunrise. Henry wore black velvet slippers (because of his foot) and every courtier had to follow suit so the king wouldn't look out of place. A pageant the next day featured Mary dressed as a Roman goddess in 'cloth of gold, with so many precious stones that the spleandour and radiance dazzled the sight'. The girl's proud parents were in the audience. However, the revelry collapsed when astonishing news came – that Rome had been sacked by mercenary troops in the pay of the Emperor, and the Pope had been taken prisoner.

Later in that same year, in November, Henry was formally invested in the Order of St Michael, the French equivalent of the Order of the Garter (in which he had already invested the French king, Francis I). The honours were exchanged after the signing of a new 'treaty of perpetual peace' between the two countries. Henry received his honour from a party of French ambassadors during a formal ceremony at Greenwich; the palace's Banqueting House was adorned with rich tapestries, and an ornamental fountain was constructed in the disguising house. Edward Hall wrote that the feasting and jousting following the ceremony continued 'until they had broken a hundred staves' while Wolsey's biographer George Cavendish thought that the masque that was performed was so brilliant that the next day memory of it seemed to be 'a fantastical dream'.

Henry and Anne Boleyn at Greenwich Palace, 1528–36

Anne Boleyn first drew Henry's gaze in in 1526. She had come to his court as a lady-in-waiting to Catherine of Aragon but by December 1528 Henry had installed her permanently at Greenwich as his mistress, 'in a very fine lodging which he has furnished very near his own,' observed the French diplomat and courtier Jean de Bellay, adding that 'Greater court is paid to her every day than has been for a long time paid to the queen.' Many were scandalized by these developments as Catherine was, of course, still queen – and during the years that Anne was Henry's mistress she still presided over the celebrations of Christmas, which must have made for a tense festive period. Anne and Henry probably married in November 1532, though as the ceremony was secret, this is a matter of some conjecture, and some historians place the date as January the following year. Whichever the case, by the spring of 1533 Henry's subjects were dying to see their new queen. According to Edward Hall, 'The King kept St George's Day at Greenwich, with great solemnity, and the court was greatly replenished with lords, knights, ladies and gentlewomen, to a great number, with all enjoyment and pleasure.' A royal baby was expected in early autumn and an air of great excitement and anticipation must have accompanied Anne's confinement at Greenwich in August. Henry took from the royal treasury 'a rich and triumphant bed' which had been part of the Duc de Longueville's ransom in 1515; he placed it in Anne's bedchamber beside a more functional pallet bed with a crimson canopy, on which she would actually be delivered. Another new bed was built in her presence chamber, where she would receive well-wishers after the birth of the longed-for prince. But a prince it was not to be; instead, Henry and Anne's first and only child, born at Greenwich on 7 September in a chamber hung with tapestries depicting the legend of St Ursula and her 11,000 virgins, was a healthy red-haired daughter who, it was said, much resembled her father. She was named Elizabeth after Henry's mother.

In the first few months of 1536 – which was to prove one of the most momentous years of Henry's reign – considerable renovations were made at Greenwich. The ceiling of Anne's presence chamber was refashioned with gilded bosses on a lattice of white battens and expensive Seville tiles were laid in the chimney grates. Five new doors were hung in Anne's bed chamber and new rush matting was laid in the passage to her robing room. Henry's own privy chamber (situated on the first floor of the donjon) was also subjected to comprehensive refurbishment, with bay windows constructed overlooking the Thames, and an antique-style ceiling patterned with timber battens with gilded lead leaves at each intersection, all fashioned by the king's master joiner Richard Ridge.

It was around this time that the first reports of Henry's interest in Jane Seymour began to surface. A very distant relation of Anne Boleyn, Catherine Howard and of Henry himself (she was a descendant of King Edward III through her maternal grandfather), Jane was born around 1508 and possibly entered the service of Catherine of Aragon in the late 1520s. After the annulment of Henry's marriage, she served in Anne Boleyn's household and gained the reputation for being gentle, diplomatic, charming and chaste, though she lacked the education of the king's other wives. In March 1536, with Henry's interest in Jane growing, Thomas Cromwell cleared out of his rooms in Greenwich Palace so that Sir Edward Seymour, Jane's older brother, and his wife could act as chaperones for Jane during Henry's visits. Cromwell's rooms adjoined Henry's privy chamber in the palace, such was his influence at this time – and it was no doubt at his suggestion that the move was made, as he was an enemy of Anne Boleyn (and her powerful uncle, the Duke of Norfolk) and was already plotting her downfall. Jane Seymour was, of course, a useful pawn in his scheming, and he sought all means of getting her closer to the king.

As Henry spent more and more time with Jane at Greenwich, it seems that his spurned wife confined herself to her chambers at York Place (later the Palace of Whitehall). In April 1536, Cromwell made known to Henry his suspicion of Anne's treasonous adultery, and on the last day of that month she was observed at a window overlooking the courtyard at Greenwich Palace, holding baby Elizabeth in her arms and pleading her case with a visibly angry Henry. Their altercation was enough to draw a small crowd to the palace, realizing 'some deep and difficult question was being discussed' according to a letter written over two decades later, in 1559, by the Scottish theologian Alexander Ales to Queen Elizabeth I. That evening Mark Smeaton, a musician in Anne's household, was arrested by Cromwell, who allegedly tortured him at his house in Stepney. The following day Henry lent his courtier and friend Sir Henry Norris a steed during the May Day jousts at Greenwich, but the pair left early, possibly after Henry had been given the news that Smeaton had confessed to having had a relationship with Anne. Henry rode with Norris to York Place and on the journey accused him too of being one of Anne's lovers. Within three weeks Anne and the five men accused of committing adultery with her (Norris, Smeaton, two other courtiers and her brother George) had all been tried and executed.

Henry's Last Years at Greenwich Palace, 1536–47

In the first few weeks of 1536, some four months before the scandal surrounding Anne Boleyn unfolded and reached its inevitable conclusion, Henry was unhorsed by a jousting opponent at Greenwich during a tournament. He was wearing full armour and when the armoured steed collapsed on top of him, he was unconscious for two hours. 'He fell so heavily that everyone thought it a miracle he was not killed,' the Spanish ambassador Eustace Chapuys reported. At one point, in fact, it was thought Henry had died, and the Duke of Norfolk hastened to the queen to break the news to her. In some ways the event, which took place on 24 January, might have been the most significant single thing to affect

Henry during the second half of his reign – if it did indeed cause the brain damage that was to affect his judgment and behaviour for the rest of his life. There is no way the truth will ever be known, and the subject is much disputed by historians, but the monstrous, egotistical, capricious, overbearing tyrant that Henry became during the last years of his life might have been the result of those events at Greenwich.

In the final decade of Henry's reign, the Palace of Whitehall and Hampton Court eclipsed Greenwich Palace as the king's favourite residence. Nonetheless it was at Greenwich on 4 June 1536 that Jane Seymour was proclaimed queen (following her marriage to Henry at Whitehall), with the whole court assembled there for the ceremony and spectacle. The chronicle written by Charles Wriothesley, officer of the College of Arms, records how during the ceremony Jane 'went in procession, after the king, with a great train of ladies following her, and also offered at Mass as queen, dining in her chamber of presence under the cloth of estate'. And even if Henry spent much of his time now at his other palaces, Greenwich remained the favourite venue for Christmas and New Year (his last recorded stay at the palace was on 22 December 1546, just five weeks before he died). One description of Greenwich during the festive season can be found among the so-called Lisle letters, which were written to Arthur Plantagenet, the first Viscount Lisle, during the time he was Governor of Calais, and which are now preserved in the National Archives at Kew. One of the letters, from the London wine merchant John Husee, describes what happened when he delivered Lisle's gift to the king during the Christmas of 1537. When Husee was admitted to the presence chamber at Greenwich, he found Henry leaning against a cupboard as courtiers came forward in turn to give their presents to him. Cromwell was with him and said, 'Here cometh my Lord Lisle's man' – at which Henry smiled warmly, and asked about the health of Lord and Lady Lisle. The gift was added to all the others, which were set out on trestle tables in the room and included a clock fashioned like a book (the gift of the Duke of Suffolk), various pictures, velvet purses full of coins, and carpets, dog collars and embroidered shirts – and even a live marmoset. Another record of unusual gifts received by Henry at Greenwich comes from 1543, when at New Year his courtier Anthony Denny presented him with a novelty called a 'clock salt' commissioned from Holbein. This was fashioned in Italian Renaissance style and was a combined clock and salt cellar that also concealed an hour glass, two sundials and a compass.

Henry With Anne of Cleves at Blackheath and Greenwich Palace

The most significant event to unfold at Greenwich during the final part of Henry's reign was his marriage to Anne of Cleves. Following the death of Jane Seymour, from complications during the birth of her son, the future Edward VI, Henry was persuaded by Thomas Cromwell to marry Anne, a protestant Rhineland princess, after Catholic Europe had turned its back on him. As we shall see later, the king's first meeting with Anne took place at Rochester, but a few days later, on 3 January 1540, Anne was formally welcomed to London in a ceremony staged just outside Greenwich Palace, at Blackheath – in those days an upland, open space where the land dropped down to Greenwich Palace and the Thames in one direction and rose to a very modest peak named Shooter's Hill in the other. The name 'Blackheath' may be derived from its 'bleak' setting or from the darkness of the soil (most historians discount as an 'urban myth' the legend that ascribes the name of the heath to the presence here of a burial pit from the time of the Black Death). Watling Street, the old Roman road between London and Dover, passes close by, and the heath has always served as a gathering point just outside London. This was where the 14-year-old Richard II met Wat Tyler and his Kentish rebels in 1381; where nearly seventy years later Jack Cade assembled 5,500 men in advance of his assault on London; and where in 1497, when Henry was just 6 years old, Cornish rebels camped during their rising against his father's tax-raising – a rebellion that was soundly defeated at a skirmish fought nearby (known as the Battle of Deptford Bridge but probably fought around a kilometre and a half from the bridge, on the northern edge of Blackheath). Now, in 1540, in the bitter midwinter chill, the heath was covered in several elaborate pavilions where the official greeting ceremony between Henry and Anne was to unfold.

It opened with Anne being welcomed by her chamberlain, the Earl of Rutland, and the officers and great ladies of her household, who kissed her hand and then escorted her into one of the pavilions, where she was robed in cloth of gold, and a pearl-embroidered caul and bonnet was placed on her head. Gathered outside were the mayor and representatives of the Corporation of London, a number of German merchants who made their home in the capital and hundreds of knights and soldiers. At noon the trumpet sounded and the King, attended by Norfolk, Suffolk and Archbishop Thomas Cranmer, along with Thomas Cromwell, the Lord Chamberlain William Sandys, the Master of Horse, the Pages of Honour and the Yeomen of the Guard, and a host of minor nobles and foreign ambassadors, arrived from Greenwich Palace, which was just over a kilometre away. The event was described in detail by Edward Hall. Henry was 'mounted on a goodly courser, trapped in rich cloth of gold, pearled on every side, the buckles and pendants all of fine gold' and wore

> a cloak of purple velvet made like a frock, all over embroidered with flat gold of damask with gold laces and tied with great buttons of diamonds, rubies and orient pearl. His sword and sword girdle were adorned with stones and emeralds … his bonnet was so rich of jewels that few men ever saw the like.

As planned, his party halted some way short of the pavilions and waited. Anne arrived on a 'richly trapped steed' and rode towards Henry who 'put off his bonnet and came forward to her, and with most lovely countenance and princely behaviour saluted, welcomed and embraced her, to the great rejoicing of the beholders'. The royal couple then rode back to Greenwich, followed by their vast retinues. As they came down the steep hill that separates Blackheath from the palace, they would have been able to see the citizens and guilds of London rowing up and down the river in gaily bedecked barges. They alighted at the outer court of the palace where Henry 'led her by the arm through the hall, and so brought her up to her privy chamber, where he left her for that time' – to be attended to by her ladies, no doubt, though that evening there was a sumptuous banquet in the Great Hall.

The wedding ceremony took place three days later, on the morning of 6 January. At Rochester, as we will see, Henry had made plain his displeasure with his new bride, and as he emerged from his privy lodgings in Greenwich on the morning of the wedding, he told Cromwell he would rather not go through with it. 'If it were not to satisfy the world and my realm, I would not do that I must do this day for none earthly thing,' he is reported to have said. Nonetheless as the clocks struck eight the next morning he appeared 'wearing a gown of cloth of gold raised with great flowers of silver, furred with black' and formally summoned his nobles. The party then proceeded to the gallery leading to the royal closets, where Henry dispatched some lords to fetch the princess, whose bridal attire consisted of 'a gown of rich cloth of gold set full of large flowers of great orient pearl, made after the Dutch fashion'. Escorted by two German lords, she came to the gallery and after three low curtseys Henry led her into the queen's closet where Cranmer married them. They then heard Mass in the small chapel in the king's closet before each went to their own privy chamber to change. Then 'with her sergeant-of-arms and all her officers before her … the king and she went openly in procession to the king's closet where they made their offerings and dined together' until, after various banquets and masques, 'the time came that it pleased the king and her to take their rest'.

Greenwich Today

After Henry's death Greenwich Palace remained an important royal residence throughout the later Tudor and early Stuart era, but it fell into disrepair during the English Civil War and was demolished in 1660 on the orders of Charles II. It was his intention to build a new palace where the old one stood, but these plans never came to fruition. Instead, the Royal Hospital for Seamen was built on the site, a Baroque extravaganza whose buildings stand to this day; however, the hospital closed in 1869, and after providing a home to the Royal Naval College the buildings now form the spectacular riverside campus of the University of Greenwich and the Trinity Laban College of Music and Dance. (The place is popular as a film location and was arguably seen to its best effect on celluloid standing in for Paris in the 2012 film of the musical *Les Misérables* – though it has also stood in for the courtyard of Buckingham Palace in the Netflix blockbuster *The Crown*.) Behind the palatial buildings stretches Greenwich Park, which rises to the summit on which the Royal Observatory stands (with its famous designation of the Greenwich Meridian marked out in the pavement). The Observatory was also commissioned by Charles II, and occupies a site where a structure known as Greenwich Castle once stood. This was formerly known as Duke Humphrey's Tower after its founder, Humphrey, Duke of Gloucester, who as we have seen constructed the first grand residence on what was to be the site of the palace. Henry VIII refurbished the castle in 1526 and renamed it Mireflore; he used it as a hunting lodge and as a residence for his mistresses, and it can be seen in the 1558 drawing of Greenwich Palace by Anton van den Wyngaerde, who portrayed it as a boxy keep surmounted by a circular tower. The Royal Observatory was built on the castle's medieval foundations, and as a result it has been postulated that this might be the reason why it is oriented very slightly the 'wrong' way for an observatory (it should be facing in a more northerly direction). That said, the orientation may be purely for aesthetic reasons.

The demolition job done by the wreckers of the Restoration era was a thorough one that virtually obliterated all above-ground vestiges of the medieval and Tudor palaces that once stood beside the river at Greenwich. In 1971, a major archaeological investigation unearthed some foundations of the palace beneath the lawns of the Grand Square, the riverside courtyard fringed by Wren's formal buildings which has its north side open to the river. The dig gave a valuable insight into the layout of the palace, though the remains were reburied and there is nothing to be seen today. Instead, a marker in the court's paving, situated on a path linking the river gate and the statue of King George II, and surrounded by manicured lawns and the imposing symmetry of Wren's buildings, reminds visitors that this was once the site of a great palace of Henry VIII. 'On this site stood the Tudor palace of Greenwich, built by King Henry VII' read the circle of words on the stone, whose centre inscription indicates that three Tudor monarchs were born in the palace – Henry himself, and his daughters Mary and Elizabeth.

Archaeologists descended on the site of the palace once again in January 2006, when a routine project to install a drain in a newly landscaped carpark at the end of Park Row, on the eastern part of the site close to the river bank, unearthed the chequer-tiled floor of the palace's chapel

The marker in the paving of the Grand Square at Greenwich that indicates the former site of the Tudor palace.

Greenwich Palace

The site of the 2006 archaeological dig that unearthed the chequered floor of the chapel of Greenwich Palace.

and vestry. This building is of considerable importance historically as it was in the private closet overlooking the chapel that Henry married Catherine of Aragon and Anne of Cleves. The floor was covered up when the dig was over and there is nothing to see now, though in the Old Royal Naval College Visitor Centre a reconstruction of the floor (and stubbly

The reconstruction in the Old Royal Naval College Visitor Centre of the chequered floor of the chapel at Greenwich Palace.

Henry VIII: A History of his Most Important Places and Events

The reconstruction in the Old Royal Naval College Visitor Centre of a window from the former palace, using original stonework.

remains of an adjacent brick wall) can be seen – along with finds from the site such as fragments of earthenware pottery, and a reconstruction (using some original stonework) of a window from the palace, with the arms of Henry VIII (with the red and white Tudor rose) and Anne Boleyn.

The quest for tangible reminders of Henry in Greenwich seems more hopeful at St Alfege Church, just a short walk from the site of the former palace, and the place where Henry was reputedly baptized. The church is built on the site where Alfege (pronounced 'Alfidge'), Archbishop of Canterbury, was killed by the Danes in the year 1012, in the process achieving sainthood. However, the medieval building that was standing in Henry's day collapsed during a storm in 1710 and the current church, which rose in its place, is a handsome Baroque structure designed by the noted English architect Nicholas Hawksmoor. A contemporary description of Henry's baptism notes that it took place on a specially built stage consisting of a tall circular wooden platform accessed by steps and decorated by Benjamin Digby, yeoman of the Queen's Wardrobe of the Beds, who covered the platform with gaily coloured cloth and set a cloth-of-gold canopy over the magnificent silver font. Tapestries were hung from the walls and rich carpets were laid on the floor, and cypress leaves were used to draught-proof the windows. At the start of the ceremony, which was conducted by Richard Foxe, Bishop of Exeter, trumpets sounded and attendants lit torches as Henry, swaddled in cloth of gold fringed with ermine and carrying a decorated candle in his hands, was brought in.

However, there is considerable dispute as to whether the medieval St Alfege Church was where the baptism took place. *The Environs of London* by Daniel Lyssons (1796) and *A Genealogical History of the Kings and Queen of England* (1707) both insist that it was, but during the legal tussles surrounding the annulment of Henry's marriage, Bishop Foxe gave evidence that he had actually baptized Henry at another Greenwich church altogether – the Church of the Observant Friars. This community had been established in 1478 by Henry's grandfather Edward IV, and during the first half of Henry's reign the Order provided several chaplains for the king and queen. Their church was adjacent to the palace; it was linked to the royal lodgings by a gallery, and was a favourite place of prayer for Catherine of Aragon (who married Henry here) and Princess Mary (later Mary I), who was (definitely) christened there (in February 1516). However, in 1534, this religious order was suppressed, the friars not having done themselves any favours by speaking out against the king's divorce and his supremacy over the church. The friary church was thereafter converted into a manufacturing workshop for the royal armouries. Had this church been the venue for Henry's baptism? We will never know – and indeed until August 2017 the exact location of this building was unclear. However, in that month a major archaeological find was made – some bee boles, or niches where beehives were stored in the winter, were discovered beneath the celebrated Painted Hall (which today forms the centrepiece of the Old Royal Naval College). The niches, along with part of a cellar floor, are visible from a gallery beside the Old Royal Naval College shop and café, and it is assumed that this was the cellar of the former friary. Those who argue that this wasn't the venue for the baptism point to a will made out by Eliot Alfons, a London vintner, who in 1493 left money for the construction of the friary church – which suggests that it had not been completed when Henry was baptized (in 1491). The other candidate church, St Alfege, remains a stopover for tourists 'doing' Greenwich – and one thing that can definitely be said about it is that it was the burial place

Henry VIII: A History of his Most Important Places and Events

Above and left:
The beehive niches unearthed in 2017 that once occupied the cellar of the friary located beside Greenwich Palace.

of Thomas Tallis, who lived in Greenwich during the last part of his life and was the leading composer of the Tudor age, though the exact site of his tomb was unfortunately lost during the eighteenth-century rebuilding of the church. After the church's windows were blown out in a wartime bomb blast, the glass artist Francis Spear, born in South London in 1902, was commissioned to fashion some new windows for it that are still in situ today – one shows Tallis, while another depicts Henry's baptism, with attendees colourfully clad in red and yellow.

Henry's baptism depicted in a window in St Alfege Church, Greenwich, where the event might have taken place.

Chapter 3

Between Greenwich and Westminster

Today the reach of the Thames between Greenwich and Central London provides for a journey of infinitely absorbing variety. Curving north along the west side of the Isle of Dogs (whose name might be derived from the fact that Henry kept his hunting dogs here) there are reminders of London's former role as the busiest port in the world, with views over the former docks of Surrey Quays on the left, while to the right is Canary Wharf, with its gleaming office towers. More docks can be seen as the river curls west past Limehouse, Wapping and St Katharine's Docks, beyond which are the iconic towers of Tower Bridge with the equally iconic turreted towers of the Tower of London immediately beyond – and this is the first building heading upstream from Greenwich that has connections with Henry VIII.

The Tower of London

The Tower of London was founded by William the Conqueror towards the end of the year 1066 and its instantly recognizable boxy keep, known as the White Tower, was built just over twenty years later. The formidable fortress was seen by Londoners as a symbol of royal oppression over them – as was William's intention. By the time of Henry's reign, some four and a half centuries later, the Tower served several purposes: it was the royal armoury and the royal treasury, but there was a royal residence here too, and the fortress also housed a menagerie of exotic beasts that was open to the public – providing the origins of London Zoo. The Tower had been a favourite residence of Edward IV, Henry's grandfather, but Henry himself rather neglected it and by the end of his reign, it was

The White Tower, the ancient heart of the Tower of London; the caps on the turrets were an architectural embellishment added by Henry.

recorded that the fortress was a malodorous place, the moat little more than a rubbish dump. Perhaps Henry's neglect of the place stemmed from its associations with the death of his mother, who died during childbirth in the royal palace when Henry was 11 years old, and her two younger brothers, Richard and Edward Plantagenet, the 'Princes in the Tower', who were very possibly murdered within its walls. In the end the place is associated much more with the people Henry executed rather than with the king himself (who did not attend any of the executions); commoners such as Thomas More and Thomas Cromwell were executed on Tower Hill, the high ground just to the north of the walls of the fortress, while Anne Boleyn, Catherine Howard and other members of the nobility were executed on Tower Green, within its precincts.

Henry's first experience of the Tower came in June 1497 when he was just 6 years old. In that year his father King Henry VII invaded Scotland in revenge for the Scottish king's support of the 'pretender' Perkin Warbeck's claim to the English throne. Raising an army meant raising taxes, something that the men of Cornwall took umbrage over. They formed a ragtag army that marched through Southwest England towards London. When they reached Farnham in Surrey, young Henry's mother brought him to the Tower for safety – something she was used to, as she had previously sought refuge here with her own mother when London was threatened during the Wars of the Roses. However, as we have already seen, the Cornish rebels were soundly defeated at Deptford Bridge, and Henry's stay in the Tower turned out to be a short one.

Henry's stay in the Tower twelve years later was under much happier circumstances. It had long been the tradition for monarchs to reside in the Tower before their Coronation; on the morning of the ceremony, they would process from there to Westminster Abbey, past throngs of cheering subjects lining the Strand and other streets along the route. Today not a trace remains of the former royal residence, a palace-within-a-fortress that was situated between the White Tower and the Wakefield Tower (which still survives, overlooking the river); the area is now covered by an extensive lawn (part of which forms the roof of the semi-submerged gift shop). However, drawings of the palace survive and show that its centrepiece was the Great Hall, which had a steeply pitched timber roof and tall windows, and was supported by stone pillars. When Henry's father died at Richmond Palace late in the evening of Saturday, 21 April 1509, Henry duly took up residence here on the following Tuesday. He was just two months short of his eighteenth birthday, and during those first couple of months of his reign, he ruled as a 'minor', with Lady Margaret Beaufort, his formidable grandmother, acting as regent. With the new king safely in residence, the Earl of Oxford, who was Constable of the Tower, placed the fortress under heavy guard. Soon afterwards, Henry's first act as king was enacted from here – a general pardon of those arrested under the

Between Greenwich and Westminster

This lawn marks the former site of the royal palace within the walls of the Tower of London.

reign of his father. However, he was not to remain in the gloomy Tower for long: his father was buried with great pomp at Westminster Abbey on 9 May and a couple of days later Henry left the Tower for the more familiar surroundings of Greenwich, where he spent most of the weeks leading up to his coronation.

During that time the royal apartments in the Tower were completely refurbished in anticipation of the joint Coronation of Henry and his wife, Catherine of Aragon, which was scheduled for Sunday, 24 June (Henry had only married Catherine on the 11th). When Henry returned to the Tower from Greenwich on 21 June, riding on horseback and approaching the fortress via London Bridge and Gracechurch Street, it was to a royal palace bedecked in red, green and white, the last two being the Tudor colours. The following night saw a remarkable ritual unfold in the Tower, namely the creation of new Knights of the Bath, which had been a traditional eve-of-coronation ceremony since it had been first instituted by Henry IV at his coronation in 1399. All the new knights were purified in ritual baths and served the king at dinner, and then kept vigil through the night at the Norman Chapel of St John in the White Tower, which prior to the Reformation boasted brilliant wall paintings, stained-glass windows and a colourful rood screen.

The following December Henry stayed briefly at the Tower as he journeyed between Greenwich and Richmond, where he would spend his first Christmas. On this occasion a delegation headed by Richard Falconer, the Tower's master gunner, approached Henry and got him to sign the 'bills' for the letters patents for their wages. This stay was fleeting – just two days – but in the summer of 1510, Henry's first as king, Henry stayed for longer, this time honouring the young men who had indulged him in formulating energetic and often violent games at Greenwich. He gave them money for a banquet which they duly consumed at Fishmongers' Hall, a building located some 400 metres upstream from the Tower that was the seat of one of the City of London's most prominent guilds (it was destroyed in the Great Fire, though a more recent building of the same name stands on the same site today). After the banquet the men, no doubt in high spirits and rather the worse for drink, walked and rode along the riverbank to the Tower to salute their king, dressed in yellow satin lashed with white: Henry, it is said, 'took pleasure to behold them'.

Although Henry visited the Tower comparatively infrequently, the royal lodgings were subject to major rebuilding works in the 1530s, when Cromwell had the old apartments gutted and the walls and ceiling decorated in antique style. A new suite of lodgings was built for Anne Boleyn near the Lanthorn Tower, with a presence chamber, dining chamber and bedchamber, a gallery leading to king's apartments, and a bridge across the moat to a private garden. At the same time St Thomas's Tower was converted into new lodgings for court officials and the White Tower was restored; this was when the distinctive decorative caps on each corner tower (that remain today) were added. The medieval Chapel of St Peter ad Vincula, where many of those executed in the Tower were buried, including Anne Boleyn and Catherine Howard, was also restored. All these building works were inspected by Henry and Anne during a visit in December 1532; they were in the company of the French ambassador Giles de la Pommeraye, and in the Tower's treasure chamber Henry presented the ambassador with a beautiful gold cup as a token of his gratitude for King Francis's recent hospitality in France.

These days it's Anne Boleyn whose presence is most felt in the Tower, rather than that of her husband. Visitors flock to the supposed site of her execution and gape at the adjacent Queen's House, which has a magnificent Tudor frontage. According to a story widely told during the Victorian era, this house was built for Anne by Henry, but unfortunately the story isn't true, as the house was actually built in the 1540s, well after Anne's death (it is, however, a remarkable building, one of the few Tudor structures to survive the Great Fire, and it's now the lodging of the Lieutenant of the Tower). Henry's most notable legacy can be found in the White Tower, where his tournament armour takes centre stage in the Royal Armouries – a collection of armour and weapons that grew out of the role of the White Tower as a military storehouse in his time, and which, remarkably, has been open to members of the public since the reign of his daughter, Queen Elizabeth.

It is appropriate that Henry's armour is so prominent in the armouries collection, as it was during the early sixteenth century that the design of armour arguably reached its apotheosis: each suit of armour was made to be as flexible and as comfortable as possible, and different suits were worn according to the occasion, be it jousting or fighting. Six of Henry's suits of armour survive, and the oldest is on show in the collection in the Tower – a splendid suit of gilded horse armour that was probably made by a Dutch craftsman, Martin van Royne, and engraved and gilded by Paul van Vrelant of Brussels. (Both these craftsmen were later 'headhunted' for Henry's armour workshop in Southwark.) The steel armour covering horse and rider is engraved with elaborate designs that incorporate the initials H and K (for Henry and Katherine – the latter being a common spelling of Catherine of Aragon's name at the time), while foliage flowering with rose blossoms and fruiting with pomegranates (the symbols respectively of Henry and Catherine) runs riot. There are also scenes of the lives of Saint Barbara, Catherine's patron saint, who was

Henry's suit of armour from 1510–15, on display in the Royal Armouries. (*Michel wal, Wikimedia Commons*)

executed by her own father for refusing to recant her Christianity. Other suits of Henry's armour held by the collection include a suit of jousting armour made by Conrad Seusenhofer of Innsbruck in 1514, which features a grotesque helmet with a snarling face and outsize ears, and a suit made for the then-outsized Henry for the May Day tournament held in the Palace of Westminster in 1540. Henry's wooden lance is also on show in the same exhibition, painted red, gold and black and sporting motifs of leaves along with fine latticework. In 2009, the 500th anniversary of Henry's accession, the Tower staged a major exhibition of all Henry's armour pieces, including the famed Wilton armour from the siege of Boulogne in 1544, made to fit the outsize frame Henry had grown into in the last years of his life, and normally on display at the Metropolitan Museum of Art in New York.

Winchester Palace and Coldharbour House

Downstream from the Tower, on the south bank of the river, is Southwark, known in medieval and Tudor times as a place of licentiousness and lawlessness, of gambling dens and brothels and later, of course, as the venue for Shakespeare's theatres. The workers in those brothels were known as Winchester Geese, so named as successive Bishops of Winchester were the major landowners hereabouts and filled their coffers with rent from the brothelkeepers. In the 1130s Henry of Blois, Bishop of Winchester and younger brother of King Stephen, had built his London townhouse beside the river here, in a spot just downstream from London Bridge. The Bishops of Winchester were amongst the most powerful and wealthy of all bishops and their London residence was built to befit their status: it had two courtyards, a riverside tennis court (or 'play' as they were known then), and a grandiose great hall that was enlarged in the fourteenth century by William of Wykeham, whose major foundations, New College, Oxford and the public school Winchester College, have fared better than the palace here. For only the skeletal, tumbledown western walls of the great hall have survived. They can be seen along a narrow lane named Pickfords Wharf and consist of a rectangular enclosure of planted flowerbeds open to the sky and hemmed in by the bars and office blocks (many of them converted from former warehouses) that characterize this part of the South Bank. The stone latticework of the rose window that William of Wykeham

A drawing of Winchester Palace from 1660 by the London-based Bohemian graphic artist, Wenceslas Hollar. (*Wikimedia Commons*)

Right: The exposed shell of the Great Hall of Winchester Palace in Southwark, where Henry first encountered Catherine Howard.

Below: The restored rose window of the Great Hall.

added has also been comprehensively restored – though the whole ensemble is rather overlooked by the hurrying office workers or weekend revellers that pass along Pickfords Wharf (indeed the ruins were only discovered in the nineteenth century, and were not fully revealed until a fire destroyed neighbouring properties in the 1980s). And the ruins are rather smothered by the contemporary and historical London that surrounds them: to the immediate west is Clink Street, named after the notorious prison that once stood here (and that, in its first incarnation, took the form of a dungeon below the palace); a few steps to the east is a reconstruction in a dry dock of Sir Francis Drake's ship the *Golden Hinde*; beyond that is Southwark Cathedral; and then comes the busy interchange of London Bridge station and the spike of the office block known as the Shard. Yet the medieval Great Hall whose shell is now exposed played an important part in Henry's story, for it was here that he met his fifth wife, the frivolous and vivacious Catherine Howard.

The occasion was a grand banquet given in March 1540 by the serving bishop, Stephen Gardiner. Catherine Howard, a cousin of Anne Boleyn, was a scion of the Howard dynasty, a diminutive, sensual, auburn-haired girl who might have been as young as 16 when Henry saw her dancing in the rainbow of light cast by the rose window that's been restored today. Contemporaries described her as attractive rather than beautiful, and though she was also described as fashionably plump she must have been overshadowed by the man-mountain that Henry had turned into by then. Nonetheless, on the rebound from the disappointment of his marriage to Anne of Cleves, Henry acted like the lovelorn romantic, and the pair were married just four months later, on the same day that Thomas Cromwell, the sworn enemy of the Howards, was beheaded on Tower Hill.

Curiously, Winchester Palace also played a part in Catherine's downfall. Accusations were made against her in an anonymous letter delivered to Henry at Hampton Court. This led to Catherine being accused of having a pre-contract of marriage with the courtier Francis Dereham, whereafter Thomas Culpeper, another ambitious courtier, took to 'succeeding him in the queen's affections'. Henry was initially in shock and disbelief at the accusations. But evidence was painstakingly collected and was presented to the king during an all-night meeting of the council held on 6 November 1541 at Winchester Palace. Henry, faced with this numbing assault on his bloated egotism and self-esteem, demanded a sword there and then with which he could slay the queen, before complaining of his misfortune in meeting with 'such ill-conditioned wives'. His anger was raw and naked, and councillors wondered whether it had driven him insane. They shrank back from his grief and rage, exchanging fearful glances. Catherine was executed three months later, less than two years after Henry watched her dancing at Winchester Palace.

Opposite Winchester Palace, on the north bank of the river, is the site of a former medieval manor house known as Coldharbour House. It has fared even less well than Winchester Palace, succumbing completely to the Great Fire, which was so all-consuming that it left no archaeological trace behind. The house was situated on Upper Thames Street, just to the east of where Cannon Street station is now, and was first mentioned in the reign of Edward II as being the property of a knight, Sir John Abel. In the late fifteenth century it came into the hands of Richard III, who gave it to the College of Arms to be used as storage space, but his successor Henry VII took it back into royal ownership and gave it to his mother, Lady Margaret Beaufort, who used it as her London townhouse. In 1497 Queen Elizabeth brought her young son Henry here when London was threatened by Cornish rebels (as we have seen, as the threat grew more intense, they moved to the Tower, just 500 metres away). This would seem to be the only connection the building had with Henry – though his experience there as a very young boy whose father's throne was under threat would have been an intense one – and little is known about the building after that. However, we do know that in 1509, when Henry acceded to the throne, Elizabeth Denton, Henry's former governess, was given the keepership of this building, along with 'a tun of Gascon wine'.

Baynard's Castle and St Paul's Cathedral

Some 300 metres further upstream from Coldharbour is the site of another important riverside manor house, Baynard's Castle. A castle was built here by William the Conqueror, who gave it to Ralph Baynard, a feudal landowner from Essex. It was later demolished by King John and the property was rebuilt in the fifteenth century as a manor house, though a rather formidable one, with battlements and two courtyards. The house served as the London residence of Richard, Duke of Gloucester (before he acceded as Richard III), and in 1501 Henry VII rebuilt the property again in advance of the wedding of his son Prince Arthur to Catherine of

Aragon. When Catherine subsequently married Henry VIII, he gave it to her on the day of their wedding, and from then on it served as the official London residence of his queens.

Like Coldharbour House the building burned down during the Great Fire and the land was subsequently used for wharves and warehouses. In the early 1970s, when land was being cleared for the new building of the City of London School, the foundations of the towers and the old river frontage of the house were revealed; the other part of the site is occupied by Baynard House, a rather brutalist office block named after the long-vanished manor house. Beneath it in a tunnel is Castle Baynard

Above and left: This office block, Baynard House, occupies the site of one of Henry's manor houses, Baynard's Castle.

Castle Baynard Street marks the location of Baynard's Castle, which once stood in this part of the City of London.

Street, an underground traffic artery that runs west–east between the river and St Paul's Cathedral.

Henry often made use of Baynard's Castle when attending services at St Paul's, which is just 100 metres to the north. In the sixteenth century 'Old St Paul's' was the largest building in England: the Romanesque-Gothic cathedral was begun by the Normans in 1087, consecrated in 1240, and extended and enlarged in the high middle ages with a ceiling of timber-ribbed vaulting above the nave, which was to seal its ultimate fate during the Great Fire. On Sunday, 14 November 1501 this enormous medieval cathedral served as the venue for the marriage of Catherine of Aragon and Arthur Tudor, Henry's older brother. Catherine was a scion of the most powerful dynasty in Europe – her parents, Ferdinand and Isabella, had driven the Arabs out of Spain and united the country – and King Henry VII wanted the marriage of their daughter to his heir to be a spectacular event that would be the talk, perhaps, of the rest of the century, which the king hoped would be dominated by a new King Arthur. At the time of the wedding Prince Henry was just a few months past his tenth birthday, but his father had ordained that he play a prominent role in the ceremony, the main part of which was to unfold on a tall, many-tiered circular platform built in the centre of the nave of the great church. The platform was linked to the west doors by a walkway built at head height – and it was along this that young Henry was to escort Catherine, from the Palace of the Bishops of London, which adjoined the north side of the cathedral (this building was also destroyed in the Great Fire, and unfortunately little is known about it). When the ceremony was over, it was Henry who led the other dignitaries to hear Mass with the bridal couple in the choir, after which he accompanied Catherine along the length of the walkway, through the West door and to the entrance to the palace, where her new husband was waiting for her, and where Henry's role as royal escort ceased.

Prince Henry and his father the king were back at St Paul's some four years later, on the eve of St George's Day, 1505, when they heard evensong on the day before Henry, then 14, was made a Knight of the Garter. On the day itself Henry walked and rode immediately behind his father, as a relic of Saint George – his leg, to be precise, encased in a chest encased in silver – was carried through the cathedral in a procession (the relic had recently been sent to London as a gift by the Holy Roman Emperor Maximilian).

Henry took centre stage in another grand ceremony staged in the cathedral in May 1514, when a sword and a cap of maintenance, consecrated by Leo X, was sent from Rome as a gift for him (in the hope that Henry would remain an ally of the Papal States). Henry accepted the gift in an elaborate ceremony that saw him ride in procession to the cathedral and then, surrounded by his courtiers, dismount at the great west door and walk to the high altar, where he knelt in front of the Papal envoy and two noblemen girded him with the sword and placed the cap on his head. Reports of this ceremony indicate that the cap was too big for him and covered his entire face. Presumably Henry adjusted it before joining a procession through the church and attending a High Mass that was accompanied by instrumentalists. The king eventually left the cathedral at one o'clock in the afternoon, at the head of a procession of ambassadors and courtiers who walked two by two to the Bishop's Palace. One Venetian estimated that 30,000 spectators had come to watch.

Just over four years later, on 3 October 1518, the cathedral was once again filled with royalty, nobles and dignitaries as Henry signed the Treaty of London at the high altar and then Cardinal Wolsey celebrated High Mass, during which Henry, seated in a throne upholstered with cloth of gold, listened to the English diplomat and cleric Richard Pace deliver a long oration in Latin. The occasion was a glorious one indeed, celebrating a treaty by which the main European powers – Burgundy, France, England, the Holy Roman Empire, the Papal States, the Netherlands and Spain – all agreed a pact of non-aggression towards each other. The peace was not to last, however, and in March 1524, Henry again travelled in state to the cathedral to give thanks for the Emperor's recent and decisive victory against the French at the Battle of Pavia.

Bridewell Palace

With the ravages of the Great Fire and London's remorseless growth, it's not surprising that so little of the Tudor city remains. Bridewell Palace is another grand structure that has bitten the dust, surviving only in drawings or written descriptions. It was situated just upstream of St Paul's and if anything of it still remains it is lost beneath a cluster of buildings immediately west and northwest of Blackfriars Station, another of London's riverside termini for suburban trains.

The original palace here was established by Cardinal Wolsey in 1515, on land he had been granted by the king close to the Dominican priory of Blackfriars, on the site of the medieval St Bride's Inn, which gave the palace its name. However, when work started on Hampton Court, Wolsey lost interest in his new residence, then only half-built, and returned the land to the king, who transformed it into a grandiose riverside palace. The palace was constructed from red brick, with octagonal towers and two courtyards; in the inner one was a donjon housing the royal lodgings, while a long gallery led to the river and the water gates. Adjacent to the palace, in what must have been a fine position overlooking the river, were terraced gardens and a tennis play, while on the 'landward' side a bridge spanned the River Fleet (which these days runs in a tunnel beneath Fleet Street) connecting with the priory, which could provide accommodation for guests. There was no great hall or chapel, and this was the first of Henry's palaces to be built without them; however, the hall or the chapel in the priory could be used when needed.

The palace was completed by June 1522, in time for Henry to show it off to the Emperor Charles V during his state visit to England. Henry even played tennis with him on the new courts; 'They departed even hands on both sides after eleven games,' the chronicler Edward Hall tells

Bridewell Palace as it appears on the map known as the Copperplate Map, drawn in the 1550s.

us. Three years later, on 18 June 1525, the king created multiple new peers in the Presence Chamber of the palace, among them his illegitimate son (by his mistress Elizabeth Blount) Henry Fitzroy, who was elevated to Duke of Richmond and Somerset and Earl of Nottingham. The boy, all of 6 years old and dressed in crimson, entered the chamber to a fanfare and knelt before his father, as the patent of creation was read out. Then the small figure took his place beside his father on the dais, indicating his precedence over every other peer in the room.

In May 1529, the Great Hall of the neighbouring priory became the venue for the court proceedings that considered the annulment of Henry's marriage to Catherine of Aragon. Famously, she began the proceedings by heading not for the chair of estate appointed for her but to the throne where Henry sat, where she fell to her knees in a dramatic gesture and claimed that when she married him, she had been a virgin 'without touch of man. And whether it be true or no, I put it to your conscience'. Her plea stemmed from Henry's claim that her marriage to his older brother Arthur must have been consummated, thereby rendering his own, later marriage to Catherine unlawful according to scripture; Catherine claimed the reverse, her insistence aided by the fact that Arthur had only been 15 years old at the time of their marriage. After her dramatic gesture she rose, curtseyed and left the court on the arms of Griffin Richards, her receiver general. The people who had gathered outside the priory cheered; the proceedings nonetheless carried on without her over the ensuing days. Bishop Fisher told the court that 'This marriage of the king and queen can be dissolved by no power, human or divine' but Henry dismissed this view as being 'but of one man'. Eventually Campeggio, the Pope's representative in England, who was acting as judge, adjourned the case, maintaining that it could only be heard in Rome.

By the 1530s Bridewell Palace was considered too small for Henry's use – and it was beset by foul smells from the River Fleet. He decided that it should be the French ambassador who should put up with the smells, not him, and between 1531 and 1539 it became the first official ambassador's residence in London. It was here that Holbein probably painted his masterpiece *The Ambassadors* (1533), one of the most famous paintings created in Henry's reign, instantly recognizable because of its famously distorted (or anamorphic) skull, a visual puzzle which the viewer must stand in a certain position to appreciate. The painting is now in the National Gallery and has been the subject of huge debate as it features several other symbols, such as a globe, some mathematical instruments and a complex sundial – though none seems to have any specific link with Henry.

Bridewell Place in the City of London marks the site of the former Bridewell Palace.

After the king's death the palace fell into the hands of his son and successor Edward VI, who passed it to the Corporation of the City of London. They turned the building over to use as an orphanage and a House of Correction for the Vagrant Poor, which later morphed into Bridewell Prison (which is why such institutions were often known thereafter as 'Bridewells'). Much of the building burned to the ground in the Great Fire though some parts remained until they were finally demolished in the 1860s. The position of the former palace is now marked by streets named Bridewell Place and Tudor Street, which run west from New Bridge Street, a major artery guiding traffic towards Blackfriars Bridge. On this street, at number 14, a rebuilt gatehouse has been incorporated into an office block, crowned by a small relief of Edward VI, and a fading plaque on the adjacent wall indicates that 'Here stood the palace of Bridewell built by Henry VIII in 1523' and outlining its subsequent history. The Crowne Plaza Hotel and Unilever House (the company's world headquarters) occupy most of the rest of the palace's former site, with the old gate onto the Fleet–Thames confluence marked by another street, Watergate.

Between Greenwich and Westminster

Right: The rebuilt gateway at 14 New Bridge Street, overlooked by a relief of Edward VI, marks the site of the former Bridewell Palace.

Below: The plaque at 14 New Bridge Street.

Watergate marks the site of the old gate onto the Thames from Bridewell Palace.

Chapter 4

The Palace of Whitehall and St James's Palace

Upstream from Bridewell Palace the Thames curves south, spanned first by Waterloo Bridge and then by Hungerford Bridge, which takes trains into Charing Cross, one of London's biggest termini. Just beyond the second bridge is the London Eye, with Waterloo station behind it; tourists on the iconic Ferris wheel who look across the Thames are confronted by the long, forbidding façade of the Ministry of Defence building, behind which runs Whitehall, the grand, straight avenue linking Trafalgar Square with Westminster. These days this street and district are synonymous with government – the Foreign and Commonwealth Office, Downing Street and the Cabinet Office all lie on the western side of Whitehall – and this association is wholly down to Henry VIII, who in the 1530s established the palace that was to become his principal royal residence in exactly the place where, four centuries later, the Ministry of Defence building was constructed. Over time the palace's former tiltyard has morphed into Horse Guards Parade, while the mandarins beavering away in the Cabinet Office building do so in the exact same spot where Henry once played tennis and watched cockfighting in the palace's specially built cockfighting pit. Over the centuries that followed Henry's initial building spurt, the palace grew to be the largest in Europe, until it was largely destroyed by fire in 1698 (by which time Versailles was actually bigger). Monarchs from Henry VIII through to James II regarded Whitehall as their principal royal residence, though nowadays only the Banqueting House (built nearly a century after Henry's time) remains intact; of Henry's palace virtually nothing survives – and any architectural hints that it once stood here are often hidden away from public view in (or under) modern-day government buildings. However, just 500 metres west of Downing Street, across the expanse of St James's Park, is an entirely separate residence of Henry's, St James's Palace – which, being largely intact and never having succumbed to the ravages of fire, provides a much richer legacy from his era, though unfortunately very little of it can be accessed by the public.

York Place

The Palace of Whitehall owes its origins to Walter de Grey, Archbishop of York, who in 1240 established his London residence in a prestigious location immediately north of the principal seat of royal power, the Palace of Westminster. The residence was known as York Place and in the 1520s it became the property of Henry's Archbishop of York, Cardinal Thomas Wolsey, who carried out extensive rebuilding on the site to create an opulent palace where he could entertain in princely style. It was built from red brick and arranged around courtyards, with a great hall and chapel, and its east side opened straight onto the river, with the water lapping at the building's outer walls. These were probably positioned exactly where the Ministry of Defence building's eastern wall is now aligned (the narrow garden that now separates this building from the river bank occupies a strip of land that has since been reclaimed from the Thames).

Henry was a frequent visitor to Wolsey's palace in the 1520s. One visit came on Shrove Tuesday in 1522, when Wolsey hosted a banquet at York Place for Imperial ambassadors that featured a pageant entitled *Le Château Vert*, a lavish spectacle that was described by the chronicler Edward Hall. The 'green castle' concerned was occupied by several noble ladies, who at the opening of the pageant were confronted by some lords who wore hats fashioned from cloth of gold and cloaks made of blue satin, and who were named Love, Nobleness, Youth, Devotion, Loyalty, Pleasure, Gentleness and Liberty. Their leader was a knight named Ardent Desire, who tempted the ladies to come down from the castle battlements. 'The lords ran to the castle, at which point there was a great sound of gunfire, and the ladies defended it with rose water and comfits,' Hall recounts. 'The lords replied with dates, oranges and other pleasurable fruits, and eventually the castle was taken … the lords took the ladies by the hands and led them out as prisoners … when they had danced their fill, everyone unmasked themselves. After this there was an extravagant banquet.' The musician, poet and playwright William Cornish produced the pageant and played the role of Ardent Desire, while among the ladies were Mary and Anne Boleyn. Henry, then aged 31, played one of the wooing lords, though Edward Hall does not mention which one.

Wolsey's abrupt fall from grace in 1529, attributable to his failure to find a way for Henry to divorce Catherine of Aragon, meant that his properties fell into Henry's hands. In November of that year Henry and Anne came by barge to York Place along with Anne's mother, to inspect the place. They found that Wolsey had been doing an inventory and the rooms were full of trestle tables laden with piles of gold plate, while several sumptuous hangings had been laid out in the long gallery. Anne liked the place and began to spend a fair amount of time there with Henry, but there were no suitable apartments in which she could lodge, as Wolsey, being a prelate, was of course unmarried – so when she visited, she would stay in a chamber beneath Wolsey's old library. On 12 January 1530 Henry and Anne held a magnificent ball in the palace in honour of the departing Jean du Bellay, the Bishop of Bayonne and the first resident French ambassador in England; this was probably the first grand event that Henry staged at what was to become the Palace of Whitehall.

Art, Architecture and Spectacle at the Palace of Whitehall

The following year the long process of developing York Place into a magnificent royal palace was begun; the name Whitehall was adopted at this time too, a reference to the colour of the ashlar or facing stone used in Wolsey's Great Hall – though it was his fall from grace that resulted in the change of name. ('You must no more call it York Place,' one gentleman tells another in the play *Henry VIII*, which Shakespeare wrote in collaboration with John Fletcher. 'That's past/For, since the Cardinal fell, that title's lost. 'Tis now the king's, and called Whitehall.') Neighbouring properties were demolished so that a spacious garden could be laid out to the north, alongside the river, while to the south an orchard was established. A crenellated gatehouse sporting chequered brickwork and an oriel window was built across the road that separated the palace from the tiltyard and tennis plays (the stately avenue currently known as Whitehall); the gateway was decorated with small decorative plates known as roundels, which were fashioned from terracotta and depicted busts of

Roman emperors. This gate was later known as the Holbein gate, though there is no evidence that the artist worked on it. Wolsey's original Great Hall and chapel were retained but new royal lodgings were built, all on one level as was the fashion by then, rather than stacked as a donjon; much of the stonework came from Kennington Palace, the fourteenth-century palace of the Black Prince, the son of Edward III, which was situated around one and a half kilometres to the southeast in Lambeth and which was demolished specifically for this purpose. Later the king annexed Durham House on the Strand, the former London residence of the Bishops of Durham, and incorporated it into the now-sprawling palace. He also built stairs down to a landing stage on the river so that he could arrive and depart by barge. It was from these steps, on 17 June 1539, that he watched an extraordinary river pageant staged on the Thames – his party being seated under a canvas canopy, lest a midsummer downpour should put a damper on the proceedings. The pageant featured a mock battle between two barges, one commanded by the 'Pope', which ended up being tipped into the Thames, and one representing the 'King's grace', which not surprisingly ended up victorious. Other barges conveyed musicians, and all the performers who took part were asked first whether they could swim.

Henry's lodgings overlooked the Thames and were sumptuously appointed. His privy chamber had an alabaster fountain, ceilings 'marvellously wrought in stone with gold' by the London grocer, theologian and decorator Clement Armstrong, and 'wainscots of carved wood representing a thousand beautiful figures'. In the bedchamber 'a great bed of walnut tree' was constructed over ten months at a cost of £83.3s.10d, and gilded by Andrew Wright, one of Henry's favoured decorative artists. The windows were designed by Galyon Hone, the Flemish craftsman who was Henry VIII's favoured glazier. The surviving Accounts of Chamber and Great Wardrobe go on to describe how there were 'many and singular commodious things' inside the palace, 'most apt and convenient to appertain only to so noble a prince for his singular comfort, pastime and solace'. Other craftsmen who worked on the palace include Lucas Horenbout, another Flemish craftsman who became court miniaturist to Henry, and the English painter John Bettes the Elder, who worked on a mural of Henry's coronation.

Thanks to the influence of Thomas Cromwell, who was his patron, Holbein established a studio within the palace some time in the early

1530s and became official painter to Henry VIII in 1536. His only surviving portrait of Henry VIII, a half-length panel painting now hanging in the Thyssen-Bornemisza Museum in Madrid, was probably painted in his studio in the palace in that year. Utilizing greys and golds, and with intricate detail of Henry's cap and tunic, it was possibly intended as a preparatory study for a larger work. In 1537 Henry commissioned Holbein to paint a vast mural of the Tudor dynasty on the wall of his privy chamber in the palace, a magnificent work which might have been twelve foot long. It was destroyed in the fire of 1698, though Remigius van Leemput's copy painted for Charles II survives in the Royal Collection, and has been copied many times since. The mural aimed to show Henry's claim to the throne by depicting his parents, Henry VII and his wife Elizabeth of York, who stand on marble steps behind Henry and his third wife Jane Seymour. The four are depicted in a splendid antique setting amidst classical roundels, engraved pillars and shell-shaped niches. This is of course the 'Holbein Henry' – showing him facing forwards, feet apart, hands on hips, and gazing at the viewer with steely authority; it was in fact the first official English state portrait, launching a royal tradition that continues to this day. Another of Holbein's portraits painted here was of Henry's 2-year-old son Edward, who was posed wearing a wide bonnet and clutching a gold rattle. Holbein gave the finished painting to Henry as a New Year's gift on 1 January 1539, during New Year celebrations at Whitehall. The solemn little boy is shown gazing at the onlooker with the gravity of an adult ruler, and the work is nowadays on display in the National Gallery of Art in Washington DC.

The palace underwent substantial redecoration after Henry married Catherine Howard. To mark the marriage Henry commissioned several Brussels tapestries on a classical theme, with the collection entitled *The Triumph of the Gods*. Two survive, *The Triumph of Hercules* and *The Triumph of Bacchus*, and can now be seen in William III's presence chamber at Hampton Court. In addition, the range of buildings fronting the river was rebuilt to include privy lodgings for Henry's daughter Mary and a new gatehouse that controlled the southern approach to the palace from Westminster. The range included a new banqueting house, designed by Nicholas Bellin of Modena and incorporating an elaborate chimney piece designed by Holbein that had antique and heraldic details along with battle scenes (only an elaborate drawing of this survives, which some have suggested shows a chimney piece that was intended for one of Henry's other palaces). The palace was refurbished throughout using furnishings from other grand houses that had been seized from disgraced subjects by Acts of Attainder; these included counterpanes (bedspreads) and bed hangings from Beddington House in Surrey, the former home of the courtier Sir Nicholas Carew who was executed for conspiracy in 1539.

In 1545 one of the most famous artworks created during Henry's reign was painted at Whitehall. *The Family of Henry VIII* was painted by an unknown artist, strongly influenced by Holbein, and is a masterful piece of dynastic propaganda. It is a panoramic work of 'widescreen' cinematic ratios and features the dominating figure of Henry at its centre, enthroned under an embroidered cloth of estate in a magnificent palatial setting. Prince Edward and his mother Jane Seymour (the latter copied from Holbein's mural) stand either side of him, while Henry's daughters Mary and Elizabeth stand to his far left and right respectively. Through an open door are tantalizing glimpses of the great gardens at Whitehall, with the King's Beasts (stylized statues of dragons, panthers, lions and bulls) mounted on columns, while in the distance a turret of the tennis court and part of the North Transept of Westminster Abbey can be seen. Also visible through the doors are a man and woman; the former, on the right, pictured with a live monkey on his shoulder, is Will Somers, Henry's fool, though it's not clear who the woman visible through the doorway on the left is. The painting was intended for the Presence Chamber at Whitehall where it is known to have been hanging in the 1580s during the reign of Elizabeth. It is now on permanent display in the atmospheric (though unfortunately rather dingily lit) passageway known as the Haunted Gallery at Hampton Court.

The Family of Henry VIII, painted at the Palace of Whitehall by an unknown artist.

Politics and Intrigue at Whitehall Palace, 1530–45

Today the word 'Whitehall' is synonymous with political intrigue, and that association arguably began in November 1532, when Henry married Anne Boleyn in secret in the chamber over the palace gatehouse. There were few witnesses – and in fact the date is a subject of some speculation, as a letter from Thomas Cranmer indicates that the wedding formally took place the following January. The ceremony was officiated either by George Brown, Prior of Austin Friars, or Dr Rowland Lee, the king's own Chaplain. The secrecy, of course, was explained by doubts about the status of the king's marriage to Catherine of Aragon. Once Archbishop Thomas Cranmer declared that marriage null and void on 23 May 1533, Anne's status was no longer contentious, and seven days later she was crowned queen consort in Westminster Abbey. After the coronation feast in Westminster Hall the assembled guests came to Whitehall to enjoy some jousting in the new tiltyard, followed by a banquet in the palace's queen's chamber. Three years later, on 20 May 1536, the day after Anne's execution, Henry married his third wife Jane Seymour at the palace. It was in this year that the palace was officially named 'The King's Palace of Westminster' (giving rise to some confusion, as the original Palace of Westminster was a different palatial residence, to the immediate south) and was designated by statute as the principal residence of the sovereign and the seat of government.

In the autumn of 1538, the palace's Great Hall was the venue for one of the most unprecedented events of Henry's reign, a public debate between a radical Lutheran, John Lambert, and Henry himself. Tiers of raked seating were erected along the lengths of the hall so that eager spectators could watch their sovereign defend the doctrines of his church (though most of the trial was conducted in Latin). The public spectacle was orchestrated by Thomas Cromwell, who as vice-regent in matters spiritual decided that a public example was needed to underline Henry's opposition to heresy. As John Lambert, the accused, had already been tried and found guilty of heresy before Thomas Cranmer the event was something of a show trial.

A comprehensive description of the trial is provided by Edward Hall, who recounts that on the first day the king appeared dressed entirely in white silk and, seated under his canopy of estate, was flanked on one side by purple-clad bishops and on the other by lords, judges and gentlemen of the privy chamber. Lambert, 'fearful and timorous' was then brought before Henry under guard. 'Ho, good fellow, what is thy name?' Henry asked him, to which Lambert replied that his name was John Nicholson but that he was also known as Lambert. 'I would not trust you, having two names, although you were my brother,' Henry scolded him. Lambert then tried to flatter Henry, commending the king for his 'great judgment and learning' but Henry simply snapped at him that he had 'not come hither to hear mine own praises!'

George Day, Bishop of Chichester and Provost of King's College, Cambridge, who was later imprisoned for opposing Edward VI's protestant reformation, was one of the bishops who tried Lambert. He explained to the court that they were not 'convened to dispute about any point of faith, but the king, being supreme head, intends openly to condemn and confute that man's heresy in all their presence' – whereupon he pointed at Lambert. This was Henry's cue to press Lambert as to whether he believed in transubstantiation, which is the belief that the bread and wine consecrated at Communion become the literal substance of the body and blood of Christ – the rejection of which is a key tenet of Protestantism. Lambert stated that he was 'with Saint Augustine, that [the bread and wine] is the body of Christ – after a certain manner' – to which Henry retorted, 'Answer me neither out of Saint Augustine, nor by the authority of any other, but tell me plainly whether you say it is the body of Christ, or no.' Lambert eventually relented, stating 'It was not his body, I deny it,' and Henry warned him he would be condemned to the stake if he persisted in the opinion, though kept the argument going for five hours in an effort to save him. 'Mark well,' said the king, 'for now you shall be condemned even by Christ's own words: This is my body.' As the hearing drew to a close 'the general applause of the hall gave victory to the king,' but Henry was still willing to give Lambert a chance: 'Wilt though live or die?' the king asked him. 'Thou hast yet free choice.' When Lambert would not recant, Henry answered, 'That being the case you must die, for I will not be a patron unto heretics.' He pointedly looked up at the ranks of spectators as his words rang around the hall. Six days later Lambert was burned at Smithfield, shouting 'None but Christ, None but Christ' into the flames as he expired.

Thomas Cranmer himself was lucky not to have ended up a victim of the battle between religious radicals and conservatives that played out during Henry's reign – and his fate was also decided by machinations that at least partly unfolded at the Palace of Whitehall. (These events were later described by the nineteenth-century antiquary John Gough Nichols in his *Narratives of the Days of the Reformation*, itself derived from the writings of the historian John Foxe.) In November 1545, the Archbishop published a primer (an illustrated book of prayers and devotions) that made him the target of religious conservatives anxious to stop what they saw as an inexorable slide towards Protestantism. The conservative faction urged Henry to have Cranmer sent to the Tower, and Henry duly agreed that his archbishop should be arrested at a meeting of the Privy Council. But it turns out that this agreement was part of a grand scheme of Henry's to humiliate the religious conservatives. On the night before the proposed arrest Henry sent Sir Anthony Denny, his Groom of the Stool, to Lambeth Palace to rouse Cranmer and bring him to Whitehall, where he met with Henry in one of the palace's galleries. There, Henry warned him of the plot. Cranmer maintained that he was happy to be tried for his beliefs as he knew Henry would not allow him to have an unfair hearing. 'What fond simplicity you have!' Henry then warned him (according to Nichols).

> If you permit yourself to be imprisoned your every enemy will take advantage of you. Do you not think that once they have you in prison three or four false naves will be procured to witness against you and condemn you … No, not so, my Lord, I have better regards towards you than to permit your enemies to overthrow you.

Henry then gave Cranmer his ring, and explained to Cranmer that when accusations were made against him, he should show it to his accusers and inform them that it signified that the matter was now in Henry's own hands.

Sure enough Cranmer was kept waiting before being admitted to the council meeting at Whitehall the following day: clearly, his fate was being decided by those inside. When the archbishop was finally brought in to confront his fellow council members, he was told that he had 'infected the whole realm with heresy' and that he would be committed to the Tower – at which point Cranmer, of course, showed the assembled men the ring that Henry had given him. The assembled council members were stunned. Sir John Russell, the Lord Privy Seal, exclaimed, 'Did I not tell you, my Lords, that the king would never permit my Lord of Canterbury to have such a blemish as be imprisoned?' That was nothing, though, compared to the show of anger that erupted from Henry himself. 'How have you handled my lord of Canterbury here?' he demanded of them.

> What makes you [treat him like] a slave, shutting him out of the council chamber among serving men? Would you be so handled yourselves? I would you should well understand that I believe Canterbury as faithful a man towards me as ever was prelate in this realm and one to whom I am in many ways beholden.

Norfolk, who had led the conspiracy against Cranmer and was the most prominent religious conservative, claimed disingenuously they never meant to harm Cranmer. But Henry was not fooled. 'There remains malice among you, one to another,' he told them. 'Let it be avoided out of hand, I would advise you.' And under the watchful eyes of their monarch, those very same councillors that had wanted to have Cranmer burned at the stake hastened to shake his hand. Henry's action was Machiavellian scheming of the highest order: he had agreed to the arrest knowing that he would then foil it, leaving the conservatives to lick their wounds. His humiliation of this faction of his council was deliberate, and was part of the wider balancing act between conservatives and radicals in the development of religious policy.

Henry's Death at Whitehall

One last act of Henry's life was yet to play out, on his grandest palatial stage.

By the time of the plot against Thomas Cranmer, Henry's health was already visibly failing. In particular, his girth was increasing at the same time as his mobility was declining. In 1542, his bed at Whitehall, made from walnut wood, had to be enlarged to cater for his increasing bulk, and at the final measurement was seven feet six inches long and almost the same measurement in width. According to the French prelate and diplomat Charles de Marillac, Henry's obesity was the result of his 'marvellous excess' in eating – although Jane Seymour's death and Catherine Howard's perfidy can't have helped either his physical or mental stability. 'The king was now overgrown with corpulency and fatness so that he became more and more unwieldy,' Edward Hall observed. 'He could not go up or down stairs unless he was raised up or let down by an engine.' There was a worry among his councillors that the same fate would befall Henry as had befallen his maternal grandfather, Edward IV, whose early death was ascribed to over-indulgence (and like Edward IV before him, Henry was also at risk of leaving a minor on the throne if he died early).

By the early 1540s his doctors were fearful that Henry would not live long. He defied them – but by the spring of 1546 his legs were perpetually swollen, making walking difficult, and he had become a semi-invalid, relying on various aids to move around his vast palaces. In July of that year the household accounts included the supply of 'two chairs called "trams" for the king's majesty to sit in, to be carried to and fro in his galleries and chambers'. It would seem that the 'trams' mentioned here were sedan chairs fitted with four horizontal poles, carried by an attendant at each corner and possibly fitted with wheels. The contrivances were kept in the king's study, also referred to as the 'chair house'. A belief grew among Victorian historians that a lift or contrivance was used to raise and lower Henry between floors, backed up by observations such as those of Edward Hall, though no such mention of any contrivance of this sort appears in household accounts, and because his apartments were mostly on one floor it is possible that Hall was mistaken in his assertion that there was one.

In the late summer of 1546 Henry was well enough to spend time hunting at Oatlands (his palace near Weybridge in Surrey) and Windsor. But by November he was back in Whitehall. He made brief visits to Greenwich Palace and Hampton Court in December but spent Christmas at Whitehall in almost total seclusion, with only a handful of councillors and gentlemen of the chamber allowed access to him. He was now destined not to leave the palace alive. On 26 December he summoned several his most trusted confidants to his privy chamber, including Edward Seymour, Earl of Hertford, who was the brother of Jane Seymour and destined to be England's Lord Protector during the minority rule of Henry's son; Sir William Paget, one of his most trusted privy councillors; and Sir Anthony Denny – and asked for the latest version of his will to be read for him. He then drew up the sixteen members of the regency council that would rule during Edward's minority.

Henry VIII: A History of his Most Important Places and Events

In early January Henry had the ulcer on his leg cauterized, which was an agonizing medical procedure in the days before anaesthetics. However, he was well enough to meet with the Imperial and French ambassadors on the 17th, when he apologized for his incapacity and admitted to the Imperial ambassador Francois van der Delft that his illness had been longer and more severe than he anticipated. This was the last time he would conduct any public business with officials outside the court. Two days later he was with his councillors planning his son's investiture as Prince of Wales when he suffered a serious relapse; his councillors sat with him during the next few nights but he could only gesture 'No! No!' with his hands when it was suggested that Sir Thomas Seymour, the brother of Edward Seymour (and later the husband of Catherine Parr), be made a privy councillor. Shortly afterwards he met with the queen and told her that it was God's will that they should part – but he was too weak to say anything more. Around this time, he dictated a farewell letter to Francis I, who was dying too, of syphilis: Europe's two great monarchs and rivals were united at last, by encroaching mortality.

Henry was again well enough to discuss state affairs on 27 January but by that evening he was fading fast. 'His servants scarcely dared speak to him to put him in mind of his approaching end,' Edward Hall wrote, 'lest he, in his angry and imperious humour, should have ordered them to be indicted.' Yet Sir Anthony Denny boldly ventured to advise his master that 'in man's judgment, he was not like to live' and that now was the time for him to remember his sins, 'as becometh every good Christian man to do'. Denny then asked Henry if he would like to speak to any 'learned man', and Henry replied that 'if he had any, it should be Dr Cranmer, but I will first take a little sleep, and then, as I feel myself, I will advise upon the matter'. These were his last known words. When Archbishop Cranmer arrived at Whitehall shortly after midnight, summoned by messenger, he found the king was beyond speech, and when the primate asked him to give some sign that he knew that he was dying in the faith of Christ, Henry 'did wring his hand in his as hard as he could', which was taken to indicate assent. Henry died just an hour or so later, probably from pulmonary embolism. He was aged 55 years and 7 months, a fairly good age for those times, particularly given his fondness for alcohol and his overindulgence at the meal table.

Henry now lay lifeless in his walnut bed in his opulent private apartments at Whitehall, his unpredictable moods, extravagant lifestyle and larger-than-life personality finally neutralized by death. As the

The Palace of Whitehall and St James's Palace

January dawn broke Cranmer led Lord Chancellor Thomas Wriothesley, Henry's chief secretary Sir William Paget, and Sir William Paulet, Lord Steward of his household, through the silent and darkened apartments to the bedchamber, to confirm that Henry was dead. Then Sir Anthony Denny along with Sir William Herbert, another gentleman of Henry's privy chamber, efficiently guarded Henry's body from the bustling world of the court. Over the next two days Henry's body lay undisturbed while palace life went on as normal – the king's meals were even brought to his lodgings with the usual flourish of trumpets. This was to give the council time to smooth the transition to the new, young king and to arrange the funeral. In this regard elaborate hearses (which were not vehicles but trestles surrounded by candles) were constructed for the lying in state of the coffin in Whitehall and at Windsor, where Henry was to be buried, and at Syon, where his coffin was to rest overnight as it was taken to Henry's final resting place. The arrangements required 33,000 yards of black cloth and 8,000 yards of black cotton to be purchased from London merchants, at an astronomical cost of £12,000 (more than £3 million in today's money). These fabrics were to be used to drape the hearses and to hang in the rooms where the coffin was to lie in state.

Then came the preparation of Henry's body – specifically, the 'spurring, cleansing, bowelling, searing, embalming, furnishing and dressing with spices' (according to the clergyman, historian and biographer John Strype, whose *Ecclesiastical Memorials* of 1822 drew on original sources). Paulet ordered the gentleman apothecary Thomas Alsop to supply unguents including cloves, oil of balm, sweet-smelling nigella and musk, and he and the yeomen apothecaries of the royal household assisted a cohort of surgeons and wax-chandlers in the embalming process. At his death Henry weighed more than twenty-eight stone (178 kilograms) and was over six feet tall so his body was not easy to manhandle. Once the bowels were removed the embalmed cadaver was wrapped in wax cerecloth and then in velvet, before being trussed up with silver cords. A label in lead was secured to the breast with the 'writing in great and small letters … containing his name and style, the day and year of his death' and then the king's sergeant plumbers and carpenters were called in to seal the body in a lead shell which was then placed in the coffin's huge outer casing of solid elm. The entrails and bowels were buried in a lead box in the chapel of Whitehall Palace and the coffin was set on trestles in the presence chamber, resting beneath a rich pall of cloth of gold with a cross on top surrounded by candles, and overlooked by the picture of Henry in his pomp on the mural painted ten years previously. Thirty of Henry's chaplains took turns to mount a twenty-four-hour watch over the body for five days.

On the evening of 2 February, the coffin was moved to the palace chapel. It was positioned beneath a hearse supported by six pillars and festooned with heraldic pensils (small pennons), escutcheons of arms, and at each corner, banners depicting saints. The ensemble was covered with a huge canopy of rich cloth of gold, the whole thing a brightly coloured spectacle illuminated in a chapel made sombre by the black cloth. A wooden rail surrounded the hearse, with seats for the twelve chief mourners, led by Henry Grey, 3rd Marquess of Dorset (the father of the ill-fated 'nine day queen' Lady Jane Grey), whose position brought with it the requirement that the holder had to organize (and sometimes personally pay for) a monarch's funeral arrangements; while at its foot was an altar, covered with black velvet, where Mass was said continuously by nominated bishops, all clad in full pontifical vestments, and led by Stephen Gardiner, as prelate of the Order of the Garter.

The coffin remained in the chapel of Whitehall Palace for twelve days. On the morning of 14 February, a solemn procession was formed to accompany the coffin from Whitehall to Windsor. The procession stretched some six and a half kilometres, the coffin at its heart covered with palls of blue velvet and cloth of gold and lying on a chariot drawn by black-caparisoned horses. On top of the coffin was a wax effigy of Henry carved by the Italian artist Nicholas Bellin and clad in crimson, with jewelled bracelets and velvet gloves adorned with rings: even in death Henry's majesty was emphasized.

Whitehall Palace Today

After Henry's time the Palace of Whitehall remained the principal residence of English monarchs for a century and a half. As the century progressed the palace began to resemble a small town, a mish-mash of buildings from different eras and in vastly different styles, some of which were to all intents and purposes standalone palatial residences in their own right. One of the most astonishing additions was James II's Catholic chapel – but it, along with everything else, was destined to be swallowed up by a catastrophic fire in 1698 that was started inadvertently by a servant

The Palace of Whitehall and St James's Palace

hanging wet linen to dry around a charcoal brazier. Sir Christopher Wren was personally ordered by William III to save the Banqueting House, the jewel of the entire palace, which he did by pulling down buildings around it to create a firebreak. Now, Inigo Jones's 1622 masterpiece is the only part that remains. Its famous ceiling was designed by Paul Rubens, a commission in 1634 from King Charles I who later stepped onto the execution scaffold through one of the room's windows.

Downing Street and the buildings on the western side of Whitehall were all built during the century after the fire. Additions and reconstructions have continued through the ages, some of which have revealed parts of the palace that stood here in Tudor and Stuart times. Building work in 1939 beside the river uncovered a flight of steps leading to a landing stage, added in 1691 by Wren, along with the river wall of the earlier Tudor palace. Both can be seen today on the river side of the Ministry of Defence building, enclosed by railings and forming part of the statue-strewn Embankment Gardens, though both sets of remains have been subject to considerable restoration. Within the Cabinet Office building

The Ministry of Defence building occupies the site of the Palace of Whitehall. In an adjacent garden (bottom right) are the scant remains of the former palace.

The wall of the former Real Tennis Court of the Palace of Whitehall within the Cabinet Office building at 70 Whitehall (*Historic England Archive*).

at 70 Whitehall, and inaccessible to the general public, are reconstructed walls of Tudor brickwork from Henry's covered tennis courts and the access passage to them (Cockpit Passage).

However, these remains are nothing compared to the most famous remnant of the Tudor palace, which lies deep beneath the Ministry of Defence building (next to its gym). This is a stone-ribbed columned cavern, with pale brick vaulting, that was originally part of Wolsey's extension to York Place, though somewhat inevitably it is known these days as Henry's wine cellar. It was discovered in 1935 during work on the building that originally stood here. In 1949, when the Ministry of Defence building was under construction, it was in danger of being demolished. However, a decision was eventually made to move the structure (it couldn't be dismantled and rebuilt because of the softness of the bricks). In an extraordinary operation the whole cellar was encased in steel and concrete and moved forty-three feet along, allowing a hole to be dug where it had formerly stood; the structure was then moved

The Palace of Whitehall and St James's Palace

This cellar beneath the Ministry of Defence building is all that remains of the interior of the Tudor Palace of Whitehall. (*POA[Phot] Amanda Reynolds/MOD*)

back thirty-three feet and lowered into the twenty-foot hole. The room, which contains some historical reconstructions of Tudor-era wine barrels, is now much restored and is used by the Ministry for some formal events, though is not generally open to the public.

St James's Palace

West of Downing Street and Horse Guards Parade – which occupy the western limits of the site of the former Palace of Whitehall – is the beautiful open space of St James's Park (with its lake), one of London's great parks. This is fringed on its northern side by The Mall, the stately processional avenue linking Trafalgar Square and Buckingham Palace. We are in the heart of 'tourist' London now – but one place not on the tourist trail is St James's Palace, which has one of its entrances on The Mall, just to the east of Buckingham Palace. This was also one of Henry's palaces – but it differs from his other palaces in Central London through its lack

Henry VIII: A History of his Most Important Places and Events

of a river frontage and, more importantly, because substantial buildings and decorations from Henry's time remain. However, the palace is today a 'working' residence, serving as the London home of several senior royals including Princess Anne (Clarence House, the official London residence of King Charles and his wife Queen Camilla while Buckingham Palace is undergoing extensive renovation, is next door). For this reason, it is not possible for members of the public to see inside St James's Palace, which is a pity, as three of the four courtyards that Henry built survive to this day, as do his 'watching' chamber and presence chamber in the state apartments, each of which has a fireplace carved with lovers' knots encasing the initials H and A (for Henry and Anne). The four-storey Great Gatehouse is, however, visible from the street, at the junction of Cleveland Row, Pall Mall and St James's Street, and looks much as it did in Henry's day, though the clock is a later addition from 1731. There

The Great Gatehouse of St James's Palace, which was originally established by Henry.

is occasionally public access to the Chapel Royal, whose Tudor ceiling survives, though the chapel itself was enlarged and repanelled in the 1830s and enemy action during the Second World War led to substantial restoration in the 1950s.

When Henry came to the throne, a leper hospital, dedicated to St James, stood on this site, surrounded by open countryside. In 1531 the king acquired the hospital, pensioned off the three remaining inmates and had the old buildings demolished. In their place rose a palace that was originally intended as a residence for Anne Boleyn, though her fall from grace meant that the half-built palace was soon repurposed. In Hilary Mantel's novel *The Mirror and the Light* the place features as

> the palace they have been carving out of the site of the old hospital. They have cleared and drained the ground, which was flooded by the Tyburn, and now a pleasant park stands all about. It is a retreat for the king and his family, away from the crowds that surge around Whitehall.

On a visit there, Thomas Cromwell is greeted by 'workmen's shouts … and the noise of chipping and hammering' as a labourer slides down a ladder and tells him they're removing all the initials of Henry and Anne, 'so fondly intertwined, like snakes breeding'. (The instances of H–A that remain celebrated Henry's later marriage to Anne of Cleves.) Inside the palace there were sumptuous lodgings, tennis courts and a tiltyard, though no great hall. The site currently occupied by St James's Park was a deer park, created from drained marshland and stocked with animals for Henry to hunt. This hunting land was extensive: a chase extended as far as Hampstead Heath and Islington, while the nearby manor of Hyde, acquired by Henry in the 1530s from the Abbot of Westminster, was also turned into a hunting park, and survives to this day as Hyde Park.

The chapel was one of the most distinctive features of the palace. It had a ceiling painted by Holbein that commemorated the marriage of Henry and Anne of Cleves, whose initials and badges and mottoes were incorporated into the design. From 1533 the chapel served as the permanent home of the Choir of the Chapel Royal, which had previously moved between the king's various palaces. This was the premier choir in the land; in 1515, the Venetian ambassador Sebastian Giustinian, who was invited by Henry to attend High Mass in the chapel, reported that it was 'gloriously sung by His Majesty's choristers, whose voices are really rather divine than human. They did not chant but sang like angels, and as for the counter-bass voices, I do not think they have their equals in the world'. The leading force in the creation of the choir was the impresario William Cornish, who personally head-hunted his dozen boy choristers, often impressing them into service with him from cathedral schools and church choirs. They were expected to dedicate their lives to training their voices, and each had to learn at least one musical instrument. Cornish was also the chief deviser of court entertainments and the boys of the choir sang, danced and acted the female roles in these (the adult choristers, who included the influential composers Robert Fayrfax and Thomas Tallis, played the male roles). Today the Choir of the Chapel Royal is still based at St James's Palace, its boy choristers traditionally comprising pupils from the City of London School.

After Henry's reign his daughter, Mary I, made much use of the palace, and died here at the end of her six-year reign. However, the palace was destined to remain in the shadow of the much larger Whitehall – until, that is, that palace burned down, whereupon St James's Palace became the sovereign's chief royal residence in London, until it was superseded by Buckingham Palace in the late eighteenth century. Soon after this, in 1809, a fair part of the old palace was unfortunately damaged by an extensive fire, though plenty remains as a place for today's royals to live and work.

Chapter 5

Westminster

If the association of Whitehall with modern British politics can be traced back five centuries to the time of Henry VIII, the association of Westminster with power and intrigue dates back much further – perhaps even a thousand years, to the time of King Canute. He reigned from 1016 to 1035, following the Danish invasion of England, and he was probably the first monarch to site a royal residence on an island on the north bank of the Thames around one and a half kilometres upstream from the ancient heart of London. The island, originally choked by thorn bushes, was known as Thorney Island, and was created by rivulets of the River Tyburn, which separated into sluggish channels where it flowed into the Thames. When Edward the Confessor restored Anglo-Saxon rule in 1042, he demolished (or possibly extended) Canute's residence, and a new palace began to rise on the island; next door, Edward built his new abbey, and the whole complex was named Westminster, to distinguish it from the East Minster downstream in the city proper (St Paul's). Over the following centuries Westminster developed as both the seat of government and the principal royal residence of the monarch – a role that remained when Henry acceded to the throne. Nowadays the Great Hall, known as Westminster Hall and built by William the Conqueror's son William II, is the only remaining part of the medieval palace. The Houses of Parliament occupy the rest of the former site: the Lords and the Commons have met here since the thirteenth century, but a disastrous fire in 1512, just three years after Henry came to the throne, saw an end to the role of the Palace of Westminster as a royal residence. Although parliament continued to meet here (and does to this day, in the nineteenth-century building still called the Palace of Westminster), after the fire Henry shifted the focus of royal power to the Palace of Whitehall, just to the north. That said, Henry has plenty of associations with Westminster Abbey, Westminster Hall and the old medieval palace – which date back to when he was a very small child.

Henry at Westminster Before His Accession

Henry's first recorded visit to Westminster came on 1 November 1494, when as a boy just three months past his third birthday, he was formally created Duke of York in a ceremony at the palace. The ceremony was spread over three days and a description of it was written by the priest Thomas Lyng, who was the London agent of the wealthy and influential Paston family of Norfolk. All parts of it unfolded at Westminster, and it was held to celebrate and champion the Tudor grip on the throne, in the face of the Plantagenet 'Pretender' Perkin Warbeck. The creation of Henry as Duke of York was a deliberate nod to his Yorkist forebears on his mother's side, and specifically to his mother's brother, Richard of Shrewsbury, who was the younger of the two Princes in the Tower; Richard's creation as Duke of York had been the first time the second son of the monarch had been styled thus (a tradition that continues to this day). Perkin Warbeck's claim to the English throne was complex and muddled but one of the claims he had made was that he was Richard of Shrewsbury, grown up – and so the rightful King of England. Henry VII was determined to put paid to that notion by creating his son Henry Duke of York.

The ceremony involved the very young Henry riding, walking and bowing, all of which he practised at Eltham before the first part of the ceremony, when he rode in procession through London on this way to Westminster, on 29 October. The route would have taken him along Fleet Street and the Strand, which in those days were lined with opulent houses with gardens that stretched down to private landing stages on the river. There followed a dinner in the king's chamber in the Palace of Westminster in which Henry (along with others who were to be knighted) performed honorific services at table for his father the king – in Henry's case this meant handing his father a towel to dry himself.

Following the formal dinner, the young Henry participated in a bathing ceremony that was supposed to represent purification, in advance of receiving a knighthood from his father the following day. The ritual involved Henry undressing and getting into a bath, whereupon the Earl of Oxford, who was Lord Great Chamberlain, read the formal admonition of knighthood to him; the same ritual was repeated for the twenty-two others who were due to be knighted the following day. When Henry was immersed, his father dipped his fingers in the water and made the sign of the cross on his son's shoulder. Henry was then lifted from the bath, dried on a bed, dressed in a simple gown and led to St Stephen's Chapel, where vigil was kept until the small hours – and when that was over there was confession, the receiving of absolution, and Mass.

The following day the Earl of Oxford helped Henry dress and rode with him across the palace yard to the Great Hall of the Palace (that is, Westminster Hall). Here Henry dismounted and was carried into the building by Sir William Sandys, who brought him before the king. At his command the Duke of Buckingham put on Henry's right spur and Thomas Grey, the first Marquess of Dorset his left (spurs being metal tools worn on the heel of riding boots to direct a horse; in this case these ceremonial spurs were fashioned from silver, giving rise to the phrase 'winning his spurs', which denotes the wearer becoming a knight). Then the king, no doubt bursting with family pride, girded his son with the sword and set him upon a table – though the symbolism of the ceremony which had played out over two days, involving cleansing and purification followed by sleep and reawakening, was probably rather lost on a 3-year-old.

And still, the ceremony was not yet over. The next day, 1 November, Henry was part of a grand procession that formed in the cloisters of St Stephen's Chapel and wended its way into the parliament chamber. It was led by heralds, with the Garter King of Arms bearing the letters patent that created each knight; then came the Earls of Suffolk, Northumberland and Derby, followed by the Earl of Shrewsbury, carrying Henry; they were followed by the Marquess of Dorset and the Earl of Arundel. Each bowed before the king, and when it was Henry's turn Oliver King, who was secretary to King Henry, read the letters patent that created him Duke of York. The king invested his son with the sword, the rod, the cap and the coronet, and then everyone repaired to St Stephen's Chapel for the solemn Mass conducted by John Morton, the Cardinal-Archbishop of Canterbury. Another grand procession followed, this one headed by Lady Margaret Beaufort, the mother of King Henry VII and the unofficial 'matriarch' of the Tudor dynasty. During the meal that followed the service, the heralds unleashed a cry at the end of the second course which confirmed Prince Henry's new royal styling and titles: 'Largesse of the most high, mighty and excellent prince, second son of the King our Sovereign Lord, Duke of York, Lieutenant-General of Ireland, Earl Marshal, Marshal of England, Lord Warden of the Cinque Ports.'

Several days of feasts and jousting followed. One spectacle was a joust between Sir Robert Curzon and Thomas Brandon, which played out in front of Henry and his father. Curzon dragged Brandon out of the saddle as he tried to extricate his sword from Brandon's gauntlet, whereupon Brandon pulled off Curzon's gauntlet before the two men broke their sword blades on each other's armour; the bout was eventually completed with new weapons. Henry's new colours, blue and tawny (the latter a browny-orange), were in abundance. After yet another feast prizes were awarded (by Henry's older sister, Margaret) 'to the noble and mighty prince, the second son of the king our sovereign lord, the Duke of York, in honour of whose creation this noble joust and tourney hath been holden'.

Some seven years later, in 1501, Westminster was again the scene of celebration, this time following the marriage of Catherine of Aragon and Prince Arthur (which took place, as we have seen, at St Paul's). The feasting and jousting began on Thursday, 18 November 1501. The following day the Great Hall was decorated with tapestries and cloth of gold and silver, and there was dancing – Arthur led out Lady Cecily, his mother's sister; Catherine and one of her ladies performed a dance in traditional Spanish costume; and Henry, then aged 10, danced with Margaret during which he 'suddenly cast off his gown and danced in his jacket' as his heavy clothes were encumbering him. Some ordinary Londoners were allowed to join in the festivities and according to *The Great Chronicle of London*, they snapped up (as souvenirs) the 'plates, spangles, roses and other conceits of silver and over gilt which fell from the garments both of lords and ladies and gentlemen whilst they leapt and danced'.

St Stephen's Chapel and Westminster Hall

The events thus described took place in the medieval Palace of Westminster. Whilst the public and private rooms of the old palace have long gone, along with its courtyards and jousting arena, two spaces, namely Westminster Hall and the undercroft of St Stephen's Chapel, remain intact from Henry's time (as does the so-called Jewel Tower, originally built in the fourteenth century to house the personal treasure of King Edward III – though it has no specific connection to Henry VIII).

St Stephen's Chapel has its origins in the late twelfth century as a private place of worship for the monarch and his family. The building was extensively remodelled by Edward III in the thirteenth century, its walls decorated with a mural of that king and his large family. The chapel survived the great inferno of 1512 and later served as the debating chamber of the House of Commons. However, it too went up in flames in 1834, during the next great fire, leaving only the crypt, known as the Chapel of St Mary Undercroft, to survive into the modern era. (Today the children of peers have a right to get married in the Chapel of St Mary Undercroft – though it's not open to the public.) In 2013, the body of Margaret Thatcher lay in state here the day before her funeral; over five centuries previously, the body of King Edward IV, Henry's maternal grandfather, had lain in state in the upper chapel for a week, prior to it being taken to Windsor for burial (though this ritual does not appear to have been repeated for any other Tudor monarchs).

Westminster Hall is remarkable for its survival. This building was (and is today) famed for its enormous size – when William Rufus built it in the 1090s, it was possibly the largest such hall in Europe – and for its astonishing hammerbeam roof commissioned in 1393 by Richard II, in advance of the wedding feast celebrating his marriage to Isabella of

The exterior of Westminster Hall, the only remaining part of the medieval Palace of Westminster.

Henry VIII: A History of his Most Important Places and Events

The interior of Westminster Hall, showing the hammerbeam roof. (*J. W. S. Lubbock / Wikimedia Commons*)

France. In her *Autobiography of Henry VIII*, Margaret George has Henry musing that it was 'a treasure I must be careful not to let time loot from me' during the feast celebrating his marriage to Anne Boleyn. 'Its dimensions are enormous, so that mounted knights can joust inside, should they so desire. Most arresting of all, its roof is a single span: the ceiling soars overhead in a graceful dance of supporting hammerbeams, scorning any supporting pillars.' Throughout the Middle Ages and beyond the Hall was a venue for celebratory feasts after coronations and weddings held in the adjacent Abbey, and today it is a grand space rich in historical resonance. Plaques on the floor commemorate the fact that this was where Kings George V and VI, Queen Elizabeth the Queen mother and Winston Churchill lay in state following their deaths; other plaques record that this is where Thomas More and Charles I were tried and condemned to death. For three days in September 2022 the Hall was the focus of worldwide attention when the coffin of Queen Elizabeth II lay in state here before her funeral at Westminster Abbey; a quarter of a million people filed past the coffin, some after queuing for more than twenty-four hours. (This, however, is a comparatively recent tradition; the first monarch to have lain in state here was Edward VII in 1910.) Outside these momentous historical occasions, however, the Hall struggles to find a purpose other than being a mightily imposing and ancient space, sandwiched between the Houses of Parliament and Westminster Abbey (though it provided a suitably grand venue where Ukraine's President Zelenskyy addressed Members of Parliament and peers when he visited London in February 2023). Access to the Hall is restricted – it's occasionally used for exhibitions, when public access is fairly straightforward, but most of the time it can only be seen by those who have organized a tour of the Houses of Parliament, which must be arranged well in advance. All of this is a shame, as, like Wolsey's wine cellar under the Ministry of Defence building, Westminster Hall is one of the few buildings in Central London that has direct links with Henry.

In addition to the grand occasions already described, which took place when Henry was a boy, the Hall was the venue for a number of similarly grand events that took place during his reign. The banquet held here after Henry's coronation in June 1509 was, according to Edward Hall, 'greater than Caesar had ever known.' One striking moment came when all the guests were seated: a fanfare sounded and the Duke of Buckingham and the Earl of Shrewsbury rode into the Hall on horseback to herald the arrival of the 'sumptuous, fine and delicate meats in plentiful abundance'. When the second course was finished the king's champion, Sir Robert Dymmocks, paraded up and down the hall on his courser before throwing down his gauntlet (a heavy protective glove) and issuing a traditional challenge – that anyone who dared contest the king's title should do so then. No one did, not surprisingly, and Henry rewarded Dymmocks with a gold cup.

The banquet that was held to celebrate Anne Boleyn's coronation on 1 June 1533 was similar in its extravagance. Henry was not present at the actual ceremony in the Abbey, but he came to the banquet afterwards – along with 800 invited guests, who were served the sumptuous dishes to the sound of trumpets; this time it was the turn of the Duke of Suffolk, as high steward, to ride up and down between the tables on a courser, overseeing everything. Anne herself sat on the king's throne at the stone dais at the south end of the hall, where she was served by eight nobles and attended to by the Countesses of Oxford and Worcester, who from time to time held a rich cloth in front of her face 'when she list to spit or do otherwise at her pleasure' – according to Edward Hall. At the end of the feast Anne was served spices from a gold cup offered by the Lord Mayor, before departing to spend the night at York Place.

In May 1517, the Hall was the venue for a very different event, when Henry appeared in person at the mass trial of 400 apprentices accused of rioting in London and attacking merchants and craftsmen. Humiliatingly, the accused were forced to wear halters, which were straps looped around the neck, attached to a 'lead', and, in a stage-managed flourish of theatricality organized by Wolsey, Queen Catherine knelt before Henry and his lords in a plea for their lives. Henry did indeed pardon them, at which point all the apprentices threw their caps in the air for joy. Henry was not present for the subsequent show trials he initiated that took place here, which saw Thomas More and Anne Boleyn condemned to the executioner's block.

Westminster Abbey and St Margaret's Church, Westminster

Not surprisingly, the origins of Westminster Abbey stretch back so far it is impossible to put a precise date to its foundation. A church (dedicated, as the Abbey is now, to St Peter) was possibly established on Thorney Island as long ago as the early seventh century. At some point the church attracted a community of monks, to what was then an isolated place consisting largely of marshes and brambles. In the 950s this community was refounded as a Benedictine monastery, and it was their church that was rebuilt by Edward the Confessor to provide himself with a royal burial church (the building was consecrated just a week before he died in 1065). His successor, Harold II, was probably crowned in the Abbey, though the first recorded coronation was that of William the Conqueror on Christmas Day 1066. Since that time every English and British monarch has been crowned here, and sixteen are also buried here.

Construction of the present church was begun in 1245 by Henry III and completed at the end of the following century during the reign of Richard II. Henry VII commissioned a chapel at the Abbey's eastern end which was finished in 1519 during the reign of his son, and which today is one of the building's most striking parts. At the start of Henry VIII's reign the Abbey was a monastic church but in 1539 the community was dissolved and Henry assumed direct royal control of the church; although a monastic community returned during the reign of Mary it has been a 'royal peculiar', responsible directly to the sovereign, since 1560.

The major association the building has with Henry is that it was the venue for his Coronation. Although his father, his mother (Elizabeth of York), his children (Mary I, Elizabeth I and Edward VI) and one of his wives (Anne of Cleves) are buried in the Abbey, Henry, unique among Tudor monarchs, was laid to rest at Windsor. Perhaps surprisingly, Henry did not attend the funeral of his father, and it also seems unlikely that he attended the funeral of his infant son, Henry, Duke of Cornwall, who died in February 1511 at the age of just 7 weeks and who was buried in a torchlit ceremony in the Abbey (when the new High Altar was being constructed in the 1860s, a small lead coffin of a child was discovered in front of it; there was no marker and the coffin wasn't disturbed, though it may well have been the coffin of this infant prince).

The Coronation began, as was traditional, with a procession from the Tower of London, through the city's streets to the Palace of Westminster. This glorious spectacle set off during the late afternoon of Saturday, 23 June 1509 – the longest day of the year (or very nearly), though the weather was typical for late June, with brilliant sunshine interrupted by occasional heavy showers. Buildings along the Coronation route were hung with tapestries while free wine flowed from fountains. Henry rode beneath a canopy borne by the Barons of the Cinque Ports, resplendent in a doublet of gold embroidered with precious stones, beneath a robe of crimson velvet furred with ermine. Heading up the procession were newly created Knights of the Bath wearing long blue gowns, and then Edward Stafford, Duke of Buckingham, the greatest nobleman in England, who carried a silver baton denoting his position as Constable of England. Following Henry was Catherine of Aragon, who famously took shelter under the awning of a humble draper's store beside a tavern known as the Cardinal's Hat, on the north side of Lombard Street, when a sudden downpour threatened to overwhelm the decorative canopy that provided her with shelter.

The couple spent the night at the Palace of Westminster, in advance of the Coronation, which took place on Sunday, 24 June: the ceremony lasted eight hours in total. Henry wore royal robes of crimson and walked to the Abbey from the Palace along a carpet of striped cloth strewn with herbs and flowers (which the crowd ripped to pieces for souvenirs afterwards). The ceremony was presided over by Archbishop Warham, who formally asked Henry,

> Will ye grant and keep to the people of England, the laws and customs to them as of old rightful and devout kings granted, and the same ratify and confirm by your oath, and specially the laws, customs and liberties granted to the clergy and people by your noble predecessor and glorious king, Saint Edward?

to which Henry replied, 'I grant and promise'. After the traditional cry of *Vivat, Vivat Rex* from the congregation, Warham anointed Henry with the holy oils of chrism and the choir sang *Te Deum Laudamus*. Catherine was also crowned, with a heavy gold diadem set with sapphires, rubies and pearls, in a ceremony that followed Henry's. When they emerged from the Abbey, to the sound of the organ playing, the bells pealing and the crowd cheering and drumming, Henry was wearing the lighter imperial or 'arched' crown, and wore a robe of purple velvet lined with ermine. 'This day consecrates a young man who is the everlasting glory of our age ... this day is the end of our slavery, the fount of our liberty, the beginning of joy,' wrote Thomas More in his *Coronation Ode*. 'Now the people, liberated, run before the king with bright faces.'

No architectural legacy from Henry's reign can be seen in the Abbey. But the same cannot be said for the smaller adjacent church, known as St Margaret's, Westminster, whose pale stonework stands in contrast to the darker stonework of the abbey. This church was founded by the abbey's monastic community in the twelfth century as a parish church

St Margaret's, Westminster; Henry and Catherine of Aragon are portrayed in the church's East Window.

where local people could worship. Its current appearance dates from extensive reconstruction initiated by Henry VII that was completed in 1523 during the reign of his son (it is now the 'parish church' of the Houses of Parliament). The legacy from Henry's time is the east window, which depicts Henry and Catherine (bottom left and right panels, respectively) kneeling in saintly contemplation as the drama of the Crucifixion unfolds before them in the central part of the window. The window was created in Holland and was commissioned specifically for the Abbey at the start of Henry's reign. However, by the time it was finished and delivered in 1533, Henry's marriage to Catherine was over and the window was seen as an unfortunate embarrassment. It was sent first to Waltham Abbey in Essex and then to Henry's palace at New Hall in the same county; in the following century it came into the possession of General Monck, a parliamentarian with some Royalist sympathies, who buried it to hide it

The East Window of St Margaret's, Westminster, with Henry and Catherine of Aragon depicted bottom left and right respectively.

from destruction by Puritans during the Civil War. Afterwards it was sold to the barrister Edward Conyers, whose residence was Copped Hall (or Copthall) in Essex – and whose son sold it to St Margaret's in 1758 amidst some controversy: the Dean and Chapter of Westminster, objecting to its Catholic imagery, filed a lawsuit which subsequently failed, and the window has been in the church ever since – although Catherine's head is a modern replacement (the original can be seen in the Abbey galleries).

The Palace of Westminster

When Henry acceded to the throne, he must have expected the Palace of Westminster to continue as the centre of English government and royal power, as it had been since the eleventh century. This was where his secretariat was based, along with his Lord Treasurer, his Lord Chancellor, his Lord Chamberlain, his Lord Steward and his Lord High Admiral. These men were the most important members of Henry's Privy Council, his most important body of advisers, which exercised its power through the Court of Star Chamber, which was also based in the palace. In the residential part of the palace Henry used the vast Painted Chamber, which dated from the reign of Henry III, as his bedchamber when the court was based here; above his bed was a mural in red, blue, silver and gold portraying the Coronation of Edward the Confessor, while on the adjacent walls were vivid depictions of Old Testament battles.

Whilst the palace lay at the heart of government it was, in the end, built on a marshy island beside the Thames, and its location meant that it was damp and difficult to heat, and tapestries had to be hung over the doors to keep out the draughts. Beggars were notorious for thronging the rubbish-strewn forecourt with its clock tower and fountain. Although Henry spent much time here during the first couple of years of his reign, the disastrous fire in April 1512 (which started in the kitchens and broke out when the court was at Greenwich) led to its abandonment and the subsequent development of the Palace of Whitehall. The parts of the medieval palace that survived the fire were put to use as parliamentary debating chambers and law courts, while the Painted Chamber became the venue for important state ceremonies. But these and most of the other parts of the medieval palace were destroyed in the second great conflagration, of 1834, with Westminster Hall only surviving as a result of the efforts of fire fighters and the fortuitous direction of the wind. To this day, though, in a deferential nod to its former role, the modern-day Palace of Westminster is still counted 'officially' as a royal residence.

Parliament had sat at Westminster since 1265, when Simon de Montfort's parliament was the first that included representatives from major towns, in the way that it still does today. Henry opened his first parliament in January 1510, looking resplendent in crimson and ermine robes and walking in procession beneath a canopy carried by the monks of Westminster Abbey; he was preceded by mitred abbots, bishops, heralds, Archbishop Warham and the Garter King of Arms. Parliament continued to sit at Westminster after the fire, and Henry addressed the last gathering of MPs in November 1545, when the Speaker gave a speech reminding him of his duties as sovereign; Henry's response acknowledged that his role was 'to endeavour myself to obtain and get such excellent qualities and necessary virtues as a prince or governor ought to have, of which I recognise myself both bare and barren. But for such small qualities as God has endowed me with, I render to his goodness my most humble thanks'. He exhorted his subjects to 'be in charity with one another, like brother and brother. Love, dread and serve God, the which I, as your sovereign lord, exhort and require you'. Edward Hall, who chronicled the event, described it as very moving. One MP wrote afterwards of the 'joy and marvellous comfort' he gained from hearing the king speak, claiming 'I reckon on this day [being] one of the happiest in my life.'

Like Greenwich, the Palace of Westminster was an arena for the high spectacle of Henry's early reign to play out, with pageants and feasts a regular occurrence during the three years before the fire. Two pageants were staged in the days following his Coronation, in a pavilion erected in the grounds of the palace that was hung with luxurious tapestries and cloth of gold. The set over which the spectacle unfolded was a castle whose battlements were made from roses and gilded pomegranates (the emblems of Henry and Catherine) and whose walls were painted white with green lozenges, each containing a rose, a pomegranate, a quiver of arrows or the letters H and K. Red and white wine poured from the mouths of gargoyles as the story of Pallas Athene, the Greek goddess of wisdom, her various knights (who were her scholars) and Cupid's golden dart, was told. The organizer of this extravagance was Thomas Howard, Earl of Surrey and 2nd Duke of Norfolk, who was grandfather to both Anne Boleyn and Catherine Howard. On the second day, Pallas's knights were challenged by those who called themselves Diana's knights (in honour of the goddess of the hunt) who came onto the scene with hounds which then set upon a live deer; afterwards the carcasses of deer were hung on poles and presented to the watching queen and her ladies.

One of the most lavish displays seen at Westminster during Henry's reign took place in the February of 1511, to celebrate the birth of his son (who was to die just ten days after the rejoicings). Against a backdrop of blue velvet, damask and cloth of gold, and costumes and pavilions covered with the letters H and K picked out in gold, Henry put on a spectacular display of horsemanship dressed as Coeur Loyall (Sir Loyal Heart). 'No man could do better,' gushed the author of the *Great Chronicle*, 'For notwithstanding the horse was very courageous and excellent in leaping, turning and exceeding flinging, [Henry] moved no more upon him than he had been holding a soft and plain trot.' Henry later appeared in the tiltyard dressed in his wife's colours with three other challengers on a pageant car drawn by a mock lion and decked out as a forest 'with rocks, hills and dales', in the midst of which was a golden castle. When the car stopped before the queen the 'foresters' on it sounded their horns and out rode the challengers from the castle: the Earl of Devon was 'Bon Valoir', Thomas Knyvet 'Bon Espoir' and Edward Neville 'Valiant Desire'. The spectacle continued the next day, when Henry Guildford, along with Thomas Grey, 2nd Marquess of Dorset, and Sir Thomas Boleyn, 'dressed like two pilgrims in black velvet tabards with pilgrims' hats over their helmets, and carrying Jacob's staffs in their hands' appeared as challengers. Course after course was run, with the queen bestowing the prizes; there was, of course, great applause when the king won the challenger's prize. *The Great Chronicle* describes how when he rode in front of the Queen's tent, he 'leapt and coursed the horse up and down in a wonderful manner' and then turned to the Queen, making 'a lowly obeisance [bow] and so passed in a demure manner into Westminster Hall'. He quickly unarmed and returned to Catherine's grandstand, where he was seen 'kissing … her in the most loving manner'.

The second day of the tournament culminated in a revel staged in the White Hall. This large hall, also known as the White Chamber (and nothing to do with the later Palace of Whitehall), was built in 1167 as a dining hall within the palace complex; surviving the first fire, it was later home to the Court of Requests and, from 1801 until the fire of 1834, it served as the debating chamber of the House of Lords. The revelry opened with a pageant, *The Garden of Pleasure*, in which Henry appeared once again as Coeur Loyall and Knyvet as Vaillaunt Desyre (with the word 'desire' adorning his codpiece). When it was over Henry called on his foreign guests and their servants to help themselves to the gold ornaments on his costume, after several people including the Spanish ambassador would not believe that the adornments were real, telling them that they should 'not fear to pull and tear the said garments from his body'. More guests joined in and Edward Hall recounts how the inevitable happened – Henry 'lost his apparel' and was stripped to his doublet and hose. Londoners who had been invited to the pageant mistook this as a general invitation to divest members of the court of their finery, and surged into the throng of merrymakers. Sir Thomas Knyvet lost all his clothes and, stark naked, was forced to shin up a pillar for safety. The ladies 'were spoiled likewise, wherefore the king's guard came suddenly and put the people back'. Henry passed it all off as a joke and 'this triumph ended with mirth and gladness' in the form of a luxurious banquet in the king's presence chamber.

Chapter 6

Chelsea and Richmond

Upstream from Westminster the Thames curves west, to take it past the wealthy London districts of Pimlico and Chelsea, before it loops around the slightly less fashionable districts of Fulham and Hammersmith, beyond which lie Kew and Richmond and a sense of open country being not far away. Close to the embankment at Chelsea a plaque on a wall is the only reminder that one of Henry's manor houses once stood beside the river here, but at Richmond there is more tangible evidence of the monarch's reign, in the form of remnants of his former riverside palace, one of the most magnificent in Tudor England. Across the Thames from the site of Richmond Palace is where Syon Abbey once stood – which also has some links with Henry, though they are rather macabre and stem from this being where his coffin rested overnight during his final journey, from the Palace of Westminster to his burial place at Windsor Castle.

Chelsea

Cheyne Walk in Chelsea is a riverside road lined with trees and exceptionally smart four-storey mansion blocks. Half way along the road is a plaque affixed to a brick wall that proclaims the site to have been 'King Henry VIII's manor house' that 'stood here until 1753 when it was demolished after the death of its last owner, Sir Hans Sloane'. A residential apartment block, which now carries the address 9–26 Cheyne Walk, was built on the site shortly after, though in a private garden there are said to be some mulberry trees that were planted when Queen Elizabeth I owned the manor house. (The plaque itself is at the junction of Cheyne Mews and Cheyne Walk, directly across from Cadogan Pier, a stop for river clippers

Chelsea and Richmond

Above: Cheyne Walk in Chelsea, the site of one of Henry's manor houses.

Right and below: The plaque on the wall at the junction of Cheyne Mews and Cheyne Walk in Chelsea, indicating that this was the location of one of Henry's manor houses.

plying this reach of the Thames.) The property that formed the historic core of Henry's palace was acquired by him in 1536 as a gift from William Sandys, 1st Baron Sandys, who served him as his Lord Chamberlain. Although the plaque installed by the Royal Borough of Kensington and Chelsea indicates that it was 'Henry's' manor house, it is actually more associated with his daughter Elizabeth, who lived here during his reign, and with Anne of Cleves, who lived in the house after Henry's death and died there in 1557 (nothing is known of its appearance, though it would clearly have had an opulent river frontage). Today Cheyne Walk is one of the most historic streets in London, on account of the luminaries from politics, the arts and sport who live and have lived here since the eighteenth century. For anyone who fancies living amidst the blue plaques, a three-bedroom flat in one of the red-brick residential blocks, with views (from gleaming whitewashed sash windows) over the same reach of the river that Anne of Cleves and the young Elizabeth I once enjoyed, costs a cool £2.5 million.

In the sixteenth century several opulent properties lined the river here. Thomas More lived just a little way upstream from Cheyne Walk, his memory evoked today by statues, formal gardens and street names. The double-courtyard house he built in 1520 (later known as Beaufort House) was surrounded by gardens and orchards, which Henry must have enjoyed during his visits to his trusted friend. In *The Autobiography of Henry VIII*, Margaret George imagines More's home as 'set far back from the river. A long, sloping green lawn led to the very riverbank', and on Henry's first visit, the king imagines that 'the colour of the grass was so deep it seemed fairly to glow … the air here seemed lighter [than at Westminster], bearing delicate smells from faraway meadows and nearby gardens'. Eschewing London for the countryside, however, had its disadvantages: in the same book, when he resigns his post as Lord Chancellor, Thomas More complains to Henry about the fees he has to pay boatmen to row him between his home and Westminster.

Syon Abbey

A few kilometres upstream from Chelsea there is, for the first time, greenery on both sides of the river. To the south is the Royal Botanic Gardens at Kew, while across from Kew is the green expanse of Syon

Park. At the centre of the park is Syon House, one of the last great houses of London, whose appearance dates largely from an eighteenth-century makeover inside and outside by Robert Adam and Lancelot 'Capability' Brown, respectively. The house serves as the London residence of the Duke of Northumberland and is open to the public. The first house here was built in 1552 by Edward Seymour, 1st Duke of Somerset and the first Lord Protector of England during the minority reign of Edward VI. He, in turn, had obtained the site from the Crown after the nunnery that stood here was dissolved. This nunnery, Syon Abbey, had occupied the site since 1431 and although Henry probably never visited the place when he was alive, it has an intimate association with him in death.

The nunnery was founded by Henry V in 1415 and originally occupied a site around two and a half kilometres downstream of the present site. It was a monastery of the Bridgettine order, founded in the fourteenth century in Sweden, and by Henry's reign it was counted as one of the most influential religious houses in the country, a home to both monks and nuns. In 2003 the TV series *Time Team* excavated the monastery's former site at Syon and discovered that the monastery's chapel had similar dimensions to Salisbury Cathedral (it is probable that Syon House is built over the foundations of the old monastery cloisters). The institution was not, however, spared the attentions of Thomas Cromwell's agents, who closed it in 1539, whereafter the buildings were used as a munitions factory during Henry's wars with France. However, the abbey church was not deconsecrated and it was chosen as the place where Henry's coffin would rest on its journey from Whitehall to Windsor – a role the building had also played when the coffin of Henry's maternal grandfather, Edward IV, had been borne on its journey from the Palace of Westminster to Windsor in 1483. The location is just slightly less than halfway between central London and Windsor – and although Whitehall Palace, Windsor Castle and Syon Abbey were all on the Thames, Henry's coffin was taken by road to his place of burial, rather than river.

The procession must have been an extraordinary sight to behold as it weaved its way through what was then the deep countryside of the county of Middlesex. Its participants gathered at Charing Cross, immediately north of Whitehall Palace, at 5am on Monday, 14 February 1547, just over two weeks after Henry's death; the eventual procession they formed stretched out for over six kilometres and included more than 1,000 horsemen as well as hundreds of people on foot, many carrying torches which must have flared brilliantly in the dim winter light. The coffin was borne on a chariot and covered with a pall of rich cloth of gold, with a funeral effigy of the dead king on top: a Spanish chronicler wrote that 'the figure looked exactly like that of the king himself and he seemed just as if he were alive'. The head of the effigy was crowned and bracelets set with pearls had been slipped onto the wrists; a sword was laid by its side, a sceptre had been placed in the right hand and an orb in the left. The chariot had a knight riding at each corner bearing banners depicting St Edward the Confessor, the Trinity, Our Lady and St George, in a conspicuous and deliberate display of the king's piety. Immediately behind the chariot were the members of the Choir of the Chapel Royal singing orations and prayers, followed by those bearing banners depicting the badge of Owen Tudor, the founder of Henry's royal house, and of the image of a greyhound, the emblem of the House of Lancaster, of which Henry's father was a scion. Also in the procession were lords, barons, viscounts, earls and bishops, and a bearded Thomas Cranmer – the Archbishop had grown it in fulfilment of a solemn vow made at Henry's death – along with Henry's household staff, down to and including those who worked in the poultry yard. Thus constituted, this extraordinary procession wended its way along the Great West Road (now the route of the A4) through the villages of Knightsbridge, Chelsea, Kensington, Fulham, Hammersmith, Chiswick and Brentford to Syon. In every village through which the cortège passed, priests came out of churches offering prayers and sprinkling holy water. (The route taken by the cortège of Queen Elizabeth II in September 2022 was similar: it started from Westminster Abbey, rather than Charing Cross, but went through Hammersmith and Chiswick and along the Great West Road through Brentford, passing just 700 metres to the north of Syon House.)

The cortège reached Syon Abbey at two in the afternoon. The chariot bearing the coffin was brought through lines of aldermen and nobles mounted on horseback, before coming to rest outside the west door of the double-aisled church. Inside it was placed within another hearse, while standards and banners were raised around it, the effigy was stored in the vestry, and an all-night watch was arranged for the night that was to come.

It was during the night that the notorious events associated with Henry's coffin supposedly unfolded. Apparently some putrid matter leaked from the coffin and dribbled onto the floor around it, to be licked up by some stray dogs that had wandered into the chapel under the cover of the winter darkness. This, apparently, was the fulfilment of a dark prophesy issued during a sermon delivered to Henry at Greenwich by a Franciscan friar named William Peyto back in 1534: 'dogs should lick his blood as they had done Ahab's,' the friar predicted. Some versions of the story maintain that the coffin's huge weight caused it to collapse from its trestle, fracturing the outer casing and cracking the lead shell within, causing fluids to leak out. A detailed account of the events that supposedly unfolded during that night was later written by the nineteenth century historian (and writer of historical fiction) Agnes Strickland. Quoting what she asserted was 'a contemporary document' (now lost, if indeed it ever existed), Strickland maintains that the leaden coffin was 'cleft by the shaking of the carriage … [resulting in] the pavement of the church [being] wetted with Henry's blood. In the morning came plumbers to solder the coffin, under whose feet was suddenly seen a dog creeping and licking up the king's blood'. What exactly happened will, of course, never be known, though it is possible that one of the soldered joints of the coffin sprung open, letting loose some fluids from the body inside that was by then in an advanced state of putrefaction. Whatever the case, the damage was fixed and the cortège resumed its slow progress between six and seven o'clock the next morning, heralded by three trumpet blasts piercing the gloomy pre-dawn winter darkness.

The Buildings of Richmond Palace

Richmond Palace must have been a veritable feast for the eyes. Its battlements and onion domes were reflected in the waters of the Thames and the whole ensemble was replete with fairytale turrets and gilded weather vanes. Henry VII's red-brick fantasy fortress rose from the south bank of the Thames around a kilometre and a half south of Syon House and was modelled on palaces that Henry had seen abroad, most particularly the ducal residence at Bruges. And it was very much Henry Tudor's palace: his son had close associations with the place before he became king and in the early years of his reign, but as he grew into middle age Henry VIII's palaces at Whitehall and Greenwich were more favoured than this distant outpost on the Thames, which was situated in what is now a very well-heeled suburb of Southwest London.

Henry Tudor's Richmond Palace was the fourth grand residence that stood here. The first was a manor house founded by the Belet family

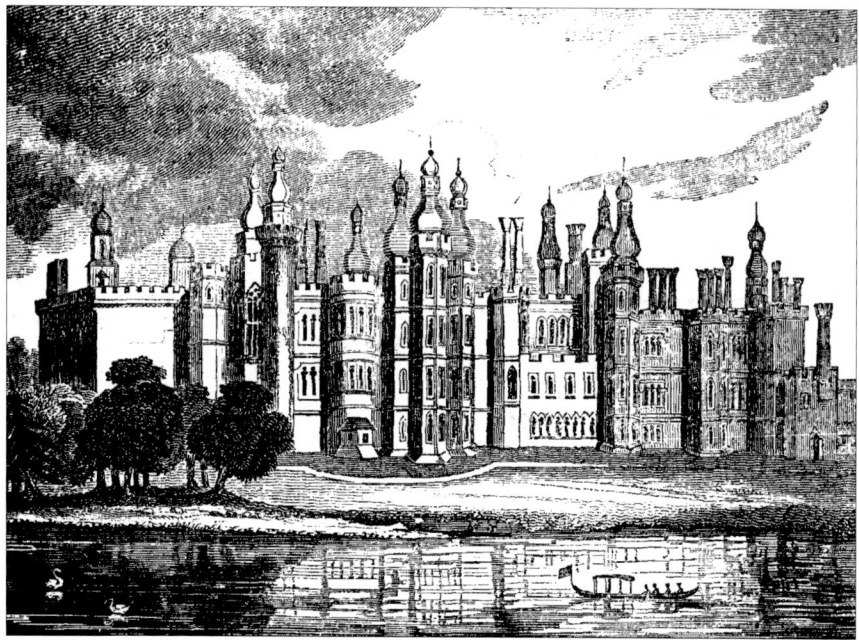

An 1836 drawing of what Richmond Palace might have looked like in Henry's time, from the periodical *The Mirror of Literature, Amusement, and Instruction*.

during the reign of Henry I; they were of Norman origin and the land for the property came to them from a king who was a son of William the Conqueror. The property was returned to the Crown in 1313 and Edward III transformed it into a royal palace, only for it to be pulled down by a griefstruck Richard II after the death of his wife, Anne of Bohemia, whose home this was. Between 1414 and the 1450s the fifth and sixth Henrys had a new palace built here, known as Sheen (or Shene). When it burned down in 1497, Henry VII took the opportunity to build a magnificent new residence in its place, which arose between 1499 and 1503 and which was named Richmond Palace after the earldom that he held before his accession. That earldom was seated at Richmond Castle in Yorkshire, which nowadays gives its name to the district of London around the former site of the palace.

Richmond Palace was based around a series of red-brick courtyards which, as with Greenwich, Westminster, Bridewell and Whitehall palaces, fronted the river, where there was a landing stage for the royal barge. In the donjon housing the royal lodgings there were beamed ceilings painted azure and studded with gold Tudor roses. Rich tapestries, panel

The River Thames at Richmond – this is where the palace's landing stage for the royal barge would have been located.

portraits and murals by, among others, Maynard the Fleming, hung everywhere; there was also a chapel and a library. The gardens were equally magnificent and were replete with fountains, orchards and statues of the King's Beasts, and intersected by timber-framed, two-storeyed gallery walks and broad paths. Beyond the gardens was a deer park. A high brick wall surrounded the complex with a tower at each corner, punctured by a gatehouse depicting the red dragon of Wales and the greyhound of Richmond, Henry's emblem. According to an account held in the College of Arms it was 'an earthly paradise, most glorious to behold'. In her novel *The Autobiography of Henry VIII* Margaret George describes Henry looking out from the palace in winter 'over the magnificent views of the frozen Thames ... People were sporting on its surface. There were young lads with bones stuck to their shoes, sliding about, playing all sorts of games [while others were] swatting stones back and forth with sticks'.

Today the gatehouse, dating from 1501 (with an upper storey added in the 1590s) is the most substantial part of the palace that remains. It fronts Richmond Green, which in Henry VIII's time was the arena for jousting, and

Henry VIII: A History of his Most Important Places and Events

Left: The former gatehouse to Richmond Palace.

Below: Richmond Green was the Palace's former jousting arena.

Chelsea and Richmond

The coat of arms of Henry VII above the former gatehouse to Richmond Palace.

which is now an elegant open space surrounded by handsome eighteenth-century town houses; the arms of Henry VII above the gate were restored in 1976. Passing through the gateway from Richmond Green brings one to Old Palace Yard, an irregularly shaped square that roughly corresponds to the outline of the Great Court of the palace and which is overlooked by a range of buildings from different eras, the oldest of which is known as the Wardrobe, where the palace's soft furnishings were stored; some Tudor elements remain in this building, though it mostly dates from the eighteenth century, as do the other buildings around the square. The site of the Chapel and the Great Hall is marked by the eighteenth-century Trumpeter's House, while the pathway linking the Old Palace Yard with Old Palace Lane preserves the former route of the entrance to the palace from the river for servants and deliverymen; at the lane's entrance are two smart, whitewashed bollards with the emblem 'EIIR' – a reminder that this area remains part of the crown estate. However, aside from the Gatehouse and parts of the Wardrobe, all the rest of the palace has gone, destroyed during Oliver Cromwell's Commonwealth, and the best 'view' of it now is via a superb model on display in the Museum of Richmond.

Henry VIII: A History of his Most Important Places and Events

Left: These bollards are a reminder that the site of Richmond Palace is still part of the crown estate.

Below: The model of Richmond Palace in Richmond Museum. (*Daniel Newman at English Wikipedia, courtesy of the Richmond Museum*)

To the northwest of the palace site is an expanse of green known as the Old Deer Park, which stretches as far as Kew Gardens, but it was created in James I's time, when the Tudors were gone - and less than a kilometre and a half to the southeast, Richmond Park, one of the great open spaces of outer London, traces its origins back to the deer park established on the high ground above the palace, but again it isn't Tudor: it was created by Charles I when he moved his court here to escape from the plague, and famously deer still graze amidst its trees today.

Henry at Richmond Palace Before His Accession

One of the most noteworthy events that took place at Richmond during Henry's boyhood occurred on Friday, 26 November 1501, when he was five months past his tenth birthday. Following the celebration of the wedding of Henry's older brother Arthur and Catherine of Aragon, which as we have seen took place at St Paul's and in which Henry had a distinct role to play, sixty barges brought members of the court upstream to Richmond in a fabulous water-borne procession. Henry, as Duke of York, had his own barge, in which his servants rode, although Henry himself rode in the royal barge with his father. The lavish celebrations that then took place at Richmond were the last time Henry or his father ever saw Arthur: when the feasting was over the heir to the throne and his new wife travelled to Woodstock Palace near Oxford, where they spent Christmas, and then Ludlow Castle in Shropshire, where Arthur died just a few months later.

Five years later, in July 1506, an alarming incident occurred at Richmond when Henry, now Prince of Wales and heir to the throne, was taking a late evening summer stroll with his father in one of the palace's newly built galleries. Just an hour later, at midnight, the gallery in which they had been walking 'fell suddenly ... the master carpenter that framed it was punished by imprisonment many days after', according to *The Great Chronicle*. Although no one was hurt, it had been a lucky escape; it's difficult to know how events might have turned out had both the king and his 14-year-old heir been killed when the gallery collapsed. By this time Henry had outgrown Eltham Palace, where he had spent his boyhood, and was spending more and more time at Richmond. In July 1508, his father had watched him joust here. The chronicler Bernard André wrote that 'very many men fought with him but he was superior to all of them', though this is probably hyperbole; at this age Henry was probably limited to running at the ring (that is, trying to catch a suspended metal ring on the end of a lance) rather than actual jousting against an opponent.

It appears that during the last year of his life Henry VII kept his son and heir under very strict supervision at Richmond. Prince Henry, then aged 17, was given no royal responsibilities, and nor was he given much training in the art of kingship, apart from lessons in history from the king; he could only leave the palace by a special private door, and even then, only in the company of specially appointed persons. The king had lost his three other sons so was concerned for Henry, in whose hands the survival of the Tudor dynasty depended; however, it seems that the king also felt threatened by his energetic and handsome son, towards whom he showed no affection – though when he died, on 21 April 1509, his son was nevertheless at his side. The words that passed between father and son during that evening are a matter of both controversy and great importance. Two members of the Royal Council later informed the Spanish ambassador that on his deathbed the king had assured his son that he was free to marry whom he chose; however, Henry informed Margaret of Savoy that he had been charged by his father 'to fulfil the old treaty with Ferdinand and Isabella of Spain by taking their daughter Catherine [of Aragon] in marriage' – so it's difficult to know whom to believe. It was against this fraught atmosphere that Henry was proclaimed King, at Richmond; he rode from there to the Tower of London to take up residence prior to his Coronation.

Henry at Richmond Palace During His Reign

For the first few years of his reign Henry often enjoyed living amidst the fantastical splendour and opulence of his father's creation beside the Thames. He spent his first Christmas as king here, watching jousts on what is now Richmond Green, and on Christmas Day he heard Mass and took communion in the palace's chapel. Later that day Will Wynesbury presented some plays in the Great Hall. Little is known of Wynesbury, aside from the fact that he was appointed as 'Lord of Misrule', that is, master of the festivities and entertainments for the Christmas period, which in Tudor times was a twelve-day festival of pageantry, merrymaking and feasting stretching from Christmas Day to the Feast of the Epiphany

(Twelfth Night) on 6 January. On New Year's Day 1510, in a glittering ceremony in the Presence Chamber of the palace, Henry gave and received gifts, which were displayed on sideboards or trestle tables for all to see.

It was now that Henry, still only 18, seemed to come of age both as a young man and as a Renaissance Prince – and the arena where he was able to emerge from the dark shadow cast by his father's dour rule was for now Richmond Palace, rather than Greenwich or Westminster. It might well have been that in the early years of Henry's reign it was Richmond that was the most opulent of his palaces: after all, its comprehensive rebuild had been completed just six years before he came to the throne. On 12 January 1510 he jousted here with his courtier William Compton, who had previously served the young Henry as a page and was his first Groom of the Stool when Henry became king. Henry jousted as a 'stranger knight' with his visor pulled down, so that no one would know his true identity. It was a furious contest that left Compton, after a joust with another courtier, Edward Neville, badly injured. Henry took that as his cue to leave the field. But as he rode away someone in the crowd cried 'God Save the King' and he had no choice but to raise his visor, revealing who he was. Compton recovered (and went on to become one of Henry's most trusted administrators and courtiers) and Henry went on to enjoy an illustrious career in the lists, though to assuage the fears of his Council, he used hollow lances to reduce the risk of serious injury. In the same month Henry demonstrated his exuberance when early one morning he and eleven companions disguised themselves as Robin Hood and his outlaws, donning short coats of green Kentish Kendal, with hoods that concealed their faces. Then, 'armed' with bows and arrows and swords and bucklers, they burst into the queen's chamber, where Catherine and her ladies – according to the chronicler Edward Hall – were much 'abashed' but agreed to dance with the visitors. Only when the dancing was finished did the king and his friends throw back their hoods and reveal who they were – to the apparent 'astonishment' of the ladies (though one suspects they might already have had an inkling of who the interlopers were).

In April 1515, it was to Richmond that Henry brought the Venetian ambassador, Sebastian Giustinian, and his entourage – in a barge fashioned like the Venetian Bucentaur (the Doge's State Barge). Giustinian left behind a remarkable account of his visit, which serves as a window into Henry's world when he was still in his early twenties. Once they had disembarked their barge, Giustinian and his party were conducted to [Henry's] presence chamber through sundry chambers all hung with the most beautiful tapestries ... we were ushered into a stately hall. At one extremity was his majesty, standing under a canopy of gold embroidered at Florence, the most costly thing I witnessed. He was leaning against his gilt throne, on which was a large gold brocade cushion, where lay the long gold sword of state.

Giustinian then describes Henry's cap of crimson velvet, his scarlet hose, a diamond 'the size of the largest walnut I ever saw' on a necklace around his neck, his cloak lined with purple velvet and white satin, and his fingers which were 'one mass of jewelled rings'. In apparent awe of all this majesty Giustinian 'delivered a Latin oration in praise of his majesty, whom we extolled with all the eloquence we could command'. This was followed by a feast, after which the party 'remained a good while with his majesty, very familiarly'. Henry was, apparently, a genial and generous host, who 'embraced us without ceremony, and conversed for a long while familiarly on various topics in good Latin and French'.

The Birth and Death of Prince Henry, Duke of Cornwall

In October 1510, it was at Richmond that Henry and Catherine took up residence in readiness for Catherine to give birth. The following month the formal preparations for the christening got under way and the Prior of Canterbury was put on notice to set up the baptismal font – the same one that had been used in Henry's own baptism. Margaret Beaufort had laid down the strict ordinances to be observed for the birth, and these were to be followed by Catherine. 'Her Highness's pleasure being understood in what chamber she will be delivered in, the same must be hanged with rich cloth of Arras, sides, roof, windows and all, except one window, which must be hanged so as she may have light when it pleaseth her,' Lady Margaret had ordained. The tapestries chosen deliberately depicted scenes from medieval romances; in this way neither the Queen nor her newborn infant would be 'affrighted by figures which gloomily stare'. The floors were laid with carpets and the curtains hung were of crimson satin embroidered with golden crowns and the Queen's coats of arms. The chamber also had an altar and a cupboard, covered with a tapestry, which contained the equipment that would be used by the midwives. It was to this chamber that Catherine was confined, awaiting the birth in seclusion; the day was marked by her hearing Mass and then hosting a banquet, after which she was escorted by two high-ranking lords to the door of her lodgings. Her chamberlain desired that all her people were to pray that 'God would send her a good hour'. The intention was that she would not be seen in public until after her birth, and that until then no man would be allowed into the chamber, not even the king.

On New Year's Eve Catherine went into labour, on a 'fair pallet bed' placed beside the great bed in her bedchamber; her son was born at half past one the following morning. This was the best New Year present Henry could wish for: the boy was healthy and the court and London went wild at the news, with free wine offered to rejoicing Londoners, cannons firing and celebratory bonfires illuminating the dark midwinter nights. The boy was named Henry and the infant must have looked very tiny in the vast painted cradle, trimmed with silver gilt with buckles fringed with gold and a scarlet counterpane furred with ermine; when visitors came, he was placed in an even bigger cradle of estate, upholstered in crimson and decorated with gold fringing, with his father's coat of arms above his head. On 5 January the boy was christened: a processional way twenty-four feet wide was created, hung with rich arras, leading to the Church of the Observant Friars next door to the palace. The ceremony was conducted 'with very great pomp and rejoicing' according to the *Venetian Calendar of State Papers*. Archbishop Warham was among the godfathers while the king of France and the Habsburg Archduchess Margaret of Austria (the daughter of Emperor Maximilian I) were cited as 'sponsors'. It was a predictably grand affair, with the ambassadors of France, Spain, Venice and the Papacy in attendance.

Devastatingly for Henry and Catherine the little prince died on 23 February at the age of 7 weeks. The infant was still at Richmond (where it was thought the air was healthier than at Greenwich or Westminster), though his parents had by then returned to the Palace of Westminster, where they received the news. The tiny coffin was conveyed to London on an elaborate hearse surrounded by wax candles, and was buried late at night at a torchlit ceremony in Westminster Abbey.

Chapter 7

Hampton Court

It was physicians who decided on the site of Hampton Court Palace. The site they chose lay on the north bank of the Thames around six and a half kilometres south of Richmond, and their decision came as a response to a request from Thomas Wolsey. The meteoric rise of this remarkable figure, from humble origins to one of the key political players in Henry's England, is comparable in some ways to that of Thomas Cromwell. His service began during Henry VII's time, when he was appointed a royal chaplain. Following Henry VIII's accession he was appointed almoner, but within the space of just five years Wolsey's administrative skill and graft (along with Henry's preference for jousting and hunting rather than poring over the details of administration) meant that he had become a key figure in the apparatus of the state – and this brought him vast rewards in terms of wealth and titles. In 1515, already Bishop of Lincoln and Archbishop of York, Wolsey was appointed Lord Chancellor by Henry, and a Cardinal by the Pope. It was in this year that the request came to his physicians as to where a new palace should be sited, based on the healthiness of the air – though another stipulation was that it must lie within a thirty-two-kilometre radius of London.

Their advice led Wolsey to purchase a lease of some land at Hampton that was owned by the Knights Hospitallers of the Order of St John of Jerusalem. Here a courtyard house built by Giles, Lord Daubeney, Lord Chamberlain to Henry VII, had already stood since 1479. Traces of the foundations of this manor house were uncovered during excavations in the 1970s, and their position is now marked out by lines of red paving slabs that twist across the uneven floor of the palace's Clock Court, in the shadow of a colonnade designed by Sir Christopher Wren; today the bell in the campanile overlooking Clock Court and Base Court is

Hampton Court

Above and below: Red paving slabs in Hampton Court's Clock Court mark out the position of the original house that stood here.

the only tangible surviving remnant of Daubeney's original house; for Wolsey demolished this building and, in its place, arose a grand, red-brick palace that nonetheless retained the original name given to it by Sir Giles Daubeney – Hampton Court. In 1525, Wolsey agreed to share the house with Henry, agreeing that it should fall to the Crown on Wolsey's death; the same agreement was made over Richmond Palace, which Wolsey then adopted as his principal residence while Henry set about developing Hampton Court as a royal palace (a pattern already established by Henry with his makeovers of Whitehall and Bridewell Palaces, which had also originally been Wolsey's).

Although Hampton Court is the building that seems most inalienably associated with Henry, it was not built by him and it was modified considerably by later owners (in fact much of Henry's palace, including the state rooms and private apartments, was lost during later renovations carried out by Sir Christopher Wren). Today it is situated in one of London's wealthiest outer suburbs, half way between Chelsea and Windsor, historically in the county of Middlesex but nowadays in the Borough of Richmond upon Thames – which on maps appears

Hampton Court today, viewed from the bridge over the Thames.

to consist as much of green open spaces as it does of the streets and houses of suburbia. The setting must have been idyllic in the sixteenth century, and some of that is still tangible today, with the lush greenery surrounding the river and pleasure craft plying the water in the shadow of shady riverside walks and pub gardens. The palace is now one of London's top tourist attractions and is the westward limit of the tourist boats that depart from Westminster Pier in Central London. These take three hours to complete the journey, stopping off at Chelsea, Kew and Richmond along the way; perhaps the journey by river between Henry's great palaces of Whitehall and Hampton Court took the same amount of time, in his day.

Thomas Wolsey at Hampton Court

Wolsey's palatial new home reflected his bloated sense of self-importance and, above all, his fabulous wealth. Hampton Court was a grand, red-brick, double-courtyard house with mullioned windows, spiky turrets, tall chimneys, a moat, gardens, a large service complex including kitchens and laundries, and an advanced system of conduits and sewers. Among its most distinctive decorative flourishes were the medallions of Roman emperors, carved in 1521 by the Florentine sculptor Giovanni di Maiano, which adorned the walls (they were based on those commissioned by the Cardinal of Amboise for his palace at Gaillon near Rouen, and many are still in situ today). Wolsey invited Henry to admire the palace for the first time in 1517, when it was only partly built; he ensured that the king and Catherine of Aragon were entertained in predictably lavish style. The following year,

One of the Roman Emperor medallions adorning the walls at Hampton Court.

in October, Henry brought some French envoys here. They were in England for the signing of the Treaty of London and were treated to a magnificent banquet, to ensure that they 'would make a glorious report in their country, to the king's honour and that of his realm'. The Cardinal's cooks worked day and night and the envoys were indeed 'rapt into a heavenly paradise' according to the 1557 biography of Wolsey by George Cavendish, his gentlemen-usher.

The palace was eventually completed in 1525, by which time it was rumoured to contain a thousand rooms. The chronicler Polydore Vergil wrote that Wolsey 'lived [here] like a glorious peacock', attended by hundreds of servants, and whenever he went forth in procession, he was 'raised up like some holy idol or other'. Wolsey did not, however, take his power and wealth for granted. He put himself through a punishing schedule and was at his desk at four every morning, often working through twelve-hour days. But there was one problem – the annulment of Henry's marriage – that Wolsey, with his close ties to the Pope, could not solve, and which eventually proved his undoing. In 1529, he was stripped of his position and property (including Hampton Court) after Anne Boleyn's faction at court managed to persuade Henry that Wolsey's involvement in the annulment arrangements was actually slowing things down. The following year Wolsey travelled north, to his Archbishopric in York. However, he was ordered to return to London to face a charge of treason, and died on the journey, at Leicester, leaving the way open for his adviser Thomas Cromwell to assume some of his power and authority.

Henry at Hampton Court

It was ironic that it was at Hampton Court, in November 1530, that Henry was informed by George Cavendish of the Cardinal's death. The story goes that Henry was at the archery butts and, seeing Cavendish leaning against a tree looking pensive, he clapped a hand on his shoulder and told him, 'I will make an end of my game, then I will talk with you.' Cavendish was later summoned to the king's privy lodgings where he spent 'an hour examining me on diverse weighty matters concerning my lord [Wolsey]'.

Hampton Court

From this time onwards Hampton Court vied with Whitehall as Henry's favoured royal palace – and it has particular associations with his wife Jane Seymour and their son, who grew up to be Henry's successor, King Edward VI. The palace also features prominently in the married lives of two of Henry's later wives, namely Catherine Howard and Catherine Parr.

Jane was brought here by barge to ecstatic acclaim on 20 May 1536, the day after the execution of Anne Boleyn. She and Henry were formally betrothed here (though they married at Whitehall) and Prince Edward was also born here. Henry and Jane did not attend Edward's baptism, in the palace chapel, but after the ceremony they received the infant in the Queen's apartments, where Henry sat beside Jane who was propped up with crimson cushions on a rich pallet bed. Henry took the young prince in his arms and invoked the names of the Virgin Mary and St George as he wept unashamedly with joy as here, at long last, was a male heir to inherit the Tudor throne. The celebrations went on until dawn and 'largesse' (in the form of coins) was distributed to those who had waited outside the palace gates in the cold October night. Although Edward survived, his mother died at Hampton Court twelve days after his birth with the king by her side. The cause of her death has been much speculated upon but it seems that she probably died of an infection contracted during labour.

Famously Catherine Howard's experiences of Hampton Court were rather different. She was 'shown off' here as Henry's new queen during a spectacular banquet on 8 August 1540, before Henry made his one and only journey to the north of England. He took his new wife with him, and it was on this 'progress' that Catherine's unwise dalliances with a courtier, Thomas Culpeper, probably took place. On 1 November of the following year Henry was informed of his wife's adulterous liaisons by Thomas Cranmer, by means of a sealed letter that Cranmer either gave him personally at Hampton Court, or left for him on his pew in the palace chapel (sources vary). The contents of the letter were explosive. Cranmer explained how he had learned of Catherine's adultery from a minor courtier named John Lassels, who in turn had received the information from his sister Mary, who (it seems) was seeking revenge after she had been overlooked for promotion in the Queen's household (though again sources differ here: some maintain that Mary Lassels was unwilling to take up a position in Catherine's household because of her knowledge of the queen's adultery).

The exact nature of Catherine's adultery revealed in the letter concerned her unchaste life before her marriage to Henry, during which time she was said to have 'lived most corruptly and sensuously'. Among her former lovers were Henry Monox, a lute player who had taught her the virginals at her grandmother's home and who had seduced her when she was 15, and Francis Dereham, who was later appointed her private secretary and the usher of her chamber. Regarding the first alleged dalliance, Agnes Dowager Duchess of Norfolk had administered 'two or three blows' to Catherine and told her to behave herself. Henry, shocked and only half-believing the allegations, asked the Lord Privy Seal, Thomas Wriothesley, to investigate, while Catherine was placed under arrest at Hampton Court. A legend tells how she briefly escaped her guards and ran through the passageway that is now known as the Haunted Gallery to plead her innocence with Henry. (This is an upper-floor passageway, now lined with paintings, that links the Great Hall and the chapel; in Henry's day it was part of the 'processional way' that he walked before services, and Catherine's ghost can apparently be seen running through the Gallery to this day.) Just over a week later, on 10 November, Henry was informed of her adultery with Culpeper, an even more explosive allegation as it apparently took place during their marriage. In disgust at his wife's behaviour, he left Hampton Court and rode to Whitehall. Four days later Catherine was taken under guard from Hampton Court to Syon Abbey, which by then had lost its religious community. Dereham and Culpeper were executed in December. Catherine would have seen their heads on spikes overlooking London Bridge when she was taken by barge from Syon to the Tower on 10 February. She was beheaded three days later.

Henry's last wife was Catherine Parr, whom he married at Hampton Court on 12 July 1543, just over sixteen months after the execution of Catherine Howard. The wedding was not a grand affair, and was celebrated in the queen's holy day closet in the palace (adjacent to the chapel) with twenty guests present, including the king's children Edward, Elizabeth and Mary, and also Lady Margaret Douglas, Henry's niece, who carried the train of Catherine's wedding dress. Catherine, of course, was to outlive Henry, though her supposedly radical religious beliefs meant she was to play a key role in the factional in-fighting between religious radicals and conservatives that characterized the 1540s, and at one point she herself came close to being arrested.

One of the most extraordinary dramas in these factional disputes played out at Hampton Court, though, did not directly involve Catherine. In August 1546, an ailing Henry arranged for his 8-year-old son Prince

Edward to deputize for him during the welcoming of Claud d'Annebault, the Lord High Admiral of France, who was in London to ratify a new peace treaty. Edward and his entourage rode to the river bank at Hounslow to meet the French delegation as they sailed up the river from London. Later Henry accompanied d'Annebault to hear High Mass in the palace chapel and then to an open-air reception, held in one of the marquees erected in the palace gardens. Henry was observed to be ailing visibly, at one point leaning heavily on the Admiral for support. John Foxe later reported that during this event Henry shocked the Admiral by telling him that Mass in both England and France should be abolished in favour of the Protestant Holy Communion. Was this wishful thinking on the part of Foxe, a protestant radical – or was Henry merely being provocative? Or was he engaged in something much more profound – an embracing of the Protestantism that was to be imposed on England during the reign of his young son, which then was only six months away? The conversation has caused debate and controversy ever since, and has been seen as being indicative of the influence of the reformist faction then in the ascendancy in Henry's council.

The Private and State Rooms at Hampton Court

In Henry's day the entrance to Hampton Court Palace took the form of an imposing five-storey gatehouse with a large oriel window and octagonal towers at each corner, each one of which was surmounted by a lead cupola. (This building was partially demolished in the early 1770s, for fear it would collapse, and rebuilt on a smaller scale with three storeys; the lead cupolas were never replaced, and the whole ensemble was refaced with new red bricks in 1882. However, it still makes for an imposing entrance to the palace for today's visitors.) The wing of the palace on the left as one faces the gatehouse housed the Counting House, where the Board of the Greencloth, the chief governing body of the Royal Household, used to meet – and whose windows allowed for a good view over the comings and goings through the gate. Beyond the gate is Base Court, which is much the same now as it was in the days of Wolsey and Henry, despite some Victorian alterations. It is linked to Clock Court, the second courtyard, by a gate known since Victorian times as Anne Boleyn's Gate the ceiling mouldings, featuring the entwined letters H and A, date from restoration work carried out then and

Henry VIII: A History of his Most Important Places and Events

The entrance to Hampton Court.

Hampton Court's main gatehouse, viewed from Base Court.

Hampton Court

Right: Anne Boleyn's Gate at Hampton Court.

Below: Anne Boleyn's Gate at Hampton Court, with the windows of the Great Hall to the left.

were installed in recognition of the fact that the rooms above were part of Anne's lodgings. (One of the original, sixteenth-century mouldings from the ceiling can be seen in the Great Hall, which is accessed by stairs from the gateway; around the size of a dinner plate, it shows Anne's emblem, a crowned falcon, carved in stone.) The rooms above the gateway were still being furnished at the time of Anne's arrest, and were later adapted for Jane Seymour (they are not accessible to the public).

When Henry inherited the palace, his lodgings were in a three-storey donjon known as the Bayne Tower that Wolsey had built specifically for his visits. This was the last royal lodgings of its type to be built in England, and it survives to this day, in Clock Court – in fact it is the only one of Henry's royal lodgings to have survived intact (although it was partly resurfaced in the nineteenth century, when the windows were replaced with Tudor-style replicas). It's not a free-standing tower as such,

The Bayne Tower, the original royal lodgings built for Henry at Hampton Court.

but a boxy protuberance that juts out a little from the Court's eastern range. In Henry's day the ground floor housed the privy chamber office and a strong room, while occupying the middle storey were the king's private bedchamber and a bathroom (hence 'bayne' from the French word '*bain*') with hot and cold running water. On the top floor were a library and a jewel house. The lodgings were in use until the 1530s when they were abandoned for a new set of rooms, most of which have since been demolished. (The tower is not open to the public, though the ground floor has in the past been used as a café.)

Henry's new lodgings, completed in 1538, were arranged around what is now Fountain Court, the third of the palace's three principal courtyards, whose current appearance dates from its complete rebuilding in Baroque style by Sir Christopher Wren between 1689 and 1694. Only one room survives from this rebuild – the Great Watching Chamber, which is accessed through a door from the Great Hall. This grand room was adapted from the Great Hall of Wolsey's original palace and was the first of the outer chambers of the king's apartments. Its name derives from the fact that the Yeomen of the Guard stood 'watch' here, controlling access to the private rooms of the palace beyond, though the room was also used for feasting after dancing or similar events in the Great Hall. Henry had an oriel window added (now furnished with stained glass, and making the room asymmetrical), and added a ceiling ornamented with a geometric lattice of gilded battens, drop pendants and leather-maché roundels bearing his badges and those of Jane Seymour – the latter taking the form of a phoenix rising from a flaming tower. A few of these roundels can still be seen on the room's ceiling, though most are nineteenth-century replacements. The room itself was much restored in Stuart times (the wood panelling is from the time of William III) and today is hung with tapestries from Henry's time, some of which were once hung in the lodgings demolished by Wren.

These rooms, situated just beyond the Great Watching Chamber, were, of course, luxuriously appointed. Several craftsmen contributed to their extravagant decoration. Antonio Toto, a Florentine artist who was later appointed Serjeant Painter to Henry, painted religious pictures and decorative panels and shields, while the London craftsman Henry Blankston ensured that all the walls shone with gold and silver. The king's presence chamber was known to be one of the wonders of the palace – and remained so for many years after his death. 'Here, everything glitters so with silver, gold and jewels as to dazzle one's eyes,' was how the German lawyer Paul Hentzner described it when he was in London in the service of Queen Elizabeth I. Persian tapestries hung on the walls while beautiful painted ceilings and a cloth-of-gold canopy of estate hung over the throne, which was positioned on a dais. Throughout these rooms the ceilings were moulded, the walls panelled and numerous tapestries were hung, including *The Triumph of Fame Over Death*, based on a work by Petrarch, which hangs in the Great Watching Chamber to this day. This had been one of Wolsey's tapestries but Henry commissioned many of his own – indeed he owned around 2,000 in total, of which around 400 had been inherited from his father. Each one took a team of skilled weavers three years to complete, and twenty-eight are displayed today at Hampton Court.

The last room in the private apartments was the bedchamber. According to the Inventory of the Goods of Henry VIII, compiled after the king's death, Henry's bed was eight foot long and had a ceiler (a canopy that hung from a wooden tester) of cloth of gold and silver, edged with silk fringes and purple velvet ribbon; the bedchamber's curtains were of purple and white taffeta bordered with gold ribbon. In the garderobe beside the bed chamber was a stool chamber (toilet) with pictures and bookshelves and a 'close stool', a pewter chamber pot set in an elaborate boxed seat that, when closed, was covered in green velvet and silk and embroidered with the king's arms and badges (by 1547 there were five such installations at Hampton Court).

The Chapel and the Great Hall

One of Henry's most important improvements at Hampton Court was the conversion, in the 1530s, of Wolsey's old chapel into a lavish masterpiece of English perpendicular style. Richard Ridge, a carver of some skill of whom little is known, created a magnificent vaulted ceiling of oak that was painted dark blue with gold stars, with the king's motto 'Dieu et mon droit' adorning the arches. Also added by Henry were stained-glass windows from Nuremberg, ornately carved choir stalls and benches, a black-and-white-chequered floor and an organ. Pews for the king and queen were set in a gallery overlooking the main body of the chapel, accessed today via rooms known as the king's and queen's holy day closets (the latter room, also known as the Lady Chapel, was the venue for the marriage ceremony between Henry and Catherine Parr). The other feature that remains from Henry's time is the glorious ceiling; the rest of the chapel was remodelled by Sir Christopher Wren, after much of the stained glass was destroyed during the Commonwealth, and the current appearance of the building dates largely from further restoration in the late nineteenth century.

The other part of the palace that is a distinct legacy of Henry is the magnificent Great Hall, work on which commenced in 1532 and took three years. It was the only Great Hall that Henry ever commissioned – all his other palaces had one already, or he chose not to build one – and it is the last such structure built in England (one of the first being of course Westminster Hall). Built like the chapel in perpendicular style, the room is 106 feet long, 40 feet wide and 60 feet high, and is surmounted by octagonal turrets bearing statues of the King's Beasts and gilded weather vanes. It's at first-floor level, with cellars below, and is reached by a processional stairway that leads up from Anne Boleyn's gateway. The most striking feature inside is the hammerbeam roof designed by the Henry's master carpenter and Clerk of Works James Needham, which incorporates elaborate drop pendants carved (once again) by Richard Ridge. He incorporated the conjoined letters H and A (for Henry and Anne) into the design of the ceiling, and some of these designs can still be seen – though in some instances the letter A was later replaced with a J for Jane Seymour, whom Henry married just after the Hall was completed. In those days the room was hung with tapestries, some of which are still there today, including one that depicts the story of Abraham, which was woven in Brussels from silk and silver-gilt thread and is thought to have been based on paintings or designs by the Flemish master Bernard von Orley. The Hall was restored in 1770 and again in the 1840s, when new stained-glass windows depicting the royal descents of Henry VIII and his wives and children were installed in place of the long-vanished Tudor glass. Today it is one of the most gloomily atmospheric interior spaces in the whole palace.

The Kitchens and Bathrooms

In Henry's day the Hampton Court kitchens, which occupied a third of the palace's ground floor space, were a vast, hot, smoky, noisy hive of activity that daily prepared food for the hundreds of people who worked in the palace – and when the court descended, they were even busier. Working in the kitchens was a sweaty and dirty job, and at one point Henry had to issue an edict that ordered the scullions to stop going about 'naked, or in garments of such vileness as they do now, nor lie in the nights and days in the kitchen or ground by the fireside'. The kitchens were last used in the eighteenth century and underwent an imaginative period of restoration between 1978 and 1991. Today they form the best surviving example of sixteenth-century service quarters anywhere in England.

The Great Kitchen comprised the 'Hall Place' kitchen, which prepared food for the household, and the 'Lord's Side' kitchen, which supplied finer dishes for household officers and courtiers. The larders were at one end and comprised a flesh larder for raw game from the royal parks such as venison, which hung for up to six weeks before it was eaten, and a dry larder, for general provisions; at the other end of the kitchens finished dishes were brought to the stone hatches, where they were checked by the Clerk of the Kitchen and garnished for the table, before being passed to the servitors queuing in the 'great space' beyond. Today only a small part of the Great Kitchen is accessible to the public. It is accessed via an atmospheric narrow lane within the palace known as Fish Court, which is aligned east–west so the sun never shines directly on the north-facing

Fish Court – the heart of Hampton Court's kitchens.

side and anything stored there remained cool. The most remarkable parts of the kitchen are the enormous ovens, which may date back to Sir Giles Daubeney's original house; the actual building housing them retains its sixteenth-century shell, though it has been much modified over the centuries (and was converted into a house at one point). Close to the Great Kitchen is the Boiling House, the only one of Henry's subsidiary kitchens to survive. Other subsidiary kitchens would have included a bakehouse, a spicery, a wafery, a confectionary, where sweet dishes were prepared, such as quince marmalade and gingerbread, a scalding house, where plucked carcasses of pheasants were plunged into huge vats of boiling water, and a poultry house for preparing poultry, lamb and mutton. Also long-vanished are the separate king's and queen's privy kitchens, which served the choicest food of all. The former were situated directly below Henry's apartments and were connected with them by a spiral staircase, so the meals always arrived hot; there were similar arrangements on the queen's side. The king's meals were taken with formality – Henry would arrive with his Lord Chamberlain to the sound of trumpets, and would eat alone at a table set up under his canopy of estate, served by his gentlemen and grooms.

Hampton Court also had a sophisticated system of pipes and drains, ensuring a fresh water supply and efficient disposal of waste. In the Tudor era such a supply system was not as new-fangled as might be imagined: water was first piped into royal palaces in 1234, when conduits were built at the Palace of Westminster, and Richard II had running water in his bathroom at Sheen, but the system of pipes and drains at Hampton Court was on a much grander scale and remained in use until 1871. The system was instigated by Wolsey and further extended by Henry; the water was piped from natural springs at Coombe Hill, some four kilometres east of Hampton Court on the other side of the river, through conduits running under the Thames. (The conduit houses still stand, and can be seen today on Coombe Lane West, the main road linking Kingston upon Thames and Wimbledon – though they are situated behind high fences, and unless you are there on one of the occasions when they are opened by members of the Kingston upon Thames Society it's not actually possible to see anything.) Waste water was simply flushed into the river through a conduit that led from the kitchens and under the moat, and which still survives. In the palace many offices and lodgings were supplied with a cold-water tap, while the king and queen had water piped into their

Coombe Conduit controlled the water supply to Hampton Court. (*Andy Scott, Wikimedia Commons*)

bathrooms, with hot water heated by a stove. In the 1530s, in a separate wing beside the gatehouse, Henry built a giant toilet block known as the Great House of Easement, a two-storey communal lavatory with fourteen seats on each floor, whose waste water emptied into palace's main drain (bypassing the moat over which the building projected), and was flushed away into the river. There were no separate stalls and no dividing walls, in common with other public toilets in England at the time; the building was remodelled in the nineteenth century and converted into apartments for palace staff.

The Gardens and Exterior of the Palace

Henry's rebuilding works in the grounds of Hampton Court Palace were as extensive as his renovation and extension of the buildings themselves. In 1536 he replaced Wolsey's original wooden bridge over the moat beside the main gatehouse with a new stone one, which visitors use today to enter the palace. (In the 1690s, when the moat was filled in, this bridge was submerged in rubble. The moat was excavated in 1909 and the bridge now forms a picturesque ensemble with the gateway – though its adornments, such as the pole-mounted statues of the 'King's Beasts', are all reconstructions.) Henry also built a new gate down by the river, which was accessed by a covered and crenellated gallery with oriel windows (all long gone).

One of Henry's most innovative and distinctive additions to the exterior of the buildings that still remains is an astronomical clock, installed on the east face of the Anne Boleyn gate, overlooking Clock Court. It was designed in 1540 by the Munich-born mathematician and horologist Nicolaus Kratzer who, with Holbein, was a member of Thomas More's circle of European intellectuals, and who became Henry's court astronomer; the builder was the Huguenot clockmaker Nicolas Oursian, who built several timepieces and sundials in England in the early sixteenth century. The clock face shows the hour and month and the number of days since the beginning of the year, in addition to the phases of the moon, movement of the constellations of the zodiac, and the time of high water

The Astronomical Clock on the wall of the Anne Boleyn's Gate at Hampton Court.

at London Bridge, which was vital information in the days of barge travel to Westminster and Greenwich. The sun is depicted as going around the earth, in keeping with the pre-Copernican world view of the time (Copernicus was to publish his revolutionary theories just three years after the clock was designed). The clock's mechanism has been replaced over the centuries but the face is original (William IV had it removed and replaced with one from a London church, but Queen Victoria had it put back). The clock was comprehensively restored in time for the 500th anniversary of Henry's accession, in 2009, though these days it is rather high up to be appreciated properly.

The 500th anniversary is also remembered elsewhere in the palace, most notably in the form of a garden that was installed in a small courtyard beside the chapel (unfortunately rather hidden away and often missed by visitors). The garden was planted with flowers and herbs that were available in sixteenth-century England, and overlooking the beds are more of the heraldic emblems known as the 'King's Beasts', here painted in the same vibrant colours that such statues would have been in Henry's time.

As far as today's visitors are concerned, the most beguiling feature of the palace gardens is the maze, which was laid out in the 1690s. The extensive gardens laid out by Henry have long gone, but apparently featured avenues lined with pillars that were topped with yet more statues of the King's Beasts, and in 1540 John Ponet, a mathematician and fellow of Queens' College Cambridge (and future Bishop of Winchester) presented the king with a marvellous sundial that depicted the phases of the moon and pattern of tides, among other phenomena. Henry also had some ornamental fish ponds dug in the gardens, and several banqueting houses built, one of which was constructed upon an artificial mound with fine views of the garden and river. Elsewhere fountains, crenellated box hedges and fantastic topiary bushes cut into the shapes of centaurs abounded. From Fish Court there was access to purpose-dug fish ponds that supplied carp and bream and which occupy the site of the present pond garden, whose walls date from 1536; in the 1690s Mary II transformed them into the sunken gardens that visitors admire today. There were also herb gardens and two orchards, one of which provided fruit for the king's table, while in the other grew 500 red rose bushes.

Henry ensured that his love of recreation – in the form of tennis, riding, jousting and bowling – was also catered for at the palace. He built a new stable block, which survives as part of the royal mews on Hampton Court Green, and a new covered tennis play, linked by a gallery to Wolsey's earlier play. One of the walls of this covered tennis court remains; however, the courts built by Henry were eventually converted into lodgings by one of his successors, James II, while the courts that can be seen today date from the 1620s. During the 1530s work on a tiltyard was begun but Henry's dwindling interest in jousting (as his health declined) meant that it was not finished during his lifetime; it eventually entered service in 1604 and occupied an area that is now formal gardens – though one of the brick viewing towers from Henry's time survives, its ground floor part of the Tiltyard Café, the main part of which occupies an adjacent pavilion; the tiled floor of a second tower was discovered by archaeologists in 2015. The covered bowling alleys, one of which incorporated ornate windows from a dissolved monastic church in Oxfordshire, have also long gone.

The 1530s saw Hampton Court transformed from a country residence into a Renaissance palace whose glories were admired by visitors from all over Europe. At the end of the decade Henry created the vast Honour

One of the brick viewing towers of Henry's tiltyard at Hampton Court – now incorporated into a café.

of Hampton Court, an enclosed royal hunting domain that covered over 9,000 hectares of countryside, from Weybridge to Thames Ditton and from Battersea to Balham and Epsom. The aim was to create a hunting ground that was easily accessible to an increasingly immobile king. Scattered throughout it were timber-framed buildings known as standings, where Henry and his hunting companions could shoot deer from a high gallery while the ladies in the party could watch while they were served refreshments. None of these have survived, but many aspects of the palace that Henry knew, including the two Tudor courtyards, the Chapel, the Great Hall, the Great Watching Chamber and the Astronomical Clock still remain – and with St James's Palace closed to the public, Hampton Court is now the closest that visitors today can get to Henry's public world. In this we are lucky: after their accession in 1689, William and Mary planned to rebuild Hampton Court in the manner of Versailles (which had just been rebuilt in its current form), and Sir Christopher Wren was tasked with knocking the old Tudor buildings down (except the Great Hall) and replacing them with a vast new Baroque palace. In the end these plans were only half enacted: Henry's old apartments went but much of what he knew was left, and today the magnificent eighteenth-century ranges that Wren built stand in contrast to the adjacent Tudor buildings. The last monarch to occupy the more recent part of the palace was George II and his wife Caroline of Ansbach (whose rooms can be seen), and when George died in 1760 the palace was turned over for use as grace-and-favour apartments (some of which were still occupied as recently as 2005); in 1838 the palace was opened to the public, and has remained so ever since.

Part II

HENRY VIII IN PROVINCIAL ENGLAND AND NORTHERN FRANCE

Chapter 8

Introduction

For medieval and Renaissance English monarchs, the arrival of summer meant a royal progress. In summer the English weather was at its kindest, the days were at their longest, the people were at their happiest (and likely to come outside and cheer their monarch) and perhaps, most importantly of all, the roads were in a good condition, having recovered from the muddy quagmire they often became after being ravaged by the rain and ice of an English winter. Henry made his first progress in 1509, the year of his accession, though it appears to have been a comparatively short one. His summer progress the following year was much more substantial, taking in Windsor Castle and then Berkshire, Hampshire, Dorset and Wiltshire, before returning to Hampshire and passing through Surrey to end at Richmond Palace. According to *The Great Chronicle*, during these progresses Henry 'exercised himself daily in shooting, singing, dancing, wrestling, casting of the bar (shot-put), playing at recorders, flutes, virginals, and in setting of songs, making of ballets'. Thus was the purpose of a royal progress: they were for Henry to enjoy hunting in England's bountiful forests, and for him to enjoy the hospitality of the nobles and monks who put him and his court up for the night (or a series of nights) in their monastery or manor house – thus allowing Henry to see something of his realm (and his subjects to see something of him). Most progresses were limited to the Southeast of England, though Henry did occasionally venture further afield – during his first progress he stayed at Old Hall in Gainsborough, the Lincolnshire home of Edward de Burgh, whose grandson was married to Catherine Parr before her marriage to Henry, and in the summer of 1511, he went to Nottingham and Coventry, where he and Queen Catherine watched the famous mystery plays performed by local guildsmen.

Introduction

Typically, a progress would last two months and would take place sometime between July and October. It was planned meticulously in advance, in detailed itineraries known as 'giests', though these could be altered if bad weather set in or a sudden outbreak of the plague meant that some places were not safe to visit (in August 1517 Henry's progress was abandoned completely because of the prevalence of the sweating sickness). The Board of the Greencloth, which supervised the Royal Household, would work out the requirements in terms of food when Henry stayed at palaces and country lodgings that he owned; if staying as a guest, Henry's hosts would lay on lavish hospitality that the king would enjoy between bouts of gambling, tennis or hunting (Henry's own hunting dogs would travel by cart with the rest of his entourage). Each move meant hundreds of courtiers relocating, while the Royal Wardrobe department organized the removal of furniture, which included the dismantling of beds, the taking down, storage and then rehanging of tapestries, and the packing of clothing, linen and valuables. Most items were packed in canvas, covered by boar hides to keep off the rain, and transported by wagons overseen by specialist sumptermen. The property to which the king was travelling had to be made ready days in advance by grooms of the privy chamber, with the Knight Harbinger responsible for the smooth completion of each move and for decisions regarding accommodation of courtiers at each location. A gentleman usher would go ahead of the party to make sure the roof of the accommodation did not leak and there were locks on the doors. At each venue local houses, barns and stables would be commandeered and tents set up in their grounds to accommodate the court. Before their dissolution, monasteries often made good places for Henry to stay; in the 1540s, when they had been dissolved, some monasteries were converted for use by Henry while on progress – after the unfortunate Abbot of Reading was hanged outside his own lodgings in 1540, Henry converted them into an occasional palace, and he even held a council meeting at Dunstable Abbey while on progress in October 1540.

Though the summer progress was the principal reason why Henry left his Thames-side palaces, there were other reasons why he travelled. He went on several pilgrimages, to Canterbury, Walsingham and elsewhere, and in 1542, he travelled with his court to the North of England for an intended meeting with the Scottish king at York – the furthest he ever travelled from London. He also travelled to Rochester to meet Anne of Cleves when she arrived in England, and to Hampshire when he accompanied the Emperor Charles V to Southampton at the end of a state visit. However, the principal reason why Henry journeyed out of London that didn't concern the royal progress was so that he could inspect his military facilities. These included Dover Castle, which stood guard over the coastline that seemed most vulnerable to invasion, and his naval facilities at Chatham and at Portsmouth, where the tragedy of the sinking of the *Mary Rose* unfolded in front of his eyes, as he watched from Southsea Castle. He also made four crossings to France during his reign – twice to indulge in diplomatic shindigs with his arch-rival Francis I, which were staged either in or just outside the English stronghold of Calais, and twice (at the beginning and end of his life) when he personally commanded English forces on assaults on towns in the Pas-de-Calais. It is with a look at these places that this chapter ends; it opens with a look at three of Henry's royal residences that lie beyond the thread of the Thames between Hampton Court and Greenwich, and which (unlike the palaces discussed so far) did not provide a home to the Court during the colder months – namely, Windsor Castle, Eltham Palace and Nonsuch Palace.

Chapter 9

Windsor Castle

When Henry came to the throne, Windsor had been a royal residence for nearly four and a half centuries. This ancient castle had been founded in 1070 by William the Conqueror and was rebuilt by Henry II in the twelfth century and then rebuilt again by Edward III, who modernized the royal lodgings and built an imposing Great Hall, known as St George's Hall, which today is the venue for dinners given by the monarch to visiting Heads of State. (Much remodelled over the centuries, this long thin hall with a hammerbeam roof covered in heraldic shields is the only one of the 'state rooms' open to the public to retain a medieval appearance.) Further improvements to the castle were made by Henry's grandfather Edward IV, who initiated the construction of St George's Chapel, where both he and Henry are buried. That Henry chose Windsor for his place of burial is perhaps surprising, as despite the lavish attention the castle had received through the centuries, it remained a medieval castle rather than a Tudor palace, and Henry tended to use it mainly in the summer months, while on progress or when he came to hunt in the extensive Forest, the forerunner to the Great Park of today (though in August 1517, he chose it as the place to sit out a virulent outbreak of the sweating sickness, and shut himself away here for a number of weeks with the Queen and a few trusted servants). The castle was also used for high-profile diplomatic extravaganzas – the distant forerunners of the state visits of today, with all their attendant theatre and pomp.

Henry at Windsor Castle

Some of the most remarkable events that unfolded at Windsor during Henry's life did so in January 1506, when Philip of Burgundy made a wholly unexpected and unplanned visit to England. At the time Henry was just a few weeks past his fourteenth birthday; with his older brother Arthur dead, he was being groomed as the successor to his then-ailing father. On the death of Isabella of Castile, the mother of Catherine of Aragon, Philip of Burgundy had claimed Castile on behalf of his wife Juana, with himself as king, and had duly set sail for Castile from the Netherlands to claim his new realm. However, his ship became caught in a storm in the western English Channel and he was forced to put ashore at Melcombe Regis, now part of the Dorset port of Weymouth. Philip's party was then lured inland on the promise of supplies. Realizing that he was essentially a prisoner, he sent his secretary to Henry VII to announce his arrival and suggest a meeting. Henry VII invited Philip to Windsor as a guest, and sent Sir Thomas Brandon to Dorset to act as his escort. The king met him outside Windsor on 31 January, with Prince Henry alongside him. A contemporary Spanish chronicler reported that the king said that Philip was 'as dear to him as my own son here present'. They then rode three abreast into Windsor, with Philip between the two Henrys, king and heir.

For several weeks Philip was entertained lavishly at Windsor, taking the opportunity to negotiate and sign a peace treaty that cemented the English alliance with the Habsburgs against France. On 9 February Philip was made a Knight of the Garter, and in turn made Prince Henry a Knight of the Golden Fleece, with Henry declaiming the oath himself – in French. The king then put the Garter round Philip's leg, while Prince Henry 'buckled it and made it fast'. A *Te Deum* was sung, trumpets blew and Philip and the two Henrys dined together in a small chamber within the castle. This was the young Prince Henry's first experience of a diplomatic summit – complete with the pageantry, food, wine and entertainment that characterized such events. Later a French embassy arrived and Henry showed off his skill with the bow and arrow by killing a deer, on which he was congratulated by the French ambassador. Henry's double-edged response was 'They were good for a Frenchman' – meaning that he would have preferred to have had Frenchmen as his target, but his guest understood him to have meant that he had shot well enough to be compared with the best French archers.

Just as American presidents are nowadays brought to Windsor to be wined and dined by the monarch, in June 1522 the Emperor Charles V came here as a guest of Henry during his state visit to England, which had already seen him tour the fleet at Dover and admire the grandeur of Westminster Abbey. Edward Hall describes how Henry and Charles signed a new peace treaty and heard Mass at St George's Chapel, after which their joint entourages gathered in St George's Hall to watch a play by William Cornish in which a 'proud horse' representing Francis I was 'tamed and bridled' by an allegorical figure, Amity – who of course represented the joint Habsburg–English alliance that had just been fomented; a sumptuous masque and banquet followed.

Anne Boleyn was known to like Windsor Castle, though her stays here with Henry were usually rather humble affairs. In March 1528, Anne brought her mother, Elizabeth Boleyn, Countess of Wiltshire, to Windsor, and the two women watched Henry hunting during the day and amused themselves with cards, dice, dancing, music and poetry recitals in the evening. One day they held a picnic at Windsor Manor, a moated royal residence in Windsor Great Park that served as a hunting lodge, and the townsfolk of Windsor lent tables and stools for the royal party to use. Plovers, partridges, larks and rabbits were on the menu, along with confections covered with rich cream. In September 1532, Anne was the focus of a more grandiose affair when Henry created her Lady Marquess of Pembroke in a glittering ceremony that also sealed the Treaty of Windsor with France. Anne was sumptuously attired for the ceremony, at which she wore 'a gown of crimson velvet completely covered with the most costly jewels' and was escorted by the Countess of Rutland and Sussex into the king's Presence Chamber, where she knelt before him as he invested her with the mantle and coronet while the Patent of Creation was read aloud by Bishop Gardiner.

Henry's principal contribution to the castle's architecture was his rebuilding of the gate through which visitors now exit. This gate, which dates from 1511, bears his coat of arms and the pomegranate emblem of Catherine of Aragon. The gateway is just across the lower ward (courtyard) from the Chapel, where Henry is buried, and used to be the symbolic entrance to the castle – there was also a moat and a drawbridge. Henry also added a tennis court at the foot of the round tower, which is shown in seventeenth-century views of the castle, though has long since been demolished. Also gone are a wooden terrace constructed in 1536 beneath the royal apartments, which gave access from his lodgings to the Little Park, and a hunting lodge named Sunninghill, which he constructed in 1511 in Windsor Forest, but whose exact location is now uncertain.

Henry VIII: A History of his Most Important Places and Events

Left and below: The Henry VIII Gate at Windsor Castle.

St George's Chapel, Windsor Castle, which Henry completed and where he is buried.

During Henry's reign the spectacular Chapel was also completed, with Henry adding a richly carved timber closet with an oriel window above Edward IV's chantry chapel so that Catherine of Aragon could watch services; her pomegranate badge features in the carving. Today there is no public access to the closet – though TV cameras are often installed here during public events as there is a good view over the altar (and the aisle under which Henry lies buried).

Henry's Funeral at Windsor

Henry's funeral is described in detail by the early-nineteenth-century clergyman and historian John Strype in his work *Ecclesiastical Memorials*, which drew heavily from contemporary sources. He relates that Henry's funeral cortège reached Windsor Castle at one o'clock in the afternoon on Tuesday, 15 February 1547, after its two-day journey from the Palace of Whitehall and the overnight stop at Syon Abbey. (Between Syon and

Windsor the route diverged from that taken by the cortège of Queen Elizabeth II in September 2022: that processional route ran through Hounslow, skirting the south of what is now Heathrow Airport, to approach Windsor Castle from the south, while Henry's funeral cortège went along what is now the Bath Road through Datchet, thereby approaching the castle from the north through Eton.) The scholars of Eton College knelt in their white surplices as Henry's cortège passed by the school; the cortège then headed up what is now Eton High Street, crossed the Thames and entered the castle through Henry's gate. In the chapel itself another hearse had been constructed to bear the coffin, 35 foot high with two storeys, fringed with black silk and surrounded by pillars topped by candles. The coffin was placed inside the hearse while the effigy was placed on top of a black velvet pall. Watching over the ceremony from the closet that Henry had constructed for Catherine of Aragon was his last wife, Catherine Parr, dressed in blue velvet robes lined with a finely woven silk, sarsenet; ambassadors and nobles also looked on from the body of the church.

The next morning Edmund Bonner, Bishop of London, and Thomas Goodrich, Bishop of Ely, began the Requiem Mass for Henry. His coat of arms and his shield, sword and helmet were reverentially laid on the altar, and Bishop Gardiner preached a sermon on the text 'blessed are the dead that die in the Lord'. He spoke of the frailty of man and the community of death, which drew in both rich and poor, great and lowly – all had suffered a 'dolorous loss' from the death of such a gracious king. Six knights removed the effigy of Henry to the vestry as the Archbishop and bishops came down to the hearse to sing the funeral canticle.

Then, with solemn ceremony, the vault accessed through the floor of the Choir was opened, and sixteen Yeomen of the Guard, using five strong linen towels, lowered the great coffin into it as Gardiner recited the burial service and threw handfuls of earth into the grave, declaiming '*Pulverem, pulveri et cinerem cineri*' – ashes to ashes, dust to dust. This was the cue for some of Henry's leading officials to break their white wands of office over their heads and hurl the fragments into the grave 'with exceeding sorrow and heaviness, not without grievous sighs and tears' – thus sending the trappings of Henry's power and authority into the vault with him. When that was done the grave was covered with planks and Christopher Barker, Garter King at Arms, dressed in a tabard, cried out:

Almighty God of his infinite goodness, give good life and long to the most high and mighty prince, our sovereign lord King Edward VI, by the grace of God, King of England, France and Ireland, defender of the Faith and on earth, under God, of the Church of England and Ireland, the supreme head and sovereign of the most noble order of the Garter.

He then declaimed 'Vive le noble Roy [i.e. Roi, or King of] England' – a cry echoed by the officers of arms. With that the trumpets in the rood loft sounded 'with great melody and courage to the comfort of all that were there present', and Henry's funeral service reached its conclusion. Many of the officials present turned back to London to arrange the Coronation of Henry's successor, the 9-year-old King Edward VI.

The Story of Henry's Tomb at Windsor

To this day Henry's coffin lies beneath the floor of the Choir in St George's Chapel, where it was lowered well over four and a half centuries ago. Yet this was meant to be a temporary arrangement. He was only buried there as it was the resting place of Jane Seymour, and Henry had indicated that they should be buried together. Not surprisingly, it was Henry's intention that he should be buried not in a dusty unmarked vault under the floor but in a magnificent tomb situated prominently within the church.

As early as 1517, Henry had made it clear that his chosen place of burial would be St George's Chapel. The first monarch buried there was Edward IV, Henry's maternal grandfather and the founder of the church. (He is buried with his wife in a tomb just outside the entrance to the Choir.) Edward had intended the building to serve as a royal mausoleum, and the following year the coffin of Henry VI, who had died in 1461 and had been buried at Chertsey Abbey, was reburied at Windsor. In making his decision to be buried here, Henry was also drawn by Windsor's historical association with the Order of the Garter, the order of chivalry founded by Edward III – and he rejected Westminster Abbey as a place of burial because there would be no room for his tomb in the great chapel founded by his father.

His father's monument was magnificent. It had cost around a million pounds in today's money and had been designed by the Italian sculptor Pietro Torrigiano. In 1519, Henry commissioned Torrigiano to construct a tomb for him and Catherine of Aragon at Windsor, which would suitably reflect the magnificence of his person and his achievements. The monument was to be fashioned from white marble and black jasper and was to be a quarter larger than Henry VII's tomb – another reason for Henry not wanting to be buried in Westminster Abbey, where many would look askance at his tomb overshadowing that of the father of the Tudor dynasty. The tomb was to be crowned with a triumphal arch bearing a statue of the king on horseback, and would be surrounded by lifesize gilt-bronze figures. Torrigiano undertook to complete the work within four years, for the sum of £2,000, and Cardinal Wolsey was put in charge of overseeing the project.

However, in 1522, a disagreement broke out between monarch and sculptor, and as a result of the row Torrigiano fled to Florence. (The sculptor had, it seems, a colourful personality – it is said he broke Michelangelo's nose while they were both students in Florence.) The argument stemmed from Torrigiano wanting to be paid in negotiable Florentine merchants' bonds rather than English pounds, which Wolsey refused to accede to. Work was abandoned on the tomb and in 1528 Henry had a simple vault made ready for him in the Choir of St George's Chapel. Around this time the Venetian architect and sculptor Jacopo Sansovino, designer of many of the prominent buildings around Venice's Piazza San Marco, was reported to be considering a commission from the English king for an astonishingly high cost of £18,750 – which might have been to create the tomb shown in a drawing owned by Nicholas Charles, the Lancaster Herald, and described a century later by John Speed in his *History of Britain*. The design of this tomb was based on a tomb originally intended for Pope Leo X, who died in December 1521. It was to be twenty-eight feet high and topped by an effigy of the king on horseback in grand Italian Renaissance style: had it ever been built it would have outshone any other sepulchral monument ever conceived.

In the event this tomb, like the first one intended for Henry, was never built. However, work was progressing on another tomb – the one that Cardinal Wolsey had commissioned for himself, for his own eventual burial at Windsor. It was begun in 1524 and the sculptor was another Florentine, Benedetto da Rovezzano. After Wolsey's fall (and his burial in Leicester), Henry purloined Wolsey's enormous sarcophagus of black marble and ordered the bronze effigy of the Cardinal to be consigned to the melting pot. The tomb, complete with nine-foot bronze pillars adorned with angels bearing candlesticks, with a cardinal's hat at its centre, was destined to be even grander than Henry VII's tomb – an extravagant exercise in hubris that probably irked Henry. He got Rovezzano to alter the design so that it could become his own tomb, with his gilded bronze effigy lying on top. There was an altar, with angels and effigies of children holding candlesticks, and the whole structure was to be surrounded by a four-foot-high bronze and black marble enclosure to form a separate chantry where priests would pray for the royal soul. Although Cromwell made regular payments for labour and supplies, it seems that Rovezzano was in poor health, possibly brought on by the fumes from smelting all the copper and bronze, and he returned to Italy in 1543, though by then the effigy of Henry had been cast and polished. The Italian military engineer Giovanni Portinari, who had worked on several reconstruction projects in England (including the city walls of Berwick-upon-Tweed), then set about completing the work. In his will Henry wrote that the tomb was 'well onward and almost made' and asked for the tombs of Henry VI and Edward IV to be embellished and 'made more princely' – so the three entombed monarchs at Windsor, and those that came after them, would be as glorious in death as they had been during their reigns.

By the time Henry died the only part of the grandiose tomb that was in place was the bronze enclosure. It had been erected in Edward IV's chapel, with the words 'Henricus Octavus Rex Angliae Franciae Doinus Hiberniae Fidei Defensor' written around it. What the enclosure lacked, of course, was an actual tomb. Portinari continued to work on it after Henry's death, as did an Italian artist, Nicholas Bellin, from 1551. Bellin was at that time living and working in the precincts of Westminster Abbey, where some parts of the tomb were still in store. In his will Edward VI asked for his father's tomb to be completed, and Bellin, who had fashioned the effigy for Henry's coffin, was commissioned to do the same for Edward's, and with this task being more urgent, Henry's tomb was neglected.

In 1553, when Mary Tudor ascended the throne, work on her father's tomb ceased. There was no desire to celebrate the life of the monarch who had ushered in such radical religious reforms. There was even a story that Cardinal Reginald Pole, Henry's arch-enemy and Mary's Catholic Archbishop of Canterbury, ordered Henry's body to be removed from his coffin and burned. This, however, did not happen, and during Elizabeth's reign work on the tomb recommenced, using the parts already created. Then in the 1570s yet another design was commissioned, this time from the English-born Dutch sculptor Cornelius Cure. However, Elizabeth was distracted by war, by money problems and by the building of the tomb for her half-brother Edward, and the consignment of marble purchased by Cure was eventually used for some new fountains at Hampton Court. In 1598, at the end of Elizabeth's reign, the German lawyer and chronicler Paul Hentzner reported that – half a century after Henry's death – the tomb was still only partially complete, and that any money available was being diverted into the building of a tomb for Elizabeth in Westminster Abbey.

It was Oliver Cromwell's Commonwealth that sounded the death-knell for the tomb. In 1645 the gilt-bronze effigy of Henry that was supposed to surmount it was sold off to raise funds for Parliament's cause in the Civil War, and four of the candlesticks were sold to the Cathedral of St Bavo in Ghent, where they can still be seen today, in the Choir of the cathedral, fronting the High Altar. (Although these enormous and incredibly ornate candle sticks, each one twice as high as an adult, may pale in significance compared to the cathedral's great artistic treasure, a glorious Renaissance altarpiece known as the Adoration of the Mystic Lamb, seeing them up close does allow for a good impression of how magnificent Henry's tomb would have been had it been completed.) As it is, what remained of the

Two of the enormous candlesticks originally made for Henry's tomb, and now in St Bavo's Cathedral in Ghent.

St Bavo's Cathedral in Ghent is now the repository for the enormous candlesticks fashioned for Henry's tomb.

tomb was removed in 1804 when there were grandiose plans made to develop the catacombs beneath the church, necessitating the uplifting of the floor. Two years later a use was finally found for the enormous black sarcophagus which had been originally intended for Wolsey, and then for Henry – it formed part of the tomb of Lord Nelson in the crypt of St Paul's Cathedral; a representation of the Admiral's viscount's coronet was placed on top of it, in the position that was originally intended for Wolsey's cardinal's hat.

By this time two other coffins had joined those of Henry and Jane Seymour in the vault beneath the Choir at St George's. In 1649, the coffin of Charles I was interred here, in an attempt by Parliament to appease those in England shocked at the execution of a monarch. Charles's supporters had heard that the exact location of the vault where Henry and Jane were buried had been lost, and discovered it by stamping on the floor and listening to the echoes. During the interment a soldier lifted the velvet palls that still covered Henry's coffin, and drilled a hole into it and retrieved a bone. Nearly forty years later, in 1686, the burial vault was investigated again when the floor of the chapel was relaid; the vault was found to be around eight feet deep and lined with brick, with the coffins of Henry and Jane stood within it on trestles. The vault was opened again just ten years later, so that the coffin of a stillborn child of Anne, Charles I's granddaughter, who from 1702 was to rule as Queen Anne, could be interred within it: the tiny coffin was placed at the feet of King Charles – the fourth and final of the oddly matched burials within this particular vault.

Well over a century later, in 1813, the vault was formally opened in the presence of the Prince Regent, later King George IV. At the time there were rumours that Charles II had ordered the reburial of the body of his father at Westminster Abbey in secret. However the coffin inscribed with Charles's name was investigated, and the head of the skeleton inside had, as expected, been severed from the body – so those rumours were firmly scotched. Henry's lead coffin was found to be encased within a shell of elm wood around two inches thick. A report on the opening of the vault indicated that the 'leaden coffin appeared to have been beaten in by violence about the middle, and a considerable opening of it exposed the skeleton of the king'. Apparently, some of Henry's beard was still attached to the skull. Jane Seymour's coffin was left undisturbed. In 1888, the then Prince of Wales deposited some relics of Charles I in the vault (the relics had previously been removed in 1813) by lowering them through a hole in the floor. Henry's coffin was again examined, this time from floor level, and it was revealed to be 'in a state of great dilapidation. The king's skull, with its very broad frontal, his thigh bones, ribs and other portions of his skeleton are exposed to view'. A later report indicated that the coffin had been 'split open by internal forces of decomposition' though this seems unlikely after such a long time; perhaps the trestles on which the coffin was sitting had collapsed, or the coffin had at last succumbed to damage caused at Syon.

Today a slab of dark marble between the choir stalls, around the length of an adult lying down, marks the position of the burial vault.

> In a vault beneath this marble slab,' the brass inscription on the slab reads, 'are deposited the remains of Jane Seymour Queen of King Henry VIII 1537, King Henry VIII 1547, King Charles I 1648 and an infant child of Queen Anne. This memorial was placed here by command of King William IV 1837.

The marble slab covering the vault where Henry VIII is buried at St George's Chapel. (*AloeVera95, Wikimedia Commons*)

Nowadays many visitors to the chapel just walk over the plaque: there are dozens just like it throughout the Chapel (though none are quite as prominently positioned) – but rather than towards the grey slab, the eyes of visitors are drawn to the beautiful choir stalls on either side of the aisle, the colourful banners of the Knights of the Garter that hang from the upper walls, the stained-glass windows, and the Choir's beautiful medieval ceiling vaulting. It's an extraordinarily mundane memorial to a king famed for his larger-than-life exploits and appearance. And, moreover, Henry's burial here did not begin a tradition: for nearly 300 years after his death most monarchs were still buried at Westminster Abbey, and it was not until George III, who died in 1820, that the tradition of royal burials at Windsor was revived. Since that time most monarchs and other senior royals have been buried here, finally fulfilling the wishes of Edward IV and his grandson Henry that this should be the royal mausoleum. Today it's the King George VI Memorial Chapel, which abuts the north wall of the Choir, that most draws the attention of visitors – Queen Elizabeth II was buried in this tiny chantry chapel on 19 September 2022, alongside her husband the Duke of Edinburgh, her sister Princess Margaret, and her parents King George VI and Queen Elizabeth the Queen Mother. The chapel was commissioned by Queen Elizabeth herself in 1962 as the resting place for her father, and was the first chantry chapel to be built at St George's since the one commissioned in 1504 for Oliver King, private secretary to Henry VII and the man who had read out the letters patent creating the infant Henry VIII Duke of York at Westminster Abbey in 1494. The two monarchs from comparatively recent times who aren't buried at St George's Chapel are Queen Victoria, who is buried in the Royal Mausoleum in Frogmore near Windsor, and Edward VIII, who abdicated the throne in 1937 and is buried in the royal burial ground beside it.

Chapter 10

Eltham Palace

If Windsor Castle holds indelible associations with the end of Henry's life, then Eltham Palace holds similar associations with its beginnings. Like all the palaces covered in the first part of this book, it's situated in Greater London, but it holds a different place in Henry's life to the Thames-side palaces and until the boundary changes of 1889, it was actually in Kent, so it makes sense to consider it separately from them. Today the palace lies within the 'Royal' Borough of Greenwich, and is situated some six and a half kilometres southeast of Greenwich Palace – though Eltham is a very different suburb to the rather more Bohemian enclave of Greenwich, with its tourists and its second-hand record shops (and both are different to upmarket Blackheath, which lies between them). In 2012 *The Independent* called Eltham an "unpretty south-east London suburb of council estates and trunk roads" in an article that looked back twenty years to the tragic racially inspired murder of black teenager Stephen Lawrence. So, the presence of a moated and palatial manor house with a thousand years of history behind it just a five-minute walk away from a pretty ordinary high street is, to say the least, somewhat surprising. The house has its origins in Eltham being on the ancient routeway from London to Maidstone and the Channel ports – and it was the place where Henry VII decided that his younger children, including his son Henry, should be brought up.

Eltham Palace Before and After Henry

The builder of the original manor house that stood here was Odo, Bishop of Bayeux, half-brother to William the Conqueror and the man who is widely considered to have commissioned the Bayeux Tapestry. (It is likely that an important dwelling stood on this spot in Saxon times, though no trace has been found of it.) By 1295 the owner of the property was Anthony Bek, Bishop of Durham, who rebuilt it as a grand manor house with a defensive wall (the remains of the Great Hall from his time, with an octagonal stone hearth and elaborate tiled floor, were unearthed in the 1970s). In 1305 he presented the house to the future Edward II, though he continued to live in it until his death six years later. Over the course of the later Middle Ages, the house was greatly expanded and became a favoured royal residence; Edward III spent much of his youth here while Henry IV spent ten of his thirteen Christmases as king here. In Henry VIII's day – as now – the magnificent Great Hall was the centrepiece of the palace. It was built in the 1470s by Henry's grandfather Edward IV, though it has been much altered and restored over the years (restoration work has kept the Hall's original hammerbeam ceiling intact, and it's the third largest in England after Westminster Hall and the Hall at Christ Church, Oxford). Edward was also responsible for the handsome stone bridge over the moat, which visitors still cross today to reach the palace.

In the 1490s, Henry VII resurfaced with red brick most of what was, by then, a substantial palace. As was traditional, the royal lodgings were situated in a stacked donjon in the Inner (or Great) Court, behind which were five smaller courtyards and a tiltyard. Although Henry VIII was to make some additions to the palace in the 1530s, it was rather neglected by subsequent Tudor monarchs, and the buildings fell into disrepair during the Stuart era; in 1656, the diarist John Evelyn described the place as being in 'miserable ruins' with the Great Hall being used as a barn. Eventually the buildings of the medieval royal palace were demolished or simply fell down. However the Great Hall remained and its roof was eventually restored in the 1890s; in the 1930s the English philanthropists Stephen and Virginia Courtauld built a modern home adjacent to it, adapting the hall itself as a venue for the private concerts they staged for their friends. Later in the twentieth century the palace was used by the Army Education Board until it was opened to the public by English Heritage in 1995. The stone bridge, the Great Hall (with its minstrels' gallery, added by the Courtaulds) and the moat remain from medieval times, but these days it's the art deco interiors of the Courtaulds' former home (particularly their distinctive circular bedroom) that provides the focus for visitors. Behind the palace the land drops down to the broad valley of the River Thames, which is overlooked by an ancient footpath, King John's Walk, which once led to the hunting

Eltham Palace

Above and right: The Great Hall at Eltham Palace.

Henry VIII: A History of his Most Important Places and Events

The Great Hall at Eltham Palace.

grounds to the south of the palace (though now it leads to nothing more exotic than an interwar local authority housing estate). The name of this path celebrates either Prince John of Eltham, the son of Edward II who was born in the palace in 1316, or King John of France (known as Jean le Bon), who was imprisoned in the palace in the 1360s by the Black Prince after the Battle of Poitiers, though given free rein to walk in the surrounding woods and fields. The lane crosses some of the highest ground in Southeast London, and affords magnificent views towards the O2 Arena (formerly the Millennium Dome) at Greenwich, and, further afield, the skyscrapers of Docklands and the City, including the distinctive profiles of the office blocks known as the 'Shard' and the 'Gherkin' – a very different view, of course, to the one King Henry enjoyed as he rode this way to hunt.

Henry's Boyhood at Eltham Palace

Henry was born just eight years after the death of his grandfather Edward IV. In the 1490s, when Henry was growing up at Eltham, many of the staff there would have remembered his grandfather, who died in 1483, and the palace would have been familiar to Henry's mother Elizabeth, Edward's daughter. So she would have felt her children were in safe and familiar hands at Eltham – and should the need arise the ride from Greenwich to Eltham could be made quickly and with ease. It was also not too arduous for Henry and his siblings when they travelled to Greenwich for events such as Christmas, which was usually celebrated there.

Henry was probably moved from Greenwich to Eltham in October 1492, when he was approaching his first birthday. By 1494 Elizabeth Denton, one of his mother's ladies, was in charge of the nursery at Eltham, which at the time Henry shared with his sister Elizabeth until she died in 1495, and with his other sister Mary and his brother Edmund who were born in 1496 and 1499 respectively. Edmund was named after Edmund Tudor, Earl of Richmond, the father of Henry VII. He died just four months past his first birthday, at Hatfield, where he had been moved with Henry and their sister because of the plague; Mary survived and grew up to marry Louis XII of France – and by her later marriage to Charles Brandon she was grandmother to Lady Jane Grey, the famous 'nine day queen' of the mid-Tudor era.

At around the age of 5, Henry began lessons with the poet laureate, John Skelton, who was to remain his teacher until he was 11 or 12. Skelton was a Cambridge man, a classicist in holy orders – 'that incomparable light and ornament of British letters', was how the great Dutch humanist and scholar Desiderius Erasmus described him. Of his young charge, Skelton once wrote that he set out to give Henry 'drink of the sugared well/Of Helicon's waters crystalline/Acquainting him with the muses nine'. Many scholars consider Skelton to be a scurrilous, indifferent poet, the author of vitriolic satires that targeted corrupt courtiers in the household of Henry VII. As far as Henry VIII is concerned, Skelton's most influential work was *Speculum Principis*, originally dated 'at Eltham, 28 August, in the year of grace 1501', though the copy that survives, in the British Museum, is a later one which Skelton presented to Henry when he became king. The text was essentially an instruction manual for kingship. 'Peruse the Chronicles, direct yourself to histories, commit them to memory,' Skelton advised the 11-year-old Henry, for he 'should exceed everybody in virtue and learning … Love poets: athletes are two a penny but patrons of the arts are rare'. A couple of the exhortations are interesting, given Henry's later habits and life. 'Above all, loathe gluttony,'

Skelton advised, and 'choose a wife for yourself, and prize her always and uniquely.' Henry, of course, had six.

Skelton seems to have been dismissed in around 1502 – though it's not clear why – and Henry's new teacher was John Holt, former Usher at Magdalen College School, Oxford, and master at Chichester Cathedral School (both still in existence today). He wrote a school textbook on Latin grammar and was a friend of Thomas More, but he died in 1504 when Henry was thirteen. Thereafter Henry's teachers were William Hone, of whom little is known, and William Blount, Lord Mountjoy, who came from a family with a long tradition of service to the Crown, and who was also an intimate of Erasmus. However, neither was with Henry for long, as when he turned 14, his formal education was over and he left Eltham for his father's court at Richmond and Greenwich – where he was to learn how to be a future king.

The most famous event in Henry's life that unfolded at Eltham was his meeting at the age of 9 with Erasmus, which took place in the Great Hall of the Palace in 1499. Erasmus was staying at Sayes Court near Greenwich, the country house of his host and former pupil Lord Mountjoy, a wealthy nobleman who had fought for Henry VII against the Cornish uprising of 1497. He was at that time acting as Henry's mentor or *socius studiorum* – that is, 'companion of studies' (as we have seen, following the departure of John Skelton he later became Henry's official tutor). Just before the meeting at Eltham Thomas More joined Erasmus as Mountjoy's guest at Sayes Court and the three then journeyed to Eltham on foot or on horseback. Erasmus wrote that 'When we came into the Hall, all the retinue was assembled; not only that of the palace but Mountjoy's as well. In the midst stood Henry, aged 9, already with a certain royal demeanour; I mean a dignity of mind combined with a remarkable courtesy'. On Henry's right was his older sister Margaret, who later married King James of Scotland, while on his left was his younger sister Mary. Hilary Mantel draws a picture of the scene in her novel *The Mirror and the Light*, which sees Henry remembering how he stood beside 'Mary, her hair white like angel's hair, and Edmund still a babe ... held in some great lady's arms, I suppose ... I [was] a bonny child and a toward wit. I sat under the canopy of state'. The scene had earlier been captured on canvas by the Pre-Raphaelite artist Frank Cadogan Cowper, whose vibrant painting from 1910 now hangs in the Palace of Westminster. As Henry stood resplendent in the Hall, Thomas More stepped forward and presented the boy with a piece of his writing. Erasmus was embarrassed by the fact that he had brought nothing similar with him. But during the dinner that followed Henry boldly sent Erasmus a note exhorting him, as Erasmus later recalled, to 'challenge something from my pen'.

Erasmus took three days to knock together something suitable: it was a short manuscript of ten leaves, illuminated to make it a fitting gift, hastily and carelessly written and apparently made up of reused materials which Erasmus made a habit of carrying with him on his travels for this sort of eventuality. There were eleven poems in the manuscript along with a new one in praise of John Skelton, and a prose letter of dedication to Henry himself: 'The debt that ancient Greece/To Homer owed … to Skelton owes Britannia/For he from Latium all the muses led/And taught them to speak English words instead/of Latin.' Erasmus did not actually speak any English, so he must have had the verses written by someone else – and indeed the writer is even unsure of Henry's schoolmaster's name: was it 'Stelkon' or 'Skelton' he was supposedly honouring? A year later Erasmus produced an ode in Latin entitled *Prosopopoeia Britannie maioris* in which he flatters and praises the island of Britain, the royal house of Tudor, King Henry VII and – in particular – his younger son: 'How much of his father shines forth in his countenance!' he gushed. Erasmus clearly spent more time on this poem, and thought it good enough to have it printed – along with the dedicatory letter with which he had prefaced his earlier poems for Henry. In this letter he doubts the value of gold as a gift – on the basis of all princes being rich but few are famous – and asserts that it is the work of poets and scholars, not wealth or statues or paintings, which confers immortality. For his part Henry did have substantial book learning and some of his later writing emulated that of Erasmus, whose meeting with him at Eltham when he was a young boy clearly inspired him to read his works widely in later life: he appears to have been artistically precocious as a child and unusually well-read for a king.

Henry at Eltham Palace During his Reign

In the early years of his kingship Henry visited Eltham frequently. The 1510s saw several improvements made to the palace, including a new chapel and tiltyard; it also seems that Henry had a hill flattened so that the views from the palace window towards Greenwich were enhanced. Wolsey was a frequent visitor during these years and the house known as the Lord Chancellor's Lodgings, opposite the entrance to the palace, was probably built for him; the building now comprises three private homes and, despite substantial renovation over the centuries, it has still retained much of its sixteenth-century appearance. It was here that Wolsey probably stayed when he took the Oath of Office of Lord Chancellor before Henry on Christmas Eve, 1515.

During Henry's reign the Great Hall at Eltham acquired something of a reputation as a dramatic venue. When the king was in residence there were frequent performances and Londoners were admitted to watch them. Eltham was also famous for a puppet show, *The Divine Motion*, which was performed in the Palace in Henry's reign and was later mentioned by Ben Johnson in his 1609 play *Epicoene, or the Silent Woman*. At Christmas 1515 the children of the Chapel Royal performed a comedy, *Troilus and Pandarus,* and later in that festive season at Twelfth Night there was a pageant with dancing and feasting, with temporary kitchens erected so that the master cooks could make jellies and gingerbreads. On the day of the feast Henry and his friend Charles Brandon, Duke of Suffolk, amused themselves by running at the ring (riding at full speed and thrusting a lance through a hanging wooden ring), during which Henry wore a wreath of green satin embroidered with the queen's pomegranate badge; at the end of the day, he generously allowed the competitors to keep the horses, armour and clothes he had provided. Courtiers watched these antics from elaborate pavilions in the grounds of the palace which were given exotic names such as White Hart, Leopard's Head and Ostrich Feather.

Henry also spent the Christmas of 1525 here – but in very different circumstances to the one ten years previously. The plague was at that time rampant in London, and Eltham was chosen over Greenwich as a place to spend the festive season because of its relatively isolated location. Few courtiers remained with Henry and according to the chronicler Edward Hall no one was allowed to 'come thither but such as were appointed by name'. Wolsey saw the plague out at Richmond Palace, which he made sure was well supplied with oranges, as they were said to ward off infection. After Christmas he journeyed to Eltham to meet with the king and draw up the famous Eltham Ordinances, which reformed the royal household, eliminating waste and cracking down on minor forms of corruption – and above all saving money, after the crisis in the exchequer caused by the wars with France. One ordinance forbade courtiers and servants from thieving 'commodities in gentlemen's houses' when the court was on its summer progress, because 'it is often seen daily that, as well as in the king's own houses, as in the places of other noblemen and gentlemen, locks, tables, forms, cupboards, trestles and other household implements be purloined and taken away, to the king's great dishonour'. Servants were pensioned off, hangers-on were ejected, the Yeomen of the Guard was reduced in number and there were tighter controls on absenteeism, though talented administrators were given a clearer career path. 'Alas, what sorrow and lamentation was made when all these persons should depart the court,' Hall observed – though Wolsey's fall from grace meant that only a few of the reforms were actually enacted.

By the 1530s Henry rarely visited Eltham; in the latter part of his reign the temptation of newer, larger and more luxurious palaces along the Thames rendered Eltham somewhat provincial. He and Anne Boleyn stayed the night here on 24 October 1532 on their way back from Henry's diplomatic shindig with Francis I outside Calais, and just over a year later, when Anne was pregnant, her apartments at Eltham were converted into a nursery; in the event Anne probably lost the baby or it died soon after birth. After that, just one more event is associated with Eltham – though it's one of the most intriguing of Henry's reign. In September 1537, Thomas Cromwell received a letter from a man named Harry Atkinson, imprisoned in the convict house in the Westminster Sanctuary, detailing a rumour that had spread throughout the prison – namely that William Webbe, the keeper of the sanctuary, was spreading false and malicious rumours about the king. The story that Webbe was supposed to have weaved is that he had been riding one day near Eltham Palace with his mistress, and they came upon the king, who took a fancy to her: according to the account preserved in the state papers from Henry's time, the king 'plucked down her muffler,' kissed her, commanded her to get off her horse, and 'had his pleasure of her'. The king of course was beyond reproach for such a crime, had it indeed been committed – though Webbe would have been guilty of treason had he spread such stories around. However, Cromwell decided not to take the matter further, possibly suspecting that the story might have been spread maliciously by someone who coveted Webbe's job and wanted him out of the way so he could succeed him.

Chapter 11

Nonsuch Palace

Nothing remains of Nonsuch Palace – which is ironic, since it was given this name because there was 'none such' building in England like it at the time it was built. It was meant to rival the Château de Chambour (or Chambord), a country residence of the French king Francis I – but today only a line of stone pillars at the western edge of Nonsuch Park in Cheam in Surrey indicates that there was once an extraordinarily lavish palace standing here. The location is only eight kilometres south of Richmond

One of a line of pillars in Nonsuch Park in Cheam that mark the location of the former palace.

Palace and a similar distance southeast of Hampton Court, and lies amidst some of the country's most well-heeled commuter-belt towns and London suburbs, namely Epsom, Chessington, Purley, Wimbledon – and Cheam itself.

The Palace and its Setting

Construction work began on the palace in April 1538; originally a site had been chosen in Waltham-in-the-Forest northeast of London but these plans were abandoned for a location in Surrey that involved the village of Cuddington being razed to the ground. The palace was built around two courts and was designed by James Needham, Henry's Clerk of Works, with some of the building material coming from the dissolved Merton Priory, which was situated nearby. Over the next three years, over 500 labourers worked around the clock to build the palace, living in tents by the construction site; however, although the inner court was complete by 1541, the outer court was still unfinished by the time of Henry's death, by which time his outlay had reached around £25,000 – £7.5 million in today's money. 'At first it seems that a modest [hunting] lodge will do,' Thomas Cromwell muses in Hilary Mantel's novel *The Mirror and the Light* as he contemplates Henry's wishes.

> But then the king decides it will be one of the wonders of the world … He orders a thousand loads of timber and begins building brick kilns. The building of the marvel goes on through the summer of 1538. When the king has a new wife he will place her in it, as a jewel in its setting.

By all accounts Nonsuch Palace was a lavish affair, both inside and out. Later on in the century, the antiquarian and historian William Camden wrote that

> Here, Henry VIII in his magnificence erected a structure so beautiful so elegant and splendid that in whatever direction the admirer of florid architecture turns his eyes he will say that it easily bears off the prize. So great is the emulation of ancient Roman art, such are its paintings, its gilding and

its decoration, that you would say that it is the sky spangled with stars.

Surviving drawings show that the outer court was festooned with elaborate turrets and battlements, while the inner court was flanked by two large octagonal pinnacled towers decorated with gilded plasterwork panels carved with Renaissance reliefs. Figures of Roman emperors adorned the gateway that led between the courts, while a massive statue of the king enthroned dominated the inner court, where the royal apartments were situated. The lower walls of were of stone, but the upper parts were covered with a variety of stucco panels showing heroic tales from history and mythology, created by Giles Goring, Nicholas Bellin of Modena and William Cure of Amsterdam.

Much of the interior was also designed by Nicholas Bellin, who entered Henry's service in 1537 after working at Fontainebleau, the country residence of the French kings outside Paris, which Francis I had rebuilt as a Renaissance palace during the 1530s. It is thought miniatures in Henry VIII's Psalter, dating from around 1540, show the interiors that Bellin designed at Nonsuch. They are Italian Renaissance in style, with marbled walls and columns and colourful floor tiles; in one room depicted in the Psalter there is a classically styled bed with a blue and gold tester (or canopy) surrounded by lavish drapes, while the ornate chimney pieces surrounded by stucco designs seem to have been taken straight from the designs of Fontainebleau. In Henry's privy chamber there was a fountain in the form of a silver serpent caught in the paws of a lion, designed by Italian craftsmen Bartholemew Penni and Antonio Toto, who had previously worked on Henry's extensive rebuilding of Hampton Court in the 1530s.

Not surprisingly, the surrounding gardens and parks were also extensive. The so-called Little Park extended over what is now Nonsuch Park, while Worcester Park stretched north towards Malden (and is the name by which the residential suburb that covers the former site is still known). A driveway lined by walnut trees linked the palace to the London Road (now the A24). The formal gardens were laid out by French garden designers and came complete with groves, fountains, rockeries, stone carvings, marble pillars, aviaries, orchards, vines and a maze. The orchards were planted with the first apricot trees in England, which yielded their exotic fruits in the final years of Henry's reign. Around 300 metres to the southwest of the palace was a banqueting hall, with a viewing platform from where Henry could watch hunts; it was excavated (along with the main site of the palace) in 1959, and a twentieth-century retaining wall (incorporating some Tudor bricks) now marks the site. Around eleven kilometres away at Cobham Henry laid out a race course one and a half kilometres long, stretching to Leigh Hill, where he raced horses – the first English monarch to indulge in what later became known as the 'sport of kings'.

The Palace During and After Henry's Reign

Despite the palace being only half-built, Henry stayed in it on a number of occasions in the 1540s, most notably in July 1545 when he spent three nights here after the shock of watching the *Mary Rose* go down off Southsea; a forest of tents was erected in the gardens for members of the court, while furnishings and tapestries were brought from Whitehall – and during his stay, Henry complained that the workmen building the remainder of the palace were being too slow with their work. He also stayed here briefly in December 1546, just a few weeks before he died, on his journey to Whitehall from his palatial manor house at Oatlands. However, it seems that no major dramas or events of his reign unfolded here, and for this reason – as well as the fact that nothing remains of the palace – over the centuries Nonsuch seems to have slipped into a sort of historical oblivion.

Henry's daughter Elizabeth stayed in the palace during her reign, but when Samuel Pepys came visiting in 1663 he found the garden in ruins, though his fellow diarist John Evelyn dined in the palace two years later and found the buildings themselves in good repair. The owner at this time was Henrietta Maria, the wife of the executed king Charles I; when she died in 1669 Charles II gave it to his mistress Barbara Villiers, and on her death he ordered the place to be demolished and the land sold off to local farms.

The site marked by the pillars – now a flat expanse of green, fringed by a pathway lined by trees – was excavated in 1959–60, when extensive foundations were unearthed, including the main well and bread ovens; they were covered up following the end of the excavations, and a plan of the palace was engraved onto a metal plate and affixed to one of the marker pillars. Today the largest building in Nonsuch Park – which is

Henry VIII: A History of his Most Important Places and Events

Above: One of the pillars that marks the location of the former Nonsuch Palace – with a metal plate depicting the palace plan.

Left: A close-up of the plan of the palace, etched onto a metal plate.

Nonsuch Palace

an expansive dog-walking area of grass and scattered glades of trees – is Nonsuch Mansion, situated 800 metres to the northeast of the palace site, built in the eighteenth century and remodelled early in the following century in Tudor Gothic style to emulate the palace. (It is now a wedding and functions venue, with a busy café spilling out onto the terrace.) Embedded into the porch, at knee-height, is an original block of building stone from the palace that bears the inscription 'IS43 HENRICV-OCTAVS 3S' – signifying '1543 Henry VIII in the 35th year of his reign'. In addition, some wood panelling from the palace has found its way to the Great Hall at Loseley Park near Guildford, a private home that is open to the public on occasions. The panels bear grotesque motifs and trompe l'oeil designs and depict mythological figures, classical urns, the Prince of Wales feathers and the cypher of Catherine Parr – a maiden issuing from a Tudor rose. Also at Loseley Park is a marble table carved with a Tudor rose and Scottish thistle, which might have come from Nonsuch; if so it was

The block of building stone from Nonsuch Palace that is built into the porch of Nonsuch Mansion.

Henry VIII: A History of his Most Important Places and Events

The porch of Nonsuch Mansion with the block of building stone from the palace.

probably made at the time Henry was thinking of marrying his son Edward to Mary Queen of Scots. Meanwhile Whitehall Historic House in Cheam, an appealingly lopsided whitewashed building with Tudor origins that stands out a little on what is otherwise a fairly unremarkable high street, and which is now a local history museum (and inevitable tearoom), displays a few pottery and other items from the palace, including the limestone base for a balustrade that lined the bowling alley, and some carved stonework from Merton Priory that was reused in the palace. The highpoint, however, in this museum is a superb model of the

The limestone base of a balustrade from Nonsuch Palace, on display in Whitehall Historic House in Cheam.

Nonsuch Palace

Above, right and overleaf: The model of Nonsuch Palace on display in Whitehall Historic House in Cheam.

Henry VIII: A History of his Most Important Places and Events

Nonsuch Palace

palace, unveiled in 2011 by Professor Martin Biddle, who had overseen the 1959 excavations as an undergraduate, and which gives a good idea of the architectural extravagance that characterized the palace (particularly in the fussy exterior decoration of the turrets). The house is around 700 metres due east of Nonsuch Mansion; a similar distance west of the palace site in Ewell is Bourne Hall Park, home to a museum that occupies the upstairs floor of a local library, and which also has some items on display from Nonsuch (though is mainly given over to displays relating to the 'derby', run at the nearby Epsom racecourse). These displays include one of the bannisters from the edge of the bowling green, a block with a carved flower (probably from Merton Priory and reused in the building of the palace), and a small 'greenware' Tudor jug (though some of the finds are from the palace's later history). There is also an inlaid wooden chest, of a type known as a 'Nonsuch chest', whose decoration (by German and Dutch craftsmen) is said to mimic that of the palace (though it didn't come from there). Other finds are distributed around other museums, including the Museum of London and Honeywood Heritage Centre in Carshalton – while a fragment of glass from the palace bearing the arms of Henry and Jane is now in the collection of the Victoria and Albert Museum.

One of the bannisters from the edge of the bowling green in Nonsuch Palace, on display in Bourne Hall Park in Ewell.

Chapter 12

Kent

Henry's principal association with Kent – certainly the Kent of the Middle Ages – came through his boyhood at Eltham Palace. Boundary changes and the spread of London have now ensured that this former palatial home that was once situated deep in the Kent countryside is now firmly in suburbia – but Henry has plenty more associations with the county, which is perhaps not surprising: not only did he have to travel through it to reach the Channel ports, for trips to France or for when he met guests who had crossed the sea to journey to his kingdom, but it was also the location of the important naval and military stronghold of Dover. Henry also visited Canterbury several times as a pilgrim and worshipper. However, it is Rochester that has the most associations with him: in Henry's day, this city on the Medway coast, with its castle and cathedral and its harbour, was an important military and religious centre – and it was also the place where one of the most intriguing dramas of his reign played out.

Rochester

At the heart of the drama that played out in Rochester was Henry's fourth wife, Anne of Cleves. Anne's father was the Duke of Kleve and Jülich, German duchies centred on the Rhineland cities of Düsseldorf (where Anne was born) and Duisburg; he was a moderate protestant who had sought to pursue a middle ground in the German Reformation, which appealed to Henry and to Thomas Cromwell, who was the 'fixer' of what turned out to be a disastrous marriage that resulted in his downfall. Following Cromwell's negotiations, Anne landed at Deal on 27 December 1537, after being delayed in Calais by winter storms. With her when she landed were a retinue of 350 courtiers and an escort of 50 English ships. Once the landing was made her party began making its slow and stately way along Watling Street towards London, via Canterbury, Faversham and Sittingbourne. On New Year's Eve Anne was escorted into Rochester by the Duke of Norfolk, England's premier nobleman.

Anne spoke no languages beside German. She was unlearned and could not sing, dance or play an instrument. She was however kind and good humoured, and amiable without being over familiar; she was probably rather innocent when it came to sexual matters. Lady Browne, the wife of Sir Anthony Browne, Henry's Master of the Horse, predicted that the king would never love Anne, as there was in her 'such fashion and manner of bringing up so gross and far discrepant from the King's Highness' appetite'. In other words, he thought Anne would not be attractive enough to rouse Henry's sexual appetite – and so it proved. Infamously, Holbein was said to have flattered Anne's appearance in the portrait he made of her for Henry at Cromwell's behest.

When Anne finally landed at Deal, Henry was spending the New Year at Whitehall. He was due to meet her officially on 3 January when her party reached Greenwich. But Henry was impatient to meet his new bride, and decided that his first meeting with her would be a surprise: he told Cromwell that he would present Anne with a New Year's Gift to 'nourish love'. It seemed that the delicate flower of romance had not yet died in his heart: the prospect of meeting Anne turned him into an ardent young lover again, not a 48-year-old with badly ulcerated legs. It seemed that it also made Henry willing to throw aside rigid court protocol in his pursuit of his planned surprise visit. So on New Year's Day he took off from London on horseback with five gentlemen of the privy chamber, and arrived at Rochester as the winter afternoon light was fading.

Unfortunately, sources differ as to where in Rochester the meeting between Anne and Henry took place. It might have been in the Bishop's Palace, long since demolished; or in the castle overlooking the Medway estuary; or in the monastic foundation located next to the Cathedral that was dissolved soon after the meeting took place. Royal lodgings had been maintained at this particular foundation since the fourteenth century (and were extended and rebuilt by Henry after the monastery was dissolved) so this seems the more likely of the three candidates. Whichever it was, though, Anne was reportedly called on in advance by Sir Anthony

Browne, who forewarned her of the king's imminent arrival. According to Strype's *Ecclesiastic Memorials* Browne was 'never more dismayed in all his life, lamenting in his heart ... to see the lady so far and unlike that was reported'. He had no time to warn Henry, however, as the impetuous bridegroom was hard on his heels.

The king duly burst into the room to surprise Anne – and an awkward and embarrassing silence followed: after failing to conceal his astonishment, Henry's attention was drawn by the bear-baiting outside in the courtyard (a common spectacle on a public holiday), which he watched from the window. Sir Anthony saw 'discontentment' in the king's expression and a 'disliking of [Anne's] person'. Henry was poor at controlling his emotions and stayed with Anne only a short time, before hastily departing amid the low bows of courtiers. He stayed the night at Rochester (probably at one of the three venues already mentioned, though it must have been a different one to Anne) and sent his present over the next morning – it was a richly garnished partlet (that is, a sleeveless garment worn over the neck and shoulders). Then he hastily and gloomily departed for London.

On the way back to London Henry spoke with Sir John Russell, a diplomat and courtier, and one of his confidantes (and later Lord Privy Seal). 'How like you this woman?' Henry asked him. 'Do you think her so fair and of such beauty as has been reported to me? I pray tell you the truth.' Sir John's reply was diplomatic and non-committal, causing Henry to fume, 'I promise you I see no such thing in her as hath been shown me of her, and am ashamed that men have so praised her as they have done. I like her not.' Similarly, the sentiments he shared with Sir Anthony Browne bristled with anger and disappointment. 'I see nothing in this woman as men report of her, and I marvel that wise men would make such reports as they have done,' he said. As we have seen, Henry formally met with Anne a few days later at Blackheath, near Greenwich; their marriage lasted a few months until he divorced her and married Catherine Howard.

Rochester today ranks as one of the most historic and picturesque cities in Southeast England, with its handsome High Street (once part of Watling Street) overlooked by the adjacent castle and cathedral. Of the three places where Henry's extraordinary meeting with Anne might have taken place, only the castle remains: its keep is nowadays open to the sky but the ruins remain substantial, and are strikingly situated overlooking the Medway Estuary, which is spanned by nineteenth-century road and rail bridges

Kent

The Great Keep of Rochester Castle, where Henry may have met Anne of Cleves for the first time.

The interior of the Great Keep is now in ruins.

Kent

and bobbing with pleasure craft, though with plenty of evidence remaining of the area's industrial heritage; to the southeast, the castle keep allows for a fabulous view over the adjacent cathedral, the second oldest in England, with the site of the former Bishop's Palace now occupied by a range of late-eighteenth-century brick and flint buildings (Southgate, Prior's Gate House and College Green). Set into the walls of the cathedral's beautiful cloistered garden is an ornately carved doorway that gave access to the monastic foundation that Henry converted into a royal residence in the 1540s, though nothing in any way substantial remains of these buildings.

The doorway that once led from Rochester Cathedral's cloistered gardens into the attached monastic foundation – another possible venue for Henry's first meeting with Anne.

The Kent Coast: Dover, Erith and Sandwich

In the late Middle Ages and into Tudor times Dover Castle was one of the most important strongholds in the kingdom. This mighty fortress, glowering over the town (and the modern freight terminal and ferry port) from a high rocky promontory, was founded by William the Conqueror, and by Henry's time it was the second largest castle in England (after Windsor). One of the earliest occasions that official business brought Henry VIII here came in October 1514, when he bade farewell to his 18-year-old sister Mary as she left England to marry the French king, Louis XII, following a treaty brokered by Wolsey. 'I betoken you to God and the fortunes of the sea, and the government of the king your husband,' were Henry's words of farewell at the harbourside. Mary then headed to

France with a fleet of fourteen ships and four maids of honour (one of whom was Anne Boleyn), and was duly married to Louis at Abbeville – though her time as queen of France was destined to be short as Louis, who was more than thirty years her senior, died just three months later.

Six years later, on 26 May 1520, Henry was once again in Dover, this time to meet the Holy Roman Emperor Charles V on his arrival in England on a state visit. The Emperor landed to the accompaniment of a thunderous salute from the English fleet. After he came ashore, he was met by Wolsey and taken to Dover Castle, passing through the same thirteenth-century gate (named Colton's Gate) that today's visitors use to enter the castle – where Henry met him the next morning. Charles then travelled with Henry to Canterbury and Sandwich, from where he sailed to the Spanish Netherlands, while Henry returned to Dover where, on 31 May, the English entourage boarded twenty-seven ships and headed over the sea to Calais for Henry's legendary meeting with Francis I at the Field of the Cloth of Gold.

The medieval Colton's Gate at Dover Castle.

In June 1522, the Emperor was once more in Dover, this time to mark the signing of a treaty and his own betrothal to Henry's daughter Mary (who at that time was only 6 years old). Charles was again met by Wolsey on the waterfront and by Henry in the castle. Henry later showed off his warship *Henry Grace à Dieu* (moored in the harbour, and later known as the *Great Harry*) to Charles, who was to stay six weeks in England on a tour that took him to Rochester and Winchester and to a number of Henry's residences, including Bridewell Palace, Hampton Court, Greenwich Palace and Windsor Castle. However, Henry was never to meet the Emperor again: their relationship soured after the failure of the planned invasion of France that their visit was meant to celebrate.

Further visits to Dover came in October 1532, when Henry and Anne Boleyn lodged in the castle on the way back from their trip to Calais and Boulogne, and 1536, when Henry inspected the castle's defences with his wife Jane Seymour. To mark their visit Henry's favoured glazier Galyon Hone created stained-glass windows in the castle that bore the queen's emblem. Today visitors can wander round the gloomily atmospheric medieval interiors of the Great Tower, where Henry always lodged during his visits, though the emphasis throughout the castle is on the life and times of an earlier Henry – namely Henry II, whose massive rebuilding work in

The medieval walls and Great Tower of Dover Castle.

the 1180s created the medieval core of the castle that Henry VIII knew and that is still intact today. The later Henry barely gets a look-in amidst all the information boards and replica furniture (all of which is aimed at families and school groups), and the nineteenth-century tunnels bored into the castle rock, famously used as command posts during the Second World War, are as big a draw as the medieval castle – as is the Roman lighthouse, which is the best-preserved free-standing Roman structure in Britain.

Dover, of course, remains as intimately associated with the sea as it did in Henry's day. But that's not the same with Erith, situated on the south bank of the Thames just before it widens into its estuary, where in June 1514 Henry proudly watched the launch of his warship the *Henry Grace à Dieu*. Erith was close enough to London for the king and queen, along with Princess Mary, to travel there by barge from Greenwich (a distance of around sixteen kilometres by river). Eyewitnesses claimed this was the greatest pageant ever seen on the River Thames: the King himself was resplendent in cloth of gold and scarlet hose, and wore a whistle on a gold chain around his neck, the insignia of the supreme commander of the navy. The ship itself had an incredible array of bronze and iron cannon, and was overlooked by a veritable forest of masts.

The medieval Great Tower of Dover Castle.

Henry maintained an affection for the ship and when she was in dock at Rye (just over the Kent border in Sussex) some years later he went to view her and dined on board; in 1531 he also inspected the fleet at the Kent port of Sandwich, staying at a late medieval building that survives to this day and is known as the King's Lodgings.

Canterbury

Canterbury was the first place to which Henry brought the Holy Roman Emperor Charles V on his May 1520 state visit to England. After the pomp and ceremony of High Mass in the Cathedral, Henry and Charles knelt in prayer at the shrine of Thomas Becket and reverentially kissed some of the saint's relics – his broken skull, the hair shirt that he was wearing on the day of his murder in 1170, and the knight's sword that had pierced it. Afterwards, on the marble staircase of the Archbishop's Palace, the Emperor was presented to his aunt, Catherine of Aragon, who was robed in ermine-lined cloth of gold with ropes of pearls around her neck. That evening a feast was held at which there were three queens present at high table – Germaine of Foix, who was the widow of Charles's grandfather Ferdinand II of Aragon, with whom it has been suggested Charles was having an affair; Catherine herself; and Henry's sister Mary, Queen of France until the death of her husband Louis XII. Apparently considerable merriment unfolded at the event: the Spanish Count of Capra got carried away and 'made love so heartily' (according to the *Venetian Calendar of State Papers*) to an English lady that he fainted and had to be carried out of the room. At the dances that followed Henry partnered his sister Mary and Charles told Wolsey that when Pope Leo died, he would support his bid to be Pope.

Nothing now remains of these two sites. The former site of Becket's shrine in the Cathedral is marked by a modern memorial, while the former Archbishop's Palace with its thirteenth-century Great Hall was demolished in the 1650s; a nineteenth-century building of the same name and purpose stands on the site, though in 1982 archaeological excavations uncovered some remains of the Great Hall.

In 1527, Canterbury was a stop for Henry on his summer progress. It was here that the first mention appears of a varicose ulcer on Henry's leg, which confined him to bed in the city; the cause might have been the constrictive garters he wore below the knee, or an injury sustained while jousting, or even syphilis (which some have speculated was the disease that eventually killed him). Thomas Vicary, a local surgeon, healed the ulcer quickly and painlessly and was promoted to sergeant-surgeon, a post he was to hold into the reigns of Mary, Edward and Elizabeth. Henry was in better health during another visit to Canterbury some ten years later, in 1537, when he again worshipped at the shrine of St Thomas, this time in the company of his new wife Jane Seymour.

Leeds and Hever Castles

With its stunning location on an island in a lake, surrounded by Kent's classically English countryside, it's not surprising that Leeds Castle ('the loveliest castle in the world', according to its marketing puff) is a popular visitor attraction as well as a wedding and functions venue. The first person to fortify this site, in the centre of the county just outside Maidstone, was a Saxon chieftain named Leed (or Led). In 1119, a Norman stronghold was built here, which the following century fell into the hands of Edward I, who developed it into a royal residence (and created the artificial lake). The castle's current fairytale-like appearance dates from a thorough Tudor-style makeover (and the addition of a major new Tudor-style wing, called the 'New Castle') in the early nineteenth century.

Between 1517 and 1523 Henry spent a considerable sum on refurbishing the castle, with an upper floor added to the castle's 'gloriette' (or keep) for Catherine of Aragon. It was during this time that the castle's medieval Great Hall was remodelled; now styled the Henry VIII Banqueting Hall, it was subject to further extensive remodelling over the centuries. The magnificent bay window that Henry installed in the Hall, overlooking the water, can still be seen, as can a fireplace he installed in the neighbouring Queen's Gallery, on which his emblem is carved into the stonework. Henry also had the so-called Maidens' Tower built to provide accommodation for the queen's ladies (nowadays it offers hotel-style accommodation for wedding guests). Henry stayed at the castle on several occasions, most notably on the night of 22 May 1520 when he was on his way to meet the French king Francis I at the Field of the Cloth of Gold. Today two paintings commemorating that event hang in the Banqueting Hall – one showing the tournament itself, the other Henry's embarkation from Dover – though both are copies of sixteenth-century paintings that now hang at Hampton

The Keep at Leeds Castle, which Henry had modified for Catherine of Aragon.

Henry VIII: A History of his Most Important Places and Events

Left: A portrait of Henry VIII in the Henry VIII Banqueting Hall at Leeds Castle.

Below: A fireplace at Leeds Castle with Henry's emblem carved into the stonework.

Kent

The Maidens' Tower at Leeds Castle, the construction of which was ordered by Henry.

Court. Towards the end of his reign, on 30 September 1544, it was at Leeds Castle that Henry was reunited with his wife Catherine Parr on his return from his military campaign in Boulogne; his glazier Galyon Hone fashioned some new decorative glass for the Banqueting Hall and Chapel in celebration of his visit, though nothing of this survives today.

Hever Castle, situated in a lush green fold of Kent countryside between Tonbridge and East Grinstead, is also more of a stop for those on the Anne Boleyn trail rather than that of her husband. Founded in the thirteenth century, from 1462 to 1539 it was the seat of the Boleyn family, and it is possible that Anne was born here (she certainly grew up here). On acquiring the property in 1462, Geoffrey Boleyn, Anne's uncle, converted it into a sumptuous residence, but in later centuries it fell into a poor state of repair until in 1903 it was acquired and restored by the American millionaire William Waldorf Astor, who had business interests in hotels and newspapers. Nowadays it's a visitor attraction playing on its Tudor roots, with jousting tournaments and archery displays in the summer. Surrounded by a moat, the castle (actually more of a manor house) is undeniably picturesque, and the rooms vividly bring the Tudor

Henry VIII: A History of his Most Important Places and Events

Above and below: Hever Castle, the former home of Anne Boleyn.

era to life; though much of the castle's interior and exterior is recreated (or heavily restored), original panelling and stonework can be seen in places. A personal door lock owned by Henry and taken with him during summer progress for security, and used while he stayed in noblemen's houses, is on view in the large room that was once the Great Hall, still attached to one of the doors (on the other door to the hall there's an exact copy); it comes complete with a coat of arms and a tiny carved face, and the drop-down mechanism still works (and is proudly demonstrated by custodians on request). That said it is the two beautiful prayer books once owned by Anne Boleyn, and reverentially displayed in one of the upstairs rooms (and inscribed by her), that draw the crowds. A bedroom in the castle was restored in Tudor style by the Astor family and is known as the Henry VIII room, though there is no evidence he ever stayed in this actual room (if he did, he would have slept under the same fifteenth-century wood-beam ceiling that today's visitors see – though he would not have awoken to see the lute-playing mannequin the castle's owners have installed as a bit of 'scene setting'). In Margaret George's fictional autobiography of Henry, his fool Will Somers recalls that Hever 'is delightful in summer. It is always so green, so cool … it was an easy day's journey from London … the king used to stand on that hill, the first one from which you could glimpse Hever, and blow his hunting horn'. However, it is entirely possible that,

Henry's personal door lock, still attached to one of the doors into the Great Hall at Hever Castle.

Left and below: Henry remembered on a pub sign in the village of Hever.

despite the presence of his door lock, Henry never actually visited Hever, and conducted all his business with the Boleyns from Bolebrook Castle, just over the county boundary in Sussex: this is also a manor house, rather than a castle, and Henry definitely stayed here when he was hunting wild boar and deer in nearby Ashdown Forest; it's now a very opulent private residence.

Kent's Manor Houses

More than any other county, Kent seems to have been peppered with grand residences owned and occasionally visited by Henry. In addition to Rochester Castle, Dover Castle and Leeds Castle were manor houses (sometimes palatial in style) at Knole, Otford and Penshurst that he owned and used as grandiose hunting lodges – not to mention the opulent abbots' lodgings of dissolved abbeys that he took over (including, as we have seen, those in Canterbury and Rochester). Of these, the house at Knole, just outside Sevenoaks, was one of the largest – and it's certainly the best known today.

Knole's medieval origins are obscure but it passed through the ownership of the Bishops of Durham and then a succession of Archbishops of Canterbury before Henry purchased it from Archbishop Thomas Cranmer in the 1540s, in exchange for the properties of some dissolved Kent priories. Declaring it to have a 'sound, perfect and wholesome situation', he enlarged the house, installing plasterwork ceilings and marble chimney pieces. A pair of cast-iron and brass andirons (also known as firedogs – metal stands for supporting wood burning in a fireplace), both bearing the badges of Henry VIII and Anne Boleyn, can be seen to this day in the Great Hall (though they are thought to have come from Hever Castle). That said, most of what can be seen today at Knole is Jacobean – and the most famous person associated with the house is not Henry at all but the writer and garden designer Vita Sackville-West, the lover of the novelist Virginia Woolf, whose 1928 novel *Orlando* was inspired in part both by Vita and by the property.

Otford was a moated manor house associated with Knole that had reputedly been built by Thomas Becket. Situated on the northern fringes of Sevenoaks it was rebuilt by Archbishop Warham, Wolsey's rival, to compete with Hampton Court, and was surrounded by luxurious gardens.

In August 1514, Henry stayed here overnight as he escorted his sister Mary to Dover for her journey to France, and in May 1520, he stayed here again on the way to the Field of the Cloth of Gold. When Henry acquired the manor from Archbishop Cranmer in 1537, he ordered some rebuilding, but in the event, he only came here once more (in March 1541) as he thought the location to be low-lying and feared it would make him prone to rheumatism. 'If I should make abode [in this part of Kent], as I do surely mind to do now and then, I will live at Knole, and most of my house[hold] shall live at Otford,' he declared during the transaction, according to Ralph Morice, Cranmer's secretary and biographer. The house decayed after his death and was sold on to a member of the Kent gentry by Elizabeth I. The only remaining Tudor parts have now been incorporated into a row of Victorian cottages while the rest of the building, extensively rebuilt, is gradually being turned into a heritage centre.

Penshurst Place, near Tonbridge, was acquired by Henry in 1521 after the fall of its owner, the Duke of Buckingham. It had been built in 1341 as a country residence by a London merchant and boasted a magnificent beamed Great Hall, which remains today, along with one of its four corner towers. In Henry's time the Penshurst estate was managed by Sir Thomas Boleyn, who lived nearby at Hever Castle, and it's thought that Henry might have used Penshurst during his affair with Thomas's daughter Mary Boleyn. After his death Edward VI granted the house to Sir William Sidney; it has been extensively rebuilt over the centuries and is now open to the public (and frequently used as a film and TV location).

When Henry was eventually married to Mary's sister Anne, the royal couple stayed at Shurland House on the Isle of Sheppey, which was owned by Sir Thomas Cheney, who extended and improved it for Henry's visit; today the former service wing is a private home (with a recent asking price of £2.5 million), while much of the rest of the manor house is in ruins. The former Archbishop's Palace in the village of Charing is in a similar condition – part ruined, part private home; it was converted into a brick courtyard house by Archbishop Morton (who died at Knole in 1500) and was used by Henry as a hunting lodge.

Stone Castle near Greenhithe is another residence associated more with Anne Boleyn than Henry. Built on the site where William the Conqueror signed a treaty with the Men of Kent, it dates from the twelfth century and in the 1520s was the home of Anne's friend Bridget, Lady Wingfield; correspondence between Anne and Bridget was later cited in Anne's trial.

Henry and Anne were her guests for two nights in October 1532, on their way to and then back from Calais. Today the building, much altered over the centuries, is a company headquarters and closed to the public. Just over three kilometres to the west is the former site of Dartford Priory, where Henry's aunt, Bridget of York, had been a nun. When it fell into his hands, he demolished most of it and built a luxurious palace on the site, complete with a great court and a processional stair to the royal apartments, which were ranged round the old cloisters. The building was demolished in stages from Elizabeth's reign onwards and only the western gatehouse remains, set into a two-storey range of brick buildings capped by chimneys. Today the building, situated a short walk from Dartford station, is owned by the local Borough Council and serves as a functions and wedding venue (the main arch has been glazed in) – and though it's rather marooned amidst retail parks and modern housing, the front garden (in which there's an informative information panel with a drawing of how the place might have looked in Henry's day) goes a little way to recreating the old Tudor ambience.

Dartford Priory, which Henry rebuilt as a palace, as it appears today; a few Tudor elements remain.

Henry VIII: A History of his Most Important Places and Events

The former entrance to Dartford Priory, which Henry adapted as a palace.

Chapter 13

Surrey and Hampshire

The southern counties of Surrey and Hampshire were prime hunting country and were frequently visited by Henry on his summer progress. His palace at Oatlands in Surrey assumed an important role in his later marriages and he was a frequent guest at the manor houses that in those days sprinkled the forests and downland that characterize this part of England. In Hampshire he was to dine in spleandour with the Emperor Charles V in the shadow of King Arthur's supposed Round Table in Winchester, while in Southsea he watched the sinking of his prized warship the *Mary Rose* from the ramparts of the castle whose construction he had commissioned himself.

Oatlands

Henry bought Oatlands (or Otelands) in 1537 and converted what had been an old moated house (named after the thirteenth-century family that originally owned it) into a sizeable palace, with three courts and an octagonal tower. The palace was situated near Weybridge, just eight kilometres to the west of Hampton Court, though its location away from the Thames would have made it more time-consuming to reach from London. Oatlands was very much a country residence, with terraced gardens sprinkled with fountains, orchards with fruit trees brought from the dissolved Chertsey Abbey, and an extensive deer park. The interior rooms were hung with fine French tapestries and Turkish carpets. Although Henry originally conceived the palace for Anne of Cleves, it was his last wife, Catherine Parr, who probably made most use of it.

Henry VIII: A History of his Most Important Places and Events

Between those two wives came Catherine Howard, whom Henry married at Oatlands in secret on 28 July 1540, with Edmund Bonner, the Bishop of London, officiating. It was the same day that Thomas Cromwell was executed; Henry's marriage to Catherine represented the triumph of Cromwell's sworn enemies, the Howards, who had engineered Cromwell's downfall. In her novel *The Autobiography of Henry VIII* Margaret George imagines the wedding feast taking place in the palace's grand dining hall – 'a high-ceilinged chamber set on the second storey, hung with hunting trophies. Stags' heads and boars' heads stared at us with their glass eyes'. Henry ordered a sumptuous 'pearl bed' to be installed at the palace for his wedding night.

In the last years of his reign Henry stayed at Oatlands in July 1543, taking refuge from the plague raging through London, and then again in the summer of 1546, which was to prove his final summer hunting season: on that occasion a ramp was built at the palace to help him mount his horse with ease. Later in that year, in December, he fell dangerously ill with a fever at Oatlands and his doctors had to battle to keep him alive; it was reported in the *Spanish Calendar of State Papers* that the Spanish ambassador travelled to see him and Henry told him that he had suffered 'a sharp attack of the fever, which lasted in the burning stage for thirty hours', but that he had been restored. Although he recovered, he remained a very sick man, with an ashen face and a body that according to his doctors had 'greatly fallen away'. He died just a few weeks later.

The palace remained popular with subsequent monarchs but was sold off and demolished during Cromwell's Commonwealth. A single brick-arched gateway (known as the Tudor Gateway) is all that remains of the palace itself; it's on a pedestrian lane called Tudor Walk, situated just 250 metres northeast of the northern end of Weybridge high street, and forms an incongruous accompaniment to the utterly unremarkable new-build homes that characterize this part of the town. A circular plaque commemorates the 're-opening' of the gateway in 1985. Other street names nearby – such as Old Palace Gardens – are nowadays the only reminder that there was once a palace here. Around 800 metres to the east, the rather smart Oatlands Park Hotel now occupies an eighteenth-century mansion built on the site of one of Henry's hunting lodges.

Surrey and Hampshire

Above: This gateway is all that remains of Oatlands Palace.

Right: Commemorative plaque beside the former gateway to Oatlands Palace.

Woking and Esher

Another of Henry's palatial homes in Surrey was Woking Palace, which first came into royal hands when it was acquired by Henry VII as a residence for his mother (and grand matriarch of the Tudor dynasty) Lady Margaret

Beaufort. The residence was originally built in around 1200 as a moated manor house, with the River Wey forming part of the moat. Henry VII had the place rebuilt, and his son made further enhancements in 1515 and then again in the early 1530s. The finished palace was arranged around a single courtyard whose gallery and cloister faced the river. There was a chapel, a gatehouse, extensive royal apartments with bay windows, and a Great Hall, and the whole ensemble was surrounded by gardens and orchards – and in 1537 Henry added a bowling alley. However, the house became ruinous during the early Stuart era and the buildings and land were gradually turned over to farming; the local council is the guardian of the solitary wall of Tudor red brick (adjacent to a more recently built stone barn) that is all that remains of the palace, though a body called the Friends of Woking Palace have erected an information board and maintain a website about the palace. Otherwise, the site, situated in open countryside some two and a half kilometres southeast of Woking's railway station, is not signposted and must be accessed via private roads, and today the tumbledown wall presents a rather forlorn appearance: it sits in a marshy field on the Wey's featureless floodplain, and all there is to see of the palace apart from the wall are some scant remains of fish ponds and the moat.

The scant remains of Woking Palace.

Henry's other Surrey residence was Esher Palace, once Wolsey's country retreat; it was where Henry was staying when he heard the news of Prince Edward's birth at Hampton Court, and later in his reign, in December 1546, he spent a night here on what was to be his final journey, from Oatlands to Whitehall. The house was originally built by William Waynefleet, Bishop of Winchester, in the late fifteenth century, and his name is remembered by Waynefleet's Tower, the original gatehouse, which is still standing, though it has been much modified (with the upper storeys added in the eighteenth century). The Tower is now a private residence; an eighteenth-century house stands on the site of the palace itself and is used by a trade union as its training college.

The Sinking of the *Mary Rose* off Southsea

There's an old schoolboy maxim that Henry VIII was the 'father of the English navy'. Certainly, by the end of his reign the English navy was an impressive fighting force – Henry had ordered the construction of forty-six warships and thirteen smaller galleys, and had purchased a further twenty-six ships and captured thirteen more. Through all this acquisition Henry had gained an encyclopaedic knowledge of naval matters, which meant he often had the upper hand when discussing tactics and strategy with his admirals. In the last years of Henry's reign his navy was put to the test when in the summer of 1545 a French armada of more than 200 ships was launched against southern England in revenge for the English capture of Boulogne. The attack was presaged by French galleys raiding and burning the fishing village of Brighton on 18 July. The following day Henry dined aboard his flagship the *Great Harry*, moored in Portsmouth harbour, with Admiral John Dudley and François van der Delft, Charles V's new ambassador to England. He had already been warned of French designs on the south coast but angrily rejected the decision to surrender Boulogne. The ship on which he and his guests dined was fifty metres long and had a complement of 1,000 men; it was the most powerful warship in Europe, and cannot fail to have impressed the Imperial Ambassador with its might.

The next day, Sunday 20th, an enemy fleet approached Portsmouth and dropped anchor threateningly off St Helen's Point on the eastern side of the Isle of Wight, near Ryde. The outnumbered English ships were sent out in two lines to engage them. Henry watched the unfolding battle from

Southsea Castle, from whose ramparts Henry watched the *Mary Rose* sink. (*N Chadwick, Wikimedia Commons*)

the ramparts of Southsea Castle, a coastal fortress which he had ordered to be constructed the previous year (its keep and angled bastions remain to this day, though the castle was modified considerably in the nineteenth century, and took on a military role as recently as the Second World War). Beside Henry stood his commander Suffolk, and the two men famously looked on in horror as the seventy-one-gun, 700-ton *Mary Rose* foundered as it approached the French fleet and sank, after being caught by a freak gust of wind which caused it to heel to starboard, whereupon seawater rushed in through the lower gun ports. The great ship had been built only the previous year, but it took all but thirty of its crew of 415 with it to the bottom of Spithead, the reach of the Solent between Ryde and Southsea. Many men were ensnared helplessly beneath the netting spread out on the decks to stop enemy soldiers boarding; their pitiable cries could be heard from the shore. 'Oh my Gentlemen!' Henry is supposed to have cried. 'Oh my gallant men!' He then turned to comfort Lady Carew, the wife of Sir George Carew, the Vice-Admiral of the Fleet, who was on the stricken ship. Despite the loss of the *Mary Rose*, the French retreated, though not before they had sacked the towns of Newhaven and Seaford on their way back home. The sinking of the *Mary Rose* was later depicted on one of the famed Cowdray engravings, prepared for Sir Anthony Browne, Master of the King's Horse, whose country residence was at Cowdray in Sussex; the paintings were unfortunately destroyed in a fire in the eighteenth century but copies remain, including one showing Henry watching the unfolding tragedy from the ramparts of Southsea Castle.

The Great Hall at Winchester Castle

Over two decades before the sinking of the *Mary Rose*, in July 1522, Henry had passed through Hampshire with Charles V during the Emperor's state visit to England. They had been on their way from Windsor, where they had signed a treaty that confirmed Charles's betrothal to Henry's daughter Mary (Charles' cousin), to Southampton, from where the Emperor would depart for Spain. Just before reaching Southampton, they signed another treaty, at Bishop's Waltham Palace, by which they agreed to support each other in an attack on France (now in ruins, the palace was a residence of the Bishops of Winchester, and dated mostly from remodelling carried out by William of Wykeham in the late fourteenth century). Prior to that they had stayed in Winchester itself – and on the 3rd they feasted in the Great Hall of Winchester Castle, where Henry was keen to show off the most famous 'relic' of Arthurian Britain.

Winchester had become identified as King Arthur's Camelot in the Middle Ages. Henry VII, eager to justify the position of a Welsh dynasty on the English throne, had emphasized his supposed descent from Arthur, and had made sure that his first-born son was named after the fabled king and, moreover, was born in Winchester. Despite Prince Arthur's early death, the Arthurian theme was to play an important part in the mythology of the Tudor dynasty, with both Henry VIII and Elizabeth I commissioning and attending pageants and plays celebrating the most famous of English heroes (who in all probability had never actually existed). Winchester itself has a long and venerable history – under King Canute (1016–35) it was even the *de facto* capital of England – and an important castle had been founded by the Normans in 1067, on a rise immediately north of what is now the city centre. The castle's heyday came during the long reign of Henry III, who in 1222 ordered the construction of the showpiece Great Hall. Eighty years later the castle's royal apartments were destroyed by fire but the Hall was saved, and today the Round Table

Henry VIII: A History of his Most Important Places and Events

Left and below: The Round Table in Winchester, whose design was ordered by Henry in 1515.

is its focus and draw. It hangs high on the wall at one end, looking for all the world like an enormous dart board, the centre occupied by a red 'bull's eye'; this turns into a Tudor Rose up close, with the segments splaying away from it picked out alternatively in green and cream. In the Middle Ages it was widely believed to be the genuine table around which King Arthur had sat with his knights but it is, in fact, a work of medieval fakery, probably constructed for a royal feast during the reign of Winchester's own Henry III, whose extraordinarily long reign was to last for another fifty years after the castle was built – though other sources claim that the table was built later, in 1290, for an Arthurian tournament to celebrate the marriages of the children of Edward I in April of that year.

During renovation work in 1976 it was discovered that all the painting on the table dated to Henry VIII's reign, and that when the table was originally constructed it was just bare wood. The designs are all thought to have been ordered by Henry during his first visit to Winchester in 1515, when he issued a writ for 'the repair of the Great Hall at Winchester and the Round Table there'. Along with the Tudor Rose, the designs include the names of twenty-four of Arthur's knights around the circumference, and a depiction of a resplendent bearded and crowned King Arthur himself. X-ray analysis has shown that at that time King Arthur's face closely resembled that of King Henry – a deliberate gesture that during the 1522 visit of Charles would have reminded the Emperor of the inheritance of the British kings and their descent from King Arthur (though repainting over the centuries has aged the figure and has rendered the resemblance less clear). The table has hung on the west wall of the Great Hall since it was moved in 1873, from the east wall – where it was probably hanging during the great feast in the Hall that was attended by Henry and Charles.

Chapter 14

Oxfordshire and Buckinghamshire

Woodstock Palace

By the time Henry VIII came to the throne, Woodstock, some ten kilometres to the northwest of Oxford, had been 'royal' for over half a millennium. King Aethelred the Unready had issued a set of legal regulations known as the 'Woodstock code' from here in 997, and in 1086 the Domesday Book recorded the area as a 'royal forest'. King Henry I had developed a hunting lodge in the forest into a royal menagerie, keeping leopards and camels in an enclosed park, while his successor Henry II had developed the lodge into a fully fledged royal residence, from which he courted his mistress, Rosamund Clifford – the 'fair Rosamund' of English folklore – and in 1179 granted a royal charter for the founding of a town nearby. Today the market town of Woodstock is a prosperous place that's part of Oxford's commuter belt. On its outskirts is the magnificent Blenheim Palace, built between 1705 and 1722 by the First Duke of Marlborough following his victory at the Battle of Blenheim – and which can claim Woodstock Palace as its distant ancestor.

Henry VII extended and rebuilt Woodstock, as had the previous Henrys, and in July 1497 brought his wife and their sons Arthur and Henry here. At that time the princes were aged 11 and 6; during their stay they had an audience with Andrea Trevisan, the Venetian ambassador, along with the king and queen. By then Woodstock took the form of a large stone house adorned with heraldic emblems. When Henry VIII inherited the property from his father, he added some sunken baths to the palace, which used water piped from a spring named Rosamund's Well (recalling the dalliances of an earlier Henry): the water from the well was apparently cool in summer and warm in winter. The palace was often used on royal progress, and on one such visit, in August 1517, it was here that Henry learned from his queen that she was pregnant: according to Richard Pace, Wolsey's secretary, Catherine 'did meet with his grace at his chamber door, and showed unto him for his welcome home her belly something great, declaring openly she was quick with child'. Subsequent visits included one in July 1543, when Henry came here with Catherine Parr.

As to the palace's later history, the buildings seem already to have been decaying when the young Princess Elizabeth was placed under house arrest here during the reign of her sister Mary. The palace was eventually destroyed during a siege in the English Civil War, but early in the next century some of its stones were used to build Blenheim Palace, in whose grounds the ruins were situated (in fact the palace's architect John Vanburgh wanted the ruins turned into a landscape feature akin to a folly, but the first Duchess of Marlborough rejected the idea, complaining it would spoil the view from the Great Court across the lakes to the great Column of Victory, and asked for what remained of the medieval palace to be removed). Today a stone plinth, installed in 1962, marks the site of the former palace. It is located just to the northeast of the northern

The stone plinth that marks the former position of the Palace of Woodstock, with Blenheim Palace in the background.

Henry VIII: A History of his Most Important Places and Events

Vanburgh's great bridge over the ornamental lake at Blenheim is built partly from stone from the Palace of Woodstock.

end of Vanburgh's great bridge over the ornamental lake (in fact some of the palace's medieval masonry ended up in the bridge's foundations). Unfortunately the plinth is rather neglected, sitting isolated on a patch of grass sloping down to the lake with no information boards to indicate what it commemorates – and the faded Latin inscriptions on its sides offer no clues, either: 'Dieu defend le Droit' is actually the motto of the Dukes of Marlborough rather than anything to do with the royal associations of the former palace. However, a reminder of the former medieval palace can also be found elsewhere in Blenheim's expansive grounds, in the form of one of the greatest concentrations of ancient oak trees found in Europe: they were planted by Henry I and subsequent monarchs (including Henry VIII) to create a deer park, and they were never cut down for timber or landscaping because of their royal origins.

Ewelme and Langley

A manor house in the village of Ewelme, situated deep in the Oxfordshire countryside midway between Henley-on-Thames and Oxford, often served as a private retreat for Henry when the court came to Woodstock. But according to the historian David Starkey, the place held much more significance for Henry than a country retreat: for his father also enjoyed coming to Ewelme, and it was here in the latter part of 1491 that Henry VIII was conceived.

At that time, the 1490s, the house was in the possession of the de la Pole family, and Henry VII must have been staying here as a guest when his younger son was conceived. Henry VII eventually took possession of the manor house in 1504 from Edmund de la Pole, the third duke of Suffolk, who was later to be executed for treason in 1513 in the early years of Henry VIII's reign. (De la Pole is character of interesting lineage: his mother was a sister to Richard III and Edward IV, making him a Yorkist claimant to the throne, and therefore a threat to the Tudors; and he was the great-great-grandson of the poet Geoffrey Chaucer, whose granddaughter Alice had married into the family and is buried in a grand tomb in St Mary's Church in Ewelme.) When Henry VIII came of age he converted the manor house into a royal residence, with a queen's side and a king's side, as was convention. However, his visits here were infrequent: one came in the summer of 1518 when the sweating sickness ravaged the county and chased him here from Woodstock. Between 1525 and 1535 Henry leased the building to Sir Charles Brandon, but he stayed here while on royal progress with both Anne Boleyn and Catherine Howard, and finally regained control of the place in 1540, using it as a hunting lodge.

The residence was reported as being in a state of decay just twenty years later, and does not appear to have been used by subsequent monarchs. A private house now stands on the site, converted from the former service wing of the Tudor palace, though its current appearance is Georgian: it last changed hands (in 2006) for a cool £10 million. Today it's barely visible behind a high wall that separates it from Ewelme's village pond – which stands at the heart of an almost unutterably English setting that includes a colony of ducks, drooping trees whose branches almost brush the water and whitewashed houses capped by thatch. In fact the pond is known as the 'King's Pool' after the tradition that Henry used to bathe in it on his visits to the manor, attracted perhaps by the traditional healing virtue of the water, which might have soothed the pain caused by his leg ulcer.

The other Oxfordshire property that has associations with Henry is Langley Manor, near Burford in the northwest of the county, which like Ewelme was a hunting lodge developed by his father. A story connected with the house tells that the 15-year-old Henry apparently lost a gold ring set with a pointed diamond somewhere in the grounds in 1507; the ring

Henry VIII: A History of his Most Important Places and Events

The King's Pool at Ewelme; tradition has it that Henry once bathed here.

was given to him by Edmund Dudley, his father's chief minister, who turned out to be one of Henry's first 'victims', executed soon after he acceded to the throne. Langley Farm now stands on the site; the buildings incorporate fragments of the hunting lodge from early Tudor times.

Henry in Buckinghamshire

In the heart of the Buckinghamshire stockbroker belt, just eight kilometres east of Amersham, Chenies Manor was built in the 1530s (on the site of a medieval manor house) by John Russell, the first Earl of Bedford, whose career as a royal minister saw him serve under Henry both as Lord High Admiral and Lord Privy Seal. Henry had given Russell land from the dissolved monasteries and Russell returned the compliment by incorporating a suite of rooms for Henry to use when he visited the property on progress. Thus flattered, Henry visited several times: it is believed he was here when Sir Thomas More was executed, and it was during another visit that Catherine Howard, accompanying him, allegedly committed adultery with Henry's courtier Thomas Culpeper. Today the building is something of a puzzle as to how much of the original Tudor dwelling survives, as there have been several rebuildings over the years (some in Tudor style); most of the current property now serves as a private house, with the remainder given over to weddings and film shoots.

In the north of the same county is North Marston, a good-looking village of handsome houses of red brick and thatch, situated midway between Aylesbury and Buckingham under the wide skies of the Vale of Aylesbury. The name of the village pub, The Pilgrim, points to an unusual past – for on the edge of the village, where the houses give way to farmland, is, surprisingly, a holy well. Its origins date to 1290, when Sir John Schorne was rector of the Parish of North Marston, and became known as a performer of miracles (on one occasion drawing the devil out of a boot – a story which somehow morphed into Schorne catching the devil *in* the boot, giving rise to the 'jack-in-the-box' legend). The well itself miraculously sprung into life during a drought, when Schorne struck the ground with his staff. Legends attached to both the well's miraculous healing water, and the curate himself, meant that from the late fourteenth to the early sixteenth century North Marston was the third most important site of pilgrimage in England, after Canterbury and Walsingham; Henry visited on two occasions, in 1511 and 1521, to give thanks for his recovery from the sweating sickness. Schorne himself was believed to be a saint of some kind: in 1478 his tomb had been moved from the village church to the exalted surroundings of St George's Chapel, Windsor, to which Henry had easy access – but nonetheless he was one of thousands of pilgrims who made an effort to travel to this remote spot. By the late twentieth century the well itself had become rather neglected, encased in something akin to a coal bunker, but following reports of disappointment expressed by visiting tourists from the Far East, in 2004 a pillared canopy was built over it – and now, when the pump is worked, a red devil rises from a lead boot at its base. The water here was meant to cure gout (hence all the legends linking Schorne with feet), and in the village church, which is as handsome (and as traditionally English) as the village it serves, is a tiny shrine at the base of a wall where the faithful once inserted their feet in the hope of a cure; the shrine was built when Schorne's tomb was moved, and it is possible that Henry even availed himself of the opportunity to have his feet blessed here.

Above and below: The ancient well in the village of North Marston, where Henry came on pilgrimage.

Chapter 15

Hertfordshire, Essex and Middlesex

Hertfordshire

There's a clutch of properties associated with Henry spread across what is now the Hertfordshire commuter belt, to the northwest of London – amidst the towns of Watford, St Albans, Hatfield and Hertford. In Henry's day, the most opulent of these was probably The More, near Rickmansworth, which the French ambassador Jean du Bellay claimed was finer even than Hampton Court. The comparisons are apt, for the palace he was describing was also one of Wolsey's exercises in self-aggrandisement. When Wolsey fell from grace, Henry purloined the building, partitioning the palace's Great Hall with a floor to create apartments on two levels; Catherine of Aragon lived here for a while after the annulment of her marriage. In the second part of his reign Henry visited the place several times while on progress, but during the following century the house fell into decay, and it was eventually demolished in 1661. The site was investigated by archaeologists in the 1950s, after which the remaining foundations were covered in earth to preserve them; two stone pillars in the grounds of Northwood Preparatory School are said to be from the manor.

Some sixteen kilometres to the northeast, Tyttenhanger House, just outside St Albans, was in medieval times the property of the Abbot of St Albans. Henry first visited the place in May 1528, chased here by an outbreak of the sweating sickness. Here he 'prepared to bide the time that God would allow him' according to the chronicler Edward Hall; the house was 'purged daily by fires and other preservatives, such as vinegar, and the king ordered the windows to be enlarged to increase the fresh air. He kept the queen with him and attended Mass and a strict devotional regime lest the plague be divine comment; in the afternoons he hunted'. Henry liked the property and made moves to acquire it in 1531, but it did not come his way until eight years later when the abbey was dissolved. Little is known about the appearance of the house, though it was moated; Henry did not make any major extensions or alterations during his tenure of the property. A seventeenth-century mansion now stands on the site. The present building incorporates none of the features from Tudor times and is divided into offices.

Hatfield House, by contrast, has survived much better. Situated just five kilometres to the northeast of Tyttenhanger, on the outskirts of the modest commuter town of Hatfield, its origins lie in the 1480s, when it was built by John Morton, Bishop of Ely and future Archbishop of Canterbury, in the style of a medieval manor house with towers, buttresses, gables and twisted chimneys. Henry acquired the house in 1538, and stayed that year when the plague was ravaging London. However, he mainly used the house as a nursery for his children – and by far the most famous event that took place here involved his daughter, Elizabeth, who received the news of her accession (following the death of her sister Mary) in the gardens of the house. A small part of the Tudor property remains, though the bulk of what is visible today was rebuilt in the Jacobean era.

Further east still is Hunsdon, situated in the countryside just east of Ware and Hertford. Henry purchased the manor house from the Duke of Norfolk in 1525 and then spent thousands on extending the place, creating a moat, building royal lodgings with heraldic windows by Galyon Hone, and partly resurfacing the house in brick. It was now a suitable place for the upbringing of a future king, and in 1539 Henry moved the court of his son Edward here – primarily because of the cleanliness of the air (a portrait of a very severe-looking 9-year-old Edward, painted in 1546 and now at Windsor, shows the house in the background, visible through a window). The house was later granted by Elizabeth I to her cousin Henry Carey, later Lord Hunsdon, and was rebuilt extensively in the nineteenth century, though one of the turrets remains from Tudor times. It is now a private residence (and very much smaller than the grand residence of Henry's time).

Even less remains of another of Henry's Hertfordshire properties, at Ashridge, near Berkhamstead, which he had converted from a dissolved thirteenth-century monastery. Like other properties in the county, it was primarily used by Henry's children, though Catherine Parr persuaded him to come here while on progress in July 1543 so that together they could visit them. By this time Henry found it difficult to visit houses such as Ashridge as they had not been adapted to his increasing bulk – unlike the riverside palaces in London. What remained of the site was cleared at the start of the nineteenth century, and a Gothic mansion was built on the site; it's now a college.

Essex

Henry's principal residence in Essex was the Palace of Beaulieu near Chelmsford. This medieval hall house, originally known as New Hall, was for a long time owned by the abbots of Waltham Abbey, and was later acquired by Edward IV. It remained in royal hands until Henry VII granted it to Thomas Butler, Earl of Ormonde, who entertained Henry VIII there in 1510 and then again in 1515. When the earl died, in that year, his daughter Margaret inherited the property and it passed into the Boleyn family: her son was Sir Thomas Boleyn, the father of Anne, and he sold it back into royal hands. Between 1515 and 1523 Henry converted the residence into a sumptuous palace and renamed it Beaulieu, although the old name stuck – and still does to this day.

One of the most noteworthy events that occurred here involved some French 'hostages' that Henry entertained at court between 1518 and 1520. They weren't really hostages as such – in fact they numbered around sixteen young noblemen whom Francis I sent to England as part of his obligations set out by the Treaty of London. The young men (some of whom might have been as young as 15) were treated by Henry as honoured guests, and were a means for the king to communicate informally with his rival: he was well aware that anything he said to them would eventually find its way to Francis's ears. According to the chronicler Edward Hall 'the king did shoot, hunt and run daily with the hostages to their great joy' – and in September 1519 the 'hostages' were treated to a sumptuous banquet at New Hall, hosted by the king and queen.

Some eight years later, in May 1527, Henry spent a month at New Hall with Anne Boleyn, who hunted with him and ate with him in his privy chamber – though Henry was still married to Catherine at the time and it is thought that his relationship with Anne was not yet consummated. By this time the palace was newly faced with Tudor brick and had a gatehouse that gave access to a main courtyard with a fountain; there was also a Hall, a chapel and a tennis court. A gilded and painted panel that once adorned the gatehouse is now at Hampton Court while (as we have seen) a window that was here, crafted by Dutch glaziers, is now at St Margaret's Church,

Westminster. Today, the building forms part of a school, named New Hall after the original house, and although much of it is Tudor, it dates principally from rebuilding during Elizabeth's time rather than Henry's. However, in 2009, archaeologists from the TV show *Time Team* excavated the grounds of the school and uncovered the foundations of the chapel and gatehouse that had been built by Henry.

Another country residence in Essex that drew Henry's eye was located at Havering-atte-Bower, which nowadays lies just inside the boundaries of Greater London. The palace is an old one, originally built by Edward the Confessor, the 'bower' being a hilltop garden that he built and that afforded views over the Thames Valley. What attracted Henry was the enormous, rambling deer park that surrounded the palace. Within the park was a smaller moated house named Pyrgo, which was a residence of Catherine of Aragon, Anne Boleyn and Jane Seymour consecutively, though little is known about its history; it appears, however, that Henry chose Pyrgo as the venue for a meeting in 1542 with his estranged daughters, Mary and Elizabeth, and, being pleased with them, made the decision to restore them to the line of succession. Both houses remained in royal hands but decayed during the Commonwealth; Pyrgo was demolished in 1770 and Havering Palace in 1814. No trace now remains of either – except for Havering Parish Church, a nineteenth-century building that has its origins in the palace chapel.

Jericho House in the village of Blackmore, near Chipping Ongar, was, in Henry's time, a small moated manor house screened by high brick walls. The water filling the moat was piped from the River Can, known locally as the Jordan, hence the name of the house. The building was adjacent to a priory and was used by the priors to accommodate visitors. During Henry's reign the place acquired a reputation as one of the king's 'houses of pleasure', where he went for trysts with his mistress Elizabeth Blount (his courtiers used to say on these occasions that he had 'gone to Jericho'). In June 1519, Elizabeth Blount gave birth to her son here, who was named Henry Fitzroy (Henry, son of the king). Today the priory church survives as the Parish Church of St Lawrence, and nearby is a Georgian brick house (known as Jericho Priory) built on the foundations of a Tudor house that might have been Jericho. Parts of the moat survive, while the Bull Inn is supposed to have once been the house's stable block.

Roydon Hall, a manor house at Harlow, has fared rather less well: it was demolished in 1864 and nothing can be seen of it today, but Henry visited a number of times, and famously after the birth of his son Edward he stood at the window and held the infant in his arms so that the crowds outside could see their future king. According to a letter written by the courtier Richard Cromwell (nephew to Thomas Cromwell and great-grandfather to Oliver), the king 'there solaced all the day with much mirth and joy, dallying with [Edward] in his arms a long space and so holding him in a window to the sight and great comfort of all the people'.

In the early sixteenth century Waltham Abbey was one of the most venerable religious houses in England: a foundation of King Canute, it was here in May 1528 that Henry sought refuge from the sweating sickness, which previously had claimed four members of Wolsey's household within the space of four hours. The abbey was the very last in England to be dissolved, in 1540, and when it was, an inventory indicated that the abbot's lodgings included a 'king's chamber' and 'queene's chamber' – so the accommodation had clearly been adapted for Henry's occasional visits. He enjoyed hunting in the neighbouring Epping Forest, in which he built a number of hunting lodges, including the Great Standing, built in 1543 and situated just five kilometres to the south. This timber building (just outside Chingford) had an open upper gallery from which the king could shoot game or watch the progress of the hunt with his companions. The structure was renovated in 1589 for Queen Elizabeth and is now (much rebuilt) a museum – where parties of schoolchildren can try on Tudor clothes and find out about Tudor kitchens, and experience the same views over Epping Forest that Henry enjoyed in his later years.

Middlesex

Henry's principal residence in Middlesex was Hanworth Palace, which has its origins in a hunting lodge that Henry's father established just a few kilometres west of Richmond Palace, on the edge of Hounslow Heath. Henry extended the property, remodelling it in Renaissance style with terracotta roundels of goddesses by Giovanni di Maiano (similar to those seen at Hampton Court), and gave it in turn to Anne Boleyn and then Catherine Parr. Bridges over the moat connected the palace to the beautiful gardens that were originally laid out by Henry VII and which included strawberry beds, orchards and an aviary, beyond which were woods where Henry VIII hunted buck and hare. After Henry's death, Elizabeth I sold the property to Francis, Lord Cottingham;

it was eventually destroyed by a fire in 1797. The site of the palace is today marked by a group of opulent buildings, of stone and red brick, set incongruously amidst gardens immediately south of St George's Church. Along a driveway leading to an eighteenth-century mansion named Tudor House two of the surviving roundels can be seen, set into walls overlooking the drive, while to the south, overlooking the main road (Elmwood Avenue/Castle Way), is a nineteenth-century mock-Tudor folly known as Tudor Court, which now contains flats, though probably occupies the site of the palace stables; to its immediate south, lining a road named Tudor Court, a sliver of unkempt woodland along a ditch is all that remains of the palace's moat. Apart from this, the only suggestion that a palace stood in what is now a fairly unremarkable west London suburb comes in the street names – there's a Moat Side and an Elizabeth Way all lined with the fairly ordinary semi-detached housing and 1960s residential blocks that characterize London's suburbs.

Henry also owned a manor house in Enfield known as Elsyng Palace, named after its first owner, Thomas Elsyng, a fourteenth-century London mercer. The king acquired the property in 1539 from Thomas Manners,

One of the roundels from Hanworth Palace.

Tudor Court in Hanworth recalls the former palace that stood here.

First Earl of Rutland, and set about converting the property into a palace, adding a covered gallery and rebuilding one of the courts. Occasionally Henry received ambassadors here, but principally this was another of his palaces that was used mainly by his children; in 1542, James Needham, Henry's Clerk of Works, was tasked with conducting an extensive renovation of the property prior to Edward, Elizabeth and Mary spending Christmas here. Five years later it was while they were staying here that Edward and Elizabeth heard of their father's death. The palace was later incorporated into the grounds of a seventeenth-century house known as Forty Hall (which still survives), and it is thought the ruins may have been retained in the grounds as a folly. However, they were eventually demolished and the bricks were used in other houses. The exact location of the palace was lost for many years until in the 1960s the local Enfield Archaeological Society unearthed remains of vaulted brick drains and associated buildings to the northeast of Forty Hall, and it has been concluded from subsequent digs (that have recently taken place every year) that in Henry's day, the palace was the size of Hampton Court and was of similar appearance to St James's Palace in central London.

Chapter 16

The West Country, the Midlands, Northern England and East Anglia

The West Country and the Midlands

Henry's principal residence in the English Midlands was the hilltop castle at Ampthill in Bedfordshire, which he purchased in 1524. The castle had a fine great hall and several stone towers overlooking a central courtyard, and was known for its fresh air and excellent deer park. Later in his reign Henry added extensive apartments which were used during the summer progress. He is known to have visited the place in the spring of 1528 to escape the sweating sickness, and in September 1540 he came here again, with Catherine Howard; on that occasion he fell ill with malaria, which led to his recurrent problems with his legs worsening – and Catherine's vice chancellor Sir Edward Baynton disgraced himself by appearing drunk in the king's presence, which led to Henry issuing a stern injunction to all household servants that such a faux pas should not happen again.

The palace fell into decay after Henry's reign and what remained of it was demolished in the seventeenth century. Today the site of the palace is marked by Catherine's Cross, erected in the 1770s to commemorate Catherine of Aragon, who lived here during her divorce proceedings. It sits in Ampthill Park, which covers a ridge of high ground overlooking the town.

Another Midlands residence of Henry's that has gone was located at Grafton in Northamptonshire. Henry's maternal grandmother Elizabeth Woodville was born in the manor house that once stood here, and in 1525 Henry requested Thomas More, Chancellor of the Duchy of Lancaster, to have the place extensively repaired. In 1528, Henry was chased here from Ampthill by the sweating sickness – which in that year was clearly rampant – and complained of pains in the head, which caused something of a panic, though he made a reasonably quick recovery. Henry's most noted visit came in July of the next year when, according to George Cavendish, Anne Boleyn, who was with him, 'kept state more like a queen than a simple maid'. Cavendish was part of Wolsey's circle (and was later his biographer) and tells an intriguing story from the time of this particular visit.

It took place just after Lorenzo Campeggio, the Papal legate, had heard Henry's nullity suit in London. Campeggio was then invited by Henry to Grafton, along with Wolsey. Cavendish claims that when the two arrived at Grafton, the Italian was taken to a comfortable set of lodgings but Wolsey was left sitting on his mule before Henry Norris offered him use of his room to change out of his riding clothes, prior to an audience with the king. This was clearly a deliberately engineered snub: however, Cavendish reports that Wolsey finally gained an audience with the king in the presence chamber of the house, and that the two men talked by a window for a long time. But the nullity suit had been lost and Wolsey's star was waning. In the fictional *Autobiography of Henry VIII* Margaret George portrays Wolsey as, in Henry's eyes, 'deferential and shaken' after their meeting – 'he lapped about my hand as a puppy, scampering about, wagging his tail to please. It sickened me and made me sad. I had no wish to witness the degradation.' The next day Anne, Wolsey's sworn enemy, insisted that Henry left early with her to see the new hunting park, and saw to it that the king was away all day – and by the time they returned, Wolsey had gone. (An account by Thomas Alward, one of Wolsey's servants, contradicts this, and maintains that the king and Wolsey went hunting after dinner that day.) Whatever the case, Henry never saw Wolsey again; that October the cardinal was stripped of his office of Lord Chancellor and in November, shortly before his death, Parliament arraigned him of 44 charges. Today, the house that now stands on the site dates almost entirely from the seventeenth century, and incorporates no part of the old Tudor house; it serves as a private hospital. However, Henry's time is remembered by a wall painting of his meeting with Campeggio that hangs in Grafton village hall, and by the village often being known as Grafton Regis – the 'Regis' being bestowed by Henry as a mark of his affection for the place.

The other properties Henry visited in the West Midlands and the counties to the south (Gloucestershire and Wiltshire) were not owned by him: he simply commandeered them for himself and his court as he was passing through. One was Moor Hall at Sutton Coldfield where he stayed in the summer of 1528 as the sweating sickness ravaged his intended destination, Woodstock (he was warned that a servant of the Duke of Suffolk, who had gone to Woodstock to prepare the palace for his arrival, had fallen ill and died from the disease). So John Vesey, Bishop of Exeter, put him up in Sutton Coldfield instead, in a house he himself had built in the 1520s on a site that is now just a few kilometres northwest of the infamous Gravely Hill motorway interchange (Spaghetti Junction). While staying at the house Henry hunted in Sutton Chase, and there is a story that a boar he was hunting turned on him, whereupon a local girl who happened to be nearby shot it dead with an arrow. The site is now occupied by an early twentieth-century house that is now a hotel.

Henry did not own property in the West Country and rarely visited this part of England. In 1535, however, his royal progress included Sudeley Castle, near Winchcombe in the Cotswolds, where he spent time with Thomas Cromwell arranging for commissioners to visit religious houses in the region. (These days Sudeley is a private home, wedding venue,

Iron Acton Court in Gloucestershire, where Henry stayed in 1535. (*Hogweard, Wikimedia Commons*)

hotel and tourist attraction in one – and it is also where Catherine Parr is buried, following her marriage to Thomas Seymour). In the same county (and on the same trip) he visited Acton Court at Iron Acton, where Sir Nicholas Poyntz constructed a lavish Renaissance-style eastern range for his house especially for Henry's visit; the range has been preserved and is considered one of the most important Tudor buildings in England – it's open to the public, who on their tour dutifully peer at the range's privy ('King Henry sat here'). During his tour of Gloucestershire Henry also visited Painswick Lodge and Berkeley Castle, and Little Sodbury Manor, where Sir John Walsh, who employed the Bible translator William Tyndale as a tutor for his grandchildren, was his host.

However, the most famous West Country property associated with Henry – thanks to the novels by Hilary Mantel – is Wolf Hall, the Wiltshire country seat of the Seymour family. Unfortunately the current house known as Wolf Hall near Burbage (which is still owned by descendants of the Seymour family) dates entirely from the seventeenth century, and only a few scant foundations of the old medieval manor house (which was in a slightly different location) remain; a barn in which King Henry and Queen Jane supposedly held a feast to celebrate their marriage burned down in the 1920s. Henry stayed three nights at Wolf Hall in 1535, during his West Country progress, and some historians maintain that the visit marks the start of his dalliance with Jane Seymour, whose father was the warden of nearby Savernake Forest, where Henry liked to hunt. In July 1543, he made another visit to Wolf Hall with his new wife, Catherine Parr, and his daughter Mary. The original house was demolished in 1723 but archaeological excavations in 2018 brought to light an extensive brick-lined sewer on the site, as well as 'ornate tiles likely to have been walked on by Henry VIII' (as one report speculated). That said, the exact size and appearance of the house as it existed in Henry's day remains a matter of some conjecture.

Norfolk and the North of England

When Henry came to the throne the village of Walsingham, forty-three kilometres northwest of Norwich, was one of Europe's great pilgrimage centres – and had been since 1061, when an Anglo-Saxon noblewoman, Richeldis de Faverches, was instructed by the Virgin Mary in a vision to recreate the house of the Holy Family that had stood in Nazareth. Henry first came on pilgrimage here as a 6-year-old in 1497, with his mother, when thanks were given for Henry Tudor's safe delivery after his showdown with the pretender, Perkin Warbeck. In 1511, he came here again to give thanks for the birth of his first son, on New Year's Day of that year (sadly the infant, christened Henry, was to live only a few weeks). Henry arrived on 20 January, dismounted a kilometre and a half away at the so-called slipper chapel, removed his shoes and walked barefoot to the shrine of the Virgin. Reverentially he knelt on the altar steps and kissed the shrine's holiest relic, the phial of the Virgin's milk, which was kept on the high altar. Then, as was the custom, the custodian held out a board for a cash offering, which in Henry's case was £1.13s.4d, which he was told gave him a remission of forty days in purgatory. Henry later arranged for the royal glazier Bernard Flower to make new stained-glass windows for Walsingham's Lady Chapel – which were destroyed later in his reign, in 1538, along with all the other monastic buildings, as well as the shrine itself.

Henry appears to have visited East Anglia only once – and the same goes for the North of England. His visit here came towards the end of his reign, in 1541, when, in the company of his wife Catherine Howard, he travelled to York. The intention was threefold: this was an extravagant 'royal progress' but Henry also planned to meet for talks with King James V of Scotland (though in the end James reneged on the invitation). The North had also risen up against Henry five years previously in a revolt known as the Pilgrimage of Grace, which had begun in Yorkshire, and Henry was anxious to overawe his subjects with a display of his military might and regal presence. The trip required vast amounts of organization and funds: never before had the court travelled in such spleandour and numbers, and by some estimates the couple were accompanied by up to 5,000 horsemen, along with 1,000 soldiers, with 200 tents and pavilions to cope with the overflow from the manor houses and palaces the party stayed in.

The party set off from London on 30 June. Catherine had recently suffered a phantom pregnancy or a miscarriage. The king was displeased with her and was probably seeking pleasures elsewhere – and so, it seems, was Catherine: it was on this trip north that she famously had dalliances with a young courtier Thomas Culpeper, which were to result in her downfall just a few months later. That said, as ornate tapestries were taken from the walls and crated up in Whitehall ready for the journey north, there was some talk that Catherine might be crowned queen in

York Minster – which might make sense, as if Catherine bore Henry a second son he would be styled Duke of York.

Slow and extravagant progress was made in the early stages of the tour, with an itinerary that took in Hatfield, Dunstable, Ampthill, Grafton and Northampton, Henry hunting and hawking along on the way. The party then entered Lincolnshire, through the ancient market town of Stamford; it had been a rising in this county that had inspired the subsequent Pilgrimage of Grace. Henry and his party passed through Lincoln (where Henry entered the town wearing Lincoln green and formally pardoned the town's citizens for their former disloyalty) and Boston, and Henry killed 400 deer in the space of two days at Hatfield Chase near Doncaster, where his party also enjoyed a picnic in the open air. Pontefract, Cawood and Hull were next on the itinerary before the party finally reached York on 16 September.

Henry entered York through the Walmgate Bar, today the most complete and preserved of all the medieval gateways into the city, and was welcomed by the Archbishop of York and the city's officials at Fulford Cross, one of the city's main streets. Two hundred men who had rebelled against the king and been pardoned came to make further submission, kneeling in the street and offering Henry purses stuffed with gold. During his time in the city Henry resided at the former abbot's house, a grand building that still survives (it's now known as King's Manor and houses departments of York University) and which was substantially rebuilt in advance of Henry's visit. It was also furnished with tapestries and

The entrance to the King's Manor in York, with its newly restored coat of arms. (*Pat Hadley, Wikimedia Commons*)

plate from Whitehall in readiness for the arrival of James V, and tents were erected in the abbey grounds to accommodate both courts. Henry waited in vain for James until 29 September, after which he moved to Hull, where he stayed in Hull Manor House, a residence that he had acquired in 1539 (of which nothing now survives). Fearful of the military intentions of France and Spain, Henry reviewed Hull's fortifications before returning to London via Kettleby, Grimsthorpe, Colleyweston, Ampthill, The More (in Hertfordshire) and Windsor. He and Catherine arrived at Hampton Court on 30 October.

Chapter 17

Across the Channel

Tournai and Thérouanne

Henry first set foot on French soil in June 1513, when he landed in Calais, at the time an English stronghold, and with the Emperor Maximilian besieged the town of Thérouanne, some thirty-two kilometres inland. The town was taken and a French army was defeated at a skirmish known as the Battle of the Spurs, fought just outside it. It marked a triumphal opening to Henry's reign. After the victory the king and his courtiers spent three days as the guests of Maximilian's daughter, Margaret of Savoy, the Regent of the Netherlands, at Lille, where the Burgundian nobility (who ruled the city at the time) hastened to be presented to the victorious Henry, and were delighted to find him 'merry, handsome, well-spoken, popular and intelligent'. Henry jousted and the Milanese ambassador commented that 'he was fresher after this exertion than before. I do not know how he can stand it'. The next day a tournament was held in the city's Palais Rihour at which the horses had to wear felt shoes to prevent them from marking the black marble floor. (The Palais still exists, though a succession of fires and rebuilds over the centuries mean that virtually nothing from Henry's time survives, bar some of the brick outer-casing, a relocated fifteenth-century staircase and the guard room, which is now the city's tourist office.) The king also impressed Margaret by 'dancing magnificently in the French style' and by playing instruments for her.

Henry also captured Tournai, which is just twenty kilometres east of Lille across the border in Belgium (along with Thérouanne, the town was later described by Thomas Cromwell as an 'ungracious doghole'). 'We entered [the city] in triumph, with a great procession' is how

Henry VIII: A History of his Most Important Places and Events

The Palais Rihour in Lille, where lavish celebrations were held following Henry's capture of the town of Thérouanne in 1513.

Margaret George has Henry recall the victory in *The Autobiography of Henry VIII*.

> The people shouted and called me 'Alexander'. My men, riding behind me, were heaped with flowers and ribbons. That day I kept my armour on far past sundown, revelling in its rigid casing and Spartan embrace. Every time I wished to bend, its stiffness reminded me that I was a warrior and a conqueror.

Henry heard Mass at the city's cathedral and staged another great tournament. In 1913, on the 400th anniversary of Henry's triumphal entry into Tournai, over 1,000 people took part in a series of pageants and processions to commemorate the event, and a round tower, dating from 1515, can still be seen today – the last remaining part of a citadel built after the invasion to house English troops. The tower is a thick-walled circular building and today sits rather neglected in an unremarkable public park (named Parc Henry VIII) in a residential district close to the railway station, and for

Above and overleaf: Tournai Cathedral, where Henry heard Mass following his conquest of the city in 1513.

The Grand-Place in Tournai, the town (now in Belgium) captured by Henry in 1513.

some years it has been shrouded in scaffolding (and steadily encroaching vegetation). These days the cathedral where Henry heard Mass, with its tremendously high nave, and the adjacent and very picturesque Grand-Place, both located just under a kilometre south of the Tower across the canalized River Scheldt, make for a more absorbing visit for the town's few tourists. For a while after its capture Tournai sent an MP to sit in the House of Commons, but Henry eventually sold this possession to Francis I in 1519.

The Field of the Cloth of Gold

Henry's most notorious and history-making visit to France came in June 1520, and had a diplomatic rather than military purpose. The mastermind of the glorious shindig known as the Field of the Cloth of Gold was Cardinal Wolsey, whose command of detail meant that 5,000 courtiers, craftsmen, administrators and servants were successfully and efficiently transported across the Channel and back again, to the greater glory of his king. In the midst of it all was Henry's meeting with the French king Francis I for a lavish fortnight of celebrations that is commemorated today by a stone memorial near the village of Balinghem, around sixteen kilometres inland from Calais. (The location, and the event, had a historical precedent: in October 1396 Charles VI of France and Richard II of England met here to celebrate Richard's betrothal to Isabella of France, during a temporary lull in the Hundred Years' War.) Henry's court would be based in Guisnes (nowadays Guînes), in the English-held Pale of Calais, while Francis would be based in Ardres, to its east, which was then in French territory (Balinghem and the site of the tournament lie between the two). There was a castle at Guisnes where courtiers and armourers were accommodated, along with an armouries workshop, but it was not nearly large enough for everyone, so 2,800 tents were set up around the castle – and even that wasn't enough: some servants and common soldiers ended up being billeted with local farmers or even sleeping in hay and straw. Richard Gibson, Master of the King's Halls, Tents and Pavilions, had magnificent marquees erected for entertainments and banquets, for which the designs survive in the British Museum: the marquees were coloured green, white, blue and gold, and all were adorned with the king's badges and mottoes. They included Henry's own dining tent (fashioned from cloth of gold) which housed his privy kitchen. Vast brick ovens were built from scratch to bake thousands of loaves of bread, while some subsidiary kitchens (making sweets and pastries) were set up in nearby houses.

An army of 6,000 labourers and craftsmen was immediately set to work to get everything built in time. Much of their work concerned the so-called 'Palace of Illusions', built next to Guisnes Castle, one of the lost treasures of Henry's reign: according to the *Venetian Calendar of State Papers* an Italian observer thought even Leonardo da Vinci could not improve on it. The structure, built from timber, stone and brick, had a square plan with gatehouse and battlements and included a dining hall with a ceiling of green silk studded with gold roses, and a floor covering of patterned taffeta; there was a king's side, a queen's side, and suites for Wolsey and for Henry's sister Mary, who was to play a prominent role in the celebrations as queen dowager of France. All had spacious chambers decorated with gilt cornices and furnished with gorgeous tapestries and hangings of cloth of gold or silver, with Galyon Hone providing the glazing. There was also a chapel painted blue and gold, and hung with cloth of gold and green velvet; on the altar was a great gold crucifix, ten candlesticks and large gold statues of the twelve apostles, plus many holy relics. Everywhere Tudor roses and heraldic devices painted by the king's serjeant painter, John Browne, abounded. The Scots poet Alexander Barclay was commissioned to write mottoes and verses to be added to the decorative scheme, while the gatehouse was surmounted by a scallop-shell pediment, the royal arms, two large Tudor roses and a golden statue of Cupid. On the lawn in front of the palace beside a gilded pillar topped with a statue of Bacchus, the god of wine, was a Roman-style fountain from which flowed white wine, Malmsey wine and claret, provided free to all comers, day and night, and consumed using silver drinking cups that were chained to the fountain. Carved into the stonework was the invitation in archaic French, '*Faicte bonne chere quy vouldra*' – whoever wants to, make good cheer. For their part, the French set up a similar 'town' of 400 tents just outside Ardres and levelled the ground for the tournaments that were to unfold.

Henry arrived in Calais at noon on 31 May, and set out for Guisnes four days later. Edward Hall observed the king and his party and thought it impossible to describe 'their rich attire, their sumptuous jewels, their diversities of beauties' – though Bishop Fisher was less impressed, and was appalled by the extravagance in view everywhere: 'Never was seen in England such excess of apparelment before.' Henry would appear each day in a series of spectacular costumes (for the previous months he had been importing great quantities of rich fabrics, including just over 1,000 yards of velvet). The queen appeared in gold, satin and damask while Mary Tudor appeared 'superbly arrayed … scintillating in her saddle'.

The festivities finally got going on 7 June with the boom of cannon fire from Guisnes and Ardres as the two kings rode from respective headquarters: Henry was dressed in cloth of gold and silver, while his horse wore gold bells that jangled as it trotted. On the edge of the field, they waited – and then, to the sound of trumpets and sackbuts, the two men galloped alone towards each other, doffed bonnets and embraced while still on horseback, before Francis invited Henry to his pavilion where, according to Polydore Vergil, they 'greeted each other like truly well-intentioned people, and then with evident satisfaction talked together in friendly fashion until evening'. The next day Francis went to Guisnes and Henry went to Ardres where he paid respect to Francis's queen, Claude. An Italian observer thought Henry 'rather fat' though the waist measurement of his armour was a reasonably respectable thirty-five inches. And then commenced two weeks of feasting, jousting and games.

Some commentators, however, remarked that the cheery bonhomie was only skin-deep. 'These sovereigns are not at peace,' commented a Venetian, 'they hate each other accordingly.' The fashion on show seemed to be as important as the tournaments: Italian observers thought the French more elegantly dressed than the English (though their dresses were sometimes too revealing), while English ladies, over-spangled with gold, were thought to be rather too fond of alcohol.

The rules for the tiltyard tournaments, in which 300 jousters participated, were agreed in advance by a committee of English and French knights. Blunted swords and lances were used so that serious injury was avoided. The two kings hung their emblems on trees set up at the end of the lists to demonstrate their equality – yet their combat was so fast and furious that sparks were seen to fly from their armour (the suit of Henry's armour preserved in the Tower of London is almost certainly the one he wore during the tournament). Henry accidentally caused the death of his own horse and was ignominiously thrown by Francis during a wrestling match. Francis, for his part, sustained a black eye, and one French knight died of wounds received in the lists from his own brother. Henry also prevented a herald from reading out the traditional proclamation that he was 'by grace of God King of England and France' – so as not to offend French sensibilities. He later told Francis that he could not be King of France 'while you are here'. The rivalry and one-upmanship reached a head on Sunday, 17 June, when Henry awoke to find Francis in his bed chamber. 'Brother, you have played me the best trick ever played, and shown me the trust I should have given you,' Henry is said to have remarked, graciously if mischievously adding, 'From now on I am your prisoner.'

June can be a variable month as far as the weather goes, and northern France was no different to London in this respect. But the *Venetian Calendar of State Papers* indicate that during the tournament it was 'hotter than St Peter's in Rome', though strong winds blew dust into people's faces and over clothing, and some of the tents were blown away, including the French king's vast marquee, forcing him to retreat to the town of Ardres. Undaunted, the jousts attracted audiences in their thousands. And the pageantry was not limited to the jousting lists. Wolsey, with five other cardinals and twenty bishops, also celebrated Mass in the Tiltyard, with music from the Chapel Royal and its French equivalent, the Chapelle de la Musique du Roi; a sour note came when a Latin oration by Richard Pace, Wolsey's secretary, was interrupted by a firework accidentally going off.

Wolsey later laid the foundation stone of a Chapel to Our Lady of Peace, founded jointly by both kings, though in the end this was never built. In fact, the whole exercise was little more than a lavish charade and an exercise in extravagance and within three years England and France were once again at war. However, in 1545, towards the end of his reign, Henry commissioned two paintings from Flemish painters that depicted the scenes that had unfolded some twenty-five years previously. One shows the king's embarkation at Dover, a tiny figure in the distance on the deck of his flagship, the *Catherine Pleasaunce*, while the other was a composite view of events that showed the king arriving in procession at Guisnes with Calais in the distance, and the meeting of the two sovereigns and fireworks bursting in the skies above them. Both paintings were probably commissioned for Whitehall Palace and remain in the royal collection today.

The festivities ended on 25 June, with Henry and Francis exchanging gifts, including jewellery and horses. After a two-week stay in Calais, Henry and Catherine rode along the coast to Gravelines, near Dunkirk, which at that time was part of Habsburg-held Flanders, and met with the regent, Margaret of Austria, and her overlord, Emperor Charles V. Diplomacy done, Henry and Catherine rode with Margaret and Charles back to Calais, where they were entertained in a temporary banqueting house of canvas that unfortunately blew over in the wind. Ironically, given the extravagance of the festivities that had unfolded on the Field of the Cloth of Gold just a few weeks previously, Henry and Charles signed an agreement not to make any new alliances with France over the following two years.

Today the event is commemorated by a simple memorial stone on the north side of the D231 road that links Guînes and Ardres (it's midway between the two villages and around 800 metres southwest of Balinghem, the traditional site of the meeting point). It's a rather bleak spot on a busy road, surrounded by featureless and undulating farm country, and the words on the plinth are now very faded: 'Camp du Drap D'Or – 1520 – Field of Cloth of Gold.' In Guînes itself nothing remains of the castle, though the village's main square corresponds to its main courtyard; close by, the Tour d'Horloge provides a family and school group-friendly tour through the town's history, with a room devoted to the Field of the Cloth of Gold, though there are no artefacts to speak of besides a very striking representation of Henry VIII as a mythical giant, which was made for the 1994 celebrations of the opening of the Channel Tunnel

The memorial stone marking the site of the Field of the Cloth of Gold.

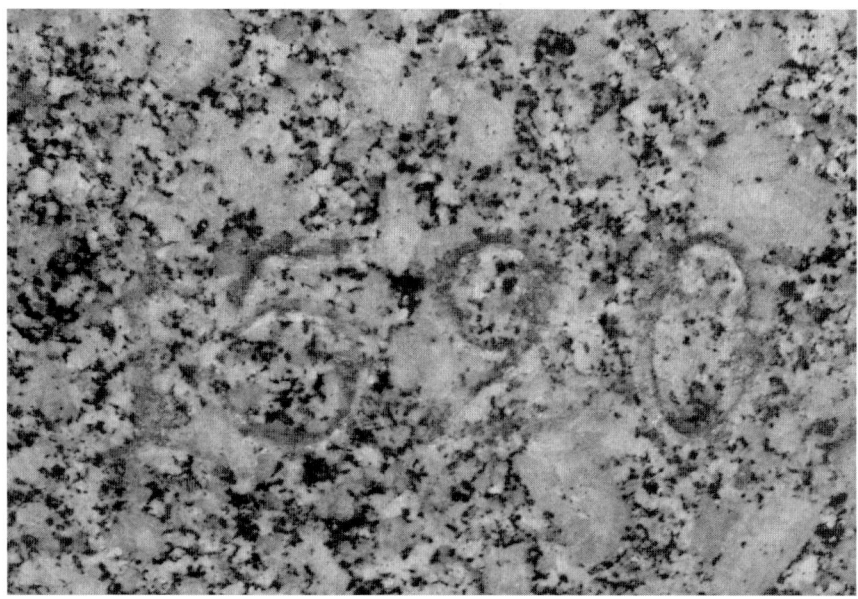

The year 1520 carved into the memorial stone marking the site of the Field of the Cloth of Gold.

Above: The main square in Guînes is located on the site of the courtyard of the former castle.

Right: Banner in Guînes commemorating the Field of the Cloth of Gold.

Mural in Guînes commemorating the Field of the Cloth of Gold.

(whose French portal lies around thirteen kilometres to the northwest). Behind the exhibition (and accessed through it) is the mound on which the Danes built the town's first castle; it's surmounted by a round turret built in 1763. Banners and murals around the town celebrate the famous event of five centuries ago. A formal celebration in June 2020, to celebrate the 500th anniversary of the event, had to be abandoned because of the Covid-19 epidemic; however, a colourful open-air pageant, performance and son et lumière display were presented the following year, for the 501st (and is easy to track down on YouTube).

Calais and Boulogne, 1532

Henry and Francis I met for a second time in France in October 1532, some twelve years after the shenanigans at the Field of the Cloth of Gold. This time the meeting took place just outside Calais, with none of the pomp and extravagance that had been the hallmark of the monarchs' first meeting. The purpose of Henry's visit was for him to garner the French king's support for his proposed marriage to Anne Boleyn. On his arrival in Calais, he was received by the town's mayor, and together they rode in a torchlit procession to hear Mass at the Church of St Nicholas. Henry lodged across the road at the Exchequer, a grand mansion that had been enlarged for this visit (and which, like the church, no longer stands). Henry's bed had already been sent ahead from England, and his lodgings had been hung with green velvet. Anne was assigned a suite of seven rooms in the same building, with a connecting door to the king's bedchamber. By this time, she had become his mistress and they were living openly together. Indeed, there was speculation Henry would secretly marry her in Calais, and Anne even hinted as much in a letter to her sister, Mary, saying that in Calais 'that which I have so long wished for will be accomplished'. But no marriage took place. Instead, Henry spent ten days at hawking, inspecting the town's defences, and gambling with the Duke of Norfolk and other courtiers.

On 16 October Henry entered France 'proper' and met Francis at the St Inglevert hospice, then known as Sandingfield and situated right on the border of the Pale of Calais. The two monarchs then rode to Boulogne, where they were met outside the walls of the town by the Dauphin and his two brothers, whom Henry embraced fondly. A 1,000-cannon salute sounded – which could be heard thirty kilometres away – as the procession entered the port. In Boulogne Henry lodged with Francis in the Abbey of Notre Dame, in a suite of chambers hung with cloth of silver and tapestries depicting Ovid's *Metamorphoses*; he attended Mass in the Abbey Church and ate in the refectory, which had been adorned with tapestries showing the story of Scipio Africanus. (The basilica that stands on the site today is almost wholly eighteenth century, with virtually nothing remaining of the old medieval abbey complex where Henry stayed.) An observer wrote that the French 'far surpassed the English in apparel': Henry, for his part, wore an outfit that Francis gave him, a crimson satin doublet encrusted with pearls beneath a long gown of white velvet embroidered in gold. The kings discussed a crusade against the Turks but Henry was more interested in getting Francis to use his influence with the Pope in his 'Great Matter' – the annulment of his marriage to Catherine. In the afternoon he watched Francis's sons playing tennis and laid bets on the outcome, made an offering at the Shrine of Our Lady of Boulogne in the church (whose miraculous statue was eventually destroyed in 1793), and hosted a sumptuous feast where he lavished gifts on Francis and his sons – indeed so lavish that Francis was ashamed at the paucity of his own intended gifts, and had to borrow funds to gift Henry six horses along with his own bed, hung with crimson velvet.

The two monarchs then headed for Calais, where on 24 October Henry was formally greeted by his illegitimate 13-year-old son, Henry Fitzroy, the Duke of Richmond; 3,000 guns sounded a salute as they rode together into the town through streets lined with English soldiers. Francis was lodged by the Calais merchants at their palatial headquarters, the Staple Inn (which like all the buildings associated with Henry in Calais has long since vanished); that evening Francis sent the Provost of Paris to Anne Boleyn bearing a costly diamond to show his esteem for her. Later on, bull and bear baiting was on offer as entertainment, and a variety of meat and game was consumed at supper, served in the banqueting hall hung with silver and gold adorned with gold wreaths that reflected the light from twenty silver chandeliers, each bearing a hundred wax candles. Anne Boleyn and seven other ladies, masked and clothed in unusual outfits of cloth of gold and crimson tinsel with gold laces, danced before the two kings, and Anne sat chatting with King Francis at a window seat for an hour afterwards. The next day Henry watched a wrestling match between the Cornish champions and the French, while Francis invited Henry Fitzroy to spend time at his court to complete his education. On 29 October Henry accompanied Francis back onto French soil, where the two monarchs said their farewells; unfortunately, his journey back to England was delayed for two weeks because of storms and fog in the Channel.

The Siege of Boulogne

Henry's final visit to France came towards the end of his reign, in 1544, when he took personal command of an invasion of France, besieging the very town he had been a guest at twelve years earlier – Boulogne. The invasion, launched with the Emperor Charles V, was part of the so-called 'enterprise of Paris' which aimed to punish Francis I for his alliance with the Turks (as well as allowing Charles to further his claims on Burgundy).

Henry's departure was delayed and his army set out before him; he finally landed in Calais on 14 July and promptly marched into French territory, riding on a great courser with an absurdly large wheel-lock pistol nonchalantly laid across the pommel of his saddle, and the banner of St George flying behind him. Ahead of him rode Charles Somerset, Lord Herbert, with his helm and lance. This was the first time Henry had worn armour into battle since 1513: the three-quarter suit (so, not protecting his feet and lower legs), beautifully etched, is now in the possession of the Metropolitan Museum of Art in New York. Thus he marched towards Boulogne, a curious blend of self-confidence and bloated immobility, while another force under Norfolk had the town of Montreuil-sur-Mer, some twenty kilometres to the south, in its sights. But bad weather meant supplies were a long time reaching the English armies, and it was early August before the full force of the English could be brought to bear on the French defenders of both towns.

Henry remained active from dawn to dusk during the six-week siege of Boulogne, directing the assault personally. His underlings had not anticipated this sudden show of stamina: it was quite an operation to winch Henry, in full armour, onto his horse, and his legs became so painful that some of the armour had to be cut away to relieve the pressure. Henry and his senior commanders set up camp to the northeast of the town, out of range of French cannons but with access to fresh water. During the operation Henry exchanged regular and affectionate letters with Catherine Parr, who had been appointed Regent in his absence and was staying at Hampton Court with Henry's children. 'The castle with the dike [defensive ditch] is at our commandment and not like to be recovered by the Frenchmen,' he wrote to her at one point. 'Castle and town are like to follow the same trade, for this day we begin three batteries ... I am too busy to write more but send blessings to all my children and recommendations to my cousin Margaret and the rest of the ladies and gentlemen and to my council.' The chronicler Edward Hall explained that Henry 'so assaulted and besieged [Boulogne] with such abundance of great ordnance that never was there a more valiant assault made. Beside the undermining of the castle, tower and walls, the town was so beaten with ordnance that there was not left one house therein.' Relentlessly pummelled, there was talk of the people of Boulogne having nothing left to eat but horses and cats. Eventually the castle was destroyed by English cannon and the French sought terms for an honourable surrender.

Henry entered the town in triumph on 18 September. According to Hall he had a sword borne before him 'by the lord marquess of Dorset' – namely Henry Grey, who was married to Henry's niece and was destined to be executed in 1554 along with his daughter, Lady Jane Grey – 'like a noble and valiant conqueror ... the trumpeters standing on the walls of the town sounded their trumpets at the time of his entering to the great comfort of all the king's true subjects'. He then spent two days riding around the town and arranging its future defence, commanding that the Church of Our Lady of Boulogne be defaced and 'plucked down' and that an earthwork be thrown up on the site 'for the great force and strength of the town'. It was, of course, hubris: the Church of Our Lady wasn't destroyed, and eventually the whole military campaign turned to tatters, with Norfolk's troops starving and Charles V being forced to withdraw with his army just eighty kilometres from Paris. Henry eventually left for England on 30 September; his prize for this exploit, the town of Boulogne, was held until 1550, when it was returned to France by his son as part of a peace treaty. No reminders of his time there, nor of the military campaign, remain.

Bibliography and Further Reading

Non-fiction

André, Bernard *The Life of Henry VII* (probably completed in 1502; most recent edition published in 2011 by Italica Press)

Betteridge, Thomas & Thomas Freeman *Henry VIII and History* (Farnham: Ashgate Publishing, 2012; most recent edition published in 2017 by Routledge)

Borman, Tracy *Henry VIII and the Men Who Made Him* (London: Hodder & Stoughton, 2018)

Bowle, John *Henry VIII: A Study of Power in Action* (London: George Allen & Unwin, 1964; most recent edition published in 2021 by Sapere Books)

Bruce, Marie Louise *The Making of Henry VIII* (London: Collins, 1977; most recent edition published in 2021 by Sapere Books)

Carradice, Phil *Rebellion Against Henry VIII* (Barnsley: Pen & Sword Books, 2023)

Collins, Linda & Siobhan Clarke, *King and Collector: Henry VIII and the Art of Kingship* (Cheltenham: The History Press, 2021)

Fabyan, Robert (attr.) *The Great Chronicle of London* (originally published in 1516; most recent edition published in 1938 by the Corporation of the City of London)

Fraser, Antonia *The Six Wives of Henry VIII* (London: Weidenfeld & Nicolson, 1992; most recent edition published in 2003 by Phoenix Press)

Guy, John *Henry VIII: The Quest for Fame* (London: Allen Lane, 2014)

Hall, Edward *Chronicle* (commonly known as *Hall's Chronicle*, originally published in 1548; most recent edition published in 2018 by Franklin Classics)

Heath, Richard *Henry VIII and Charles V: Rival Monarchs, Uneasy Allies* (Barnsley: Pen & Swords Books, 2023)

Hutchinson, Robert *Henry VIII: The Decline and Fall of a Tyrant* (London: Weidenfeld & Nicolson, 2019)

Hutchinson, Robert *The Last Days of Henry VIII: Conspiracy, Treason and Heresy at the Court of the Dying Tyrant* (London: Weidenfeld & Nicolson, 2005)

Hutchinson, Robert *Thomas Cromwell: The Rise and Fall of Henry VIII's Most Notorious Minister* (London: Weidenfeld & Nicolson, 2007)

Kendall, Paul *Henry VIII in 100 Objects* (Barnsley: Pen & Sword Books, 2021)

Leland, Thomas *Itinerary* (first published by Thomas Hearne 1710–12 from original notebooks compiled between 1538 and 1543; most recent edition published in 2011 by Nabu Press)

Licence, Amy *1520: The Field of the Cloth of Gold* (Stroud: Amberley Publishing, 2020)

Lipscomb, Suzannah *1536: The Year that Changed Henry VIII* (Oxford: Lion Books, 2009)

Lisle, Arthur Plantagenet, *The Lisle Letters* (original letters written between 1533 and 1540 and published in the *Calendar of Letters and Papers, Foreign and Domestic, of Henry VIII* edited by J. S. Brewer, J. Gairdner and R. H. Brodie [London 1862–1930]; most recent complete edition published in 1981 by University of Chicago Press, edited by Muriel St Clare Byrne; abridged edition published in 1997 by Secker & Warburg [London])

Lloyd, Christopher & John Thurley *Henry VIII: Images of a Tudor King* (London: Phaidon Press, 1990)

Matusiak, John *Henry VIII: The Life and Rule of England's Nero* (Stroud: The History Press, 2014)

Morris, Sarah & Natalie Grueninger *In the Footsteps of the Six Wives of Henry VIII* (Stroud: Amberley Publishing, 2016)

Nichols, John Gough *Narrative of the Days of the Reformation* (London: Camden Society, 1859; most recent edition published in 2022 by Legare Street Press)

Rimer, Graeme (ed.) *Arms and the Man* (Barnsley: Pen & Sword Books, 2009)

Scarisbrick, J. J. *Henry VIII* (London: Eyre Methuen, 1968; most recent edition published in 1997 by Yale University Press)

Schroder, Timothy *A Marvel to Behold: Gold and Silver at the Court of Henry VIII* (Martlesham, Suffolk: Boydell & Brewer, 2020)

Starkey, David *Henry: Virtuous Prince* (London: HarperCollins, 2008)

Starkey, David *The Reign of Henry VIII: The Personalities and Politics* (London: Hamlyn, 1985; most recent edition published in 2002 by Vintage)

Strype, John *Ecclesiastical Memorials* (Oxford: Clarendon Press, 1822; most recent edition published in 2007 by Kessinger Publishing)

Weir, Alison *Henry VIII: King and Court* (London: Jonathan Cape, 2001; most recent edition published by Vintage, 2008)

Weir, Alison *The Six Wives of Henry VIII* (London: The Bodley Head, 1991; most recent edition published in 2007 by Vintage)

Wooding, Lucy *Henry VIII* (Abingdon: Routledge, 2015, second edition)

Wriothesley, Charles *A Chronicle of England During the Reign of the Tudors, from AD 1485 to 1559* (completed around 1560; most recent edition, edited by William Douglas Hamilton, published in 1875 by the Camden Society)

Fiction & Plays

Beattie, Andrew *The Prince and the Pauper: A Full-Length Historical Drama* (Los Angeles: Youth Plays, 2021)

Bolt, Robert *A Man for All Seasons* (London: Heinemann, 1960; most recent edition published in 2013 by Bloomsbury Methuen Drama)

Castor, H. M. *VIII* (London: Templar, 2011)

Fletcher, John & William Shakespeare *Henry VIII* (First published 1623; multiple modern editions)

George, Margaret *The Autobiography of Henry VIII* (London: Macmillan, 1986; most recent edition published in 2012 by Pan Macmillan)

Gregory, Philippa *The Other Boleyn Girl* (London: HarperCollins, 2001; most recent edition published in 2007 by HarperCollins)

Mantel, Hilary *The Wolf Hall Trilogy: Wolf Hall* (London: Fourth Estate, 2009); *Bring Up the Bodies* (London: Fourth Estate, 2019); *The Mirror and the Light* (London: Fourth Estate, 2021)

Sansom, C. J. *Dissolution* (London: Macmillan, 2003; most recent edition published in 2015 by Pan)

Sansom, C. J. *Sovereign* (London: Macmillan, 2006; most recent edition published in 2015 by Pan)

Twain, Mark *The Prince and the Pauper* (Boston: James R. Osgood & Co, 1881; most recent edition published in 2020 by Pan Macmillan)

Weir, Alison *Henry VIII: The Heart and the Crown* (London: Headline, 2023)

Acknowledgements

Many thanks to Elaine Galloway for her suggestions regarding the text and for an informative tour of the site of Greenwich Palace – and to the staff and volunteers at the Old Royal Naval College for some valuable information regarding the artefacts that can be seen there.

Index

Abbeville 162
Abel, Sir John 37
Acton Court 202–203
Adam, Robert 85
Aethelred the Unready 186
Ales, Alexander 17
Alfege 24
Alfons, Eliot 25
Alsop, Thomas 59
Amersham 190
Ampthill 200, 205, 206
André, Bernard 8, 93, 223
Anne, Queen 22, 134, 135
Anne of Cleves 19–21, 23, 36, 65, 75, 84, 121, 156–160, 177
Ardres 212–15
Armin, Robert 14
Armour (Henry VIII's) viii, 17, 25, 28, 33–34, 70, 144, 208, 212, 213, 214, 221
Armstrong, Clement 50
Arthur, King 39, 177, 183, 185
Arthur Tudor (Henry's brother) *see* Tudor, Arthur
Ashridge, Hertfordshire 194
Astor, William Waldorf 169
Atkinson, Harry 145
Autobiography of Henry VIII vii, 72, 84, 89, 171, 178, 201, 208, 225

Balinghem 212, 215
Banqueting House (Whitehall) 47, 61
Barclay, Alexander 213
Barker, Christopher (Garter-at-Arms) 128
Bayeux Tapestry 137
Baynard House 38
Baynard's Castle 37–39
Baynton, Sir Edward 200
Beaufort, Lady Margaret 30, 37, 69, 96, 179–180
Beaulieu Palace, Essex (formerly New Hall) 77, 195
Beddington House 52
Bek, Anthony (Bishop of Durham) 138
Bellay, Jean du 15, 49, 193
Bellin, Nicholas 51, 60, 131, 148
Bettes the Elder, John 50
Biddle, Professor Martin 155
Bishop's Waltham Palace 183
Blackfriars station 41
Blackheath 19–20, 137, 158
Blackmore, Essex 196
Blenheim Palace 186–8
Blount, Elizabeth 11, 42, 196
Blount, William (Lord Mountjoy) 142
Bolebrook Castle 173
Boleyn, Anne places: in Calais 220; at Dover Castle 163; at Eltham Palace

145; at Ewelme 189; at Grafton 201; at Greenwich Palace 15–17, 24; at Hampton Court x, 105, 107, 111, 115; at Hanworth Palace 197; at Hever Castle 169–171; at Knole 173; at New Hall/Beaulieu 195; at Pyrgo 196; at Stone Castle, 174; at St James's Palace, 65; at the Tower of London 32 (*see also* execution); at Windsor Castle 125; at York Place, 49; events: Coronation 2, 73; execution 3, 15, 74, 103; in popular history vii; maid of honour 162; marriage 72, 219; relationship to Duke of Norfolk and Catherine Howard 10, 17, 19; relations with Thomas Wolsey 102

Boleyn, Elizabeth 125
Boleyn, Geoffrey 169
Boleyn, George 17
Boleyn, Mary 49, 174, 225
Boleyn, Thomas 80, 195
Bolt, Robert vii, 225
Bonner, Edmund (Bishop of London) 128, 178
Bonnivet, Guillaume Gouffier de 12–13
Boulogne 34, 163, 169, 181, 218–222
Brandon, Charles, Duke of Suffolk 10, 11, 13, 18, 19, 73, 141, 144, 182, 202
Brandon, Sir Thomas 70, 124
Brentford 86
Bridewell Palace 3, 41–47, 88, 100, 163
Bridewell Place 44
Brown, George (Prior of Austin Friars) 53
Brown, Lancelot ('Capability') 85
Browne, Sir Anthony 157–158, 183
Browne, John (Henry's Sergeant Painter) 213
Bruges 87
Buckingham Palace 21, 63, 64, 66
Burgh, Edward de 120

Cabinet Office 47, 61-62
Cade, Jack 19
Calais 11, 18, 122, 145, 157, 162, 163, 175, 207, 212–213, 215, 218–221
Cambridge 54, 116, 141
Camden, William 147
Campeggio, Lorenzo 12, 43, 201
Canary Wharf 28
Cannon Street station 37
Canterbury (Archbishop of) 24, 56, 69, 131, 194; *see also* Alfege, Cranmer *and* Morton
Canterbury (City of) 121, 156, 157, 162, 165–166, 173, 191
Canute, King 67, 183, 197
Carew, Elizabeth 10–11
Carew, Sir George 182
Carew, Nicholas 10–11, 13, 52
Carey, Henry 194
Carry on Henry vi
Carshalton 155
Castor, H. M. vii, 225
Catherine of Aragon wedding/marriage 9, 31, 53, 75, 94; marriage annulment 43, 49, 53, 200
Cavendish, George 15, 102, 201
Chapel Royal 14, 65, 66, 86, 144, 214
Charing (village in Kent) 174
Charing Cross (district of London) 85, 86
Charing Cross station 47
Charles, Archduke of Austria 8
Charles I 61, 93, 134–135, 149
Charles II 21, 51, 149
Charles V (Emperor) 5, 13, 41, 122, 124, 162, 181, 183, 215, 220, 222, 223
Cheam 146–147, 152–153
Chelsea 82–84, 86, 100, 101
Cheney, Sir Thomas 174
Chenies Manor 190
Chertsey Abbey 129, 177
Chichester Cathedral School 142

Index

Chieregato, Francesco vi
Chingford 197
Christmas celebrations 3, 9–11, 13, 15, 18, 32, 57, 93, 94, 138, 141, 144, 199
Churchill, Sir Winston 72
Church of the Observant Friars, Greenwich 25, 97
City of London School 38, 66
Civil War 5, 21, 78, 132, 187
Clifford, Rosamund ('Fair Rosamund') 186
Cobham 149
Coldharbour House 37, 38
Compton, William 95
Conyers, Edward 78
Coombe Hill 113–114
Copperplate Map 42
Copthall, Essex 78
Cornish, William 10, 48, 66, 125
Courtauld, Stephen and Virginia 138
Cowdray House 183
Cowper, Frank Cadogan 142
Cranmer, Thomas 20, 21, 53–56, 58–59, 86, 103, 173, 174
Cromwell, Oliver 5, 91, 132, 178
Cromwell, Richard 197
Cromwell, Thomas vii, ix, 16–20, 30, 32, 36, 53, 85, 98, 102, 131, 145, 147, 156–157, 178, 197, 202, 207, 224
Crown, The (Netflix TV series) 21
Crowne Plaza Hotel, City of London 44
Cuddington 147
Culpeper, Thomas 36, 103–104, 191, 204
Cure, Cornelius 131–132
Cure, William 148
Curzon, Sir Robert 70
Cutty Sark 4

d'Annebault, Claud 105
Dartford Priory 175–176
Daubeney, Giles 98, 100, 113

Day, George (Bishop of Chichester) 54
Deal 156–157
Delft, Francois van der 58, 181
Denny, Anthony 18, 55, 57–59
Denton, Elizabeth 37, 141
Deptford Bridge, Battle of 19, 30
Dereham, Francis 36, 104
Digby, Benjamin 24
Donjon xi, 5, 6, 16, 50, 88, 108, 138
Douglas, Lady Margaret 104
Dover 19, 125, 156, 166, 174, 215
Dover Castle 122, 161–164, 173
Downing Street 47, 61, 63
Draughton, Margaret 7
Dudley, Edmund 190
Dudley, Admiral John 181
Dunstable 121, 205
Durham House 50
Düsseldorf 156
Dymmocks, Sir Robert 73

East Grinstead 169
Edmund (Henry's brother) 141, 142
Edward I 185
Edward II 37, 138, 140
Edward III 70, 71, 88, 123, 129, 138
Edward IV 7, 28, 57, 71, 85, 123, 129, 131, 136, 138, 140, 189, 195
Edward VI 19, 44–45, 54, 74, 85, 103, 129, 131, 174
Edward VII 72
Edward VIII 136
Edward the Confessor 67, 74, 78, 86, 196
Elizabeth (Henry's daughter, later Elizabeth I) ix, 16, 17, 22, 33, 52, 74, 82, 84, 104, 110, 131, 132, 149, 166, 174, 175, 183, 187, 194, 196, 197, 198, 199
Elizabeth II 72, 86, 136
Elizabeth of York (Henry's mother) 7, 51
Elsyng Palace 198

Eltham Palace ix, xi, 93, 122, 136–145, 156
Elton, Geoffrey vii
Enfield 198, 199
Epping Forest 197
Erasmus, Desiderius 141–143
Erith 161, 164
Esher Palace 179, 181
Eton College 128
Ewell 155
Ewelme 188–190

Fabyan, Robert *see also* Great Chronicle of London 9, 223
Falconer, Richard 32
Family of Henry VIII (painting) xii, 52
Faverches, Richeldis de 203
Fayrfax, Robert 66
Ferdinand and Isabella of Spain 39, 94
Fermer, Richard 14
Field of the Cloth of Gold 162, 166, 174, 211–218
Fishmongers' Hall 32
Fitzroy, Henry 42, 196, 220
Fleet, River 41, 43, 44
Fleet Street 41, 68
Fletcher, John vii, 49, 225
Flower, Bernard 204
Fontainbleau, Palace of 148
Foxe, John (English historian) 55, 105
Foxe, Richard (Bishop of Exeter) 25
Francis I (of France) 12, 15, 26, 32, 58, 122, 125, 145, 146, 148, 162, 166, 195, 197, 211–215, 218–220
François (French Dauphin) 12, 13, 219
Friar's Church, Greenwich *see* Church of the Observant Friars, Greenwich
Fulham 82, 86

Gainsborough, Lincolnshire 120
Gardens (of palaces) xii, 5, 32, 41, 49, 52, 68, 84, 89, 101, 105, 114, 116–117, 148, 149, 161, 173, 175, 177, 178, 180, 194, 196, 197, 198
Gardiner, Stephen 36, 125, 128
George II 22
George IV 134
George V 72
George VI 136
George, Margaret vii, 72, 84, 89, 171, 178, 208
Ghent 5, 132, 133
Gibson, Richard 212
Giustinian, Sebastian 11, 12, 65, 95, 96
Golden Hinde 36
Goodrich, Thomas (Bishop of Ely) 128
Gracechurch Street 31
Grafton 200–201, 205
Gravelines 215
Great Chronicle of London 9, 223
Great Fire of London 32, 33, 37, 39, 40, 41, 44
Great Hall vi, viii, xi, xii, 10, 13, 20, 30, 34, 36, 41, 43, 48, 49, 53, 65, 67, 69, 70, 91, 94, 104, 107, 108, 109–111, 118, 123, 138–140, 142, 151, 165, 166, 171, 173, 174, 180, 183–185, 193, 200
Great Harry 163, 181
Great Standing, Essex 197
Greenwich (district of London) 4, 24–28, 137, 140, 143
Greenwich, University of 5, 21
Greenwich Castle 21
Greenwich Meridian 5, 21
Greenwich Observatory 4, 21
Greenwich Palace viii, ix, xi, 2–24, 31, 32, 57, 79, 87, 88, 95, 97, 116, 122, 141, 142, 144, 157, 163, 164
Greenwich Park 21
Grey, Henry (3rd Marquess of Dorset) 60, 222
Grey, Lady Jane 60, 141, 222

Index

Grey, Thomas (1st Marquess of Dorset) 69
Grey, Thomas (2nd Marquess of Dorset) 80
Grey, Walter de 48
Guildford, Sir Henry 10, 11, 80
Guisnes/Guînes 212–213, 215, 217–218

Hall, Edward 3, 9–11, 13–15, 20, 42, 48–49, 53, 57, 58, 73, 79, 81, 95, 125, 193, 195, 213
Hammersmith 82, 86
Hampton Court viii, x, xii, 3, 18, 36, 41, 51, 52, 57, 98–122, 132, 147, 148, 163, 173, 177, 181, 195, 197, 199, 206, 221
Hanworth Palace 197–199
Harlow 196
Harrison, William ix
Hatfield Chase 205
Hatfield House 194
Havering-atte-Bower 196
Hawksmoor, Sir Nicholas 5, 24
Henry I 186, 188
Henry II 123, 163, 186
Henry III 74, 78, 185
Henry IV 31, 138
Henry V 85
Henry VI 131
Henry VII 5, 7, 30, 37, 68, 69, 74, 88, 91, 94, 124, 136, 137, 138, 142, 143, 179, 180, 189, 195, 197, 223
Henry VIII baptism 24–27; birth 7; childhood and education 7–8, 140–143; conception 189; coronation 73–76; death 56–60; first meeting with Anne of Cleves 157–158; first meeting with Catherine Howard, 36; funeral 85–87, 127–129; historians' views on, vii–viii; living arrangements, x–xii; magnificence of court vi; marriage to Anne Boleyn 53; marriage to Anne of Cleves 20–21, 23; marriage to Catherine of Aragon 9, 23; proclaimed king, 94; representation in fiction, plays and films, vii; palaces viii–xii; tomb 129–136

Henry VIII (play by William Shakespeare and John Fletcher) vii, 49, 225
Henry, Duke of Cornwall (Henry's son) 75, 96–97
Hentzner, Paul 110, 132
Herbert, Sir William 59
Hever Castle 169–174
Holbein, Hans vi, vii, 14, 18, 50–52, 65, 115, 157
Hollar, Wenceslas 35
Holt, John 142
Hone, Galyon 50, 163, 169, 194, 212
Hone, William 142
Hood, Robin 11–12, 95
Horenbout, Lucas 50
Horse Guards Parade 47, 63
Hounslow 105, 128, 197
Howard, Catherine 16, 30, 32, 36, 51, 56, 103, 104, 158, 178, 189, 191, 200, 204
Howard, Thomas (2nd Duke of Norfolk) 79
Howard, Thomas (3rd Duke of Norfolk) 10, 17, 19, 56, 157, 194, 219, 221, 222
Hull 205–206
Humphrey, Duke of Gloucester 5, 21
Hunsdon 194
Husee, John 18
Hyde Park 65

Iron Acton 202–203
Isle of Dogs 28

James I and VI 93
James II 47, 60, 117
James IV of Scotland 7, 142
James V of Scotland 204, 206
Jericho House 196
Jewel Tower, Westminster 70
John, King of England 37
John (Jean le Bon) King of France 140
John, Prince (Prince John of Eltham) 140
Johnson, Ben 144
Jones, Inigo 61
Jousting viii, 8–11, 13–15, 17, 33, 34, 53, 70, 72, 89, 90, 94, 95, 98, 117, 166, 207, 213, 214
Juana 'the Mad' 13

Kennington Palace 50
Kensington 84, 86
Kew 82, 84, 93, 101
King, Oliver 69, 136
Kingston upon Thames 113
Knights of the Bath 31, 75
Knole 173–174
Knyvet, Thomas 80
Kratzer, Nicolaus 115

Lambert, John *see* Nicholson, John
Langley Manor 189–190
Lassels, John and Mary 103
Laughton, Charles vi
Lee, Dr Rowland 53
Leeds Castle 166–169, 173
Leemput, Remigius van 51
Leicester 102, 130
Leland, John 6, 224
Leo X, Pope 130, 165
Lille 207–208

Limehouse 28
Linacre, Thomas xii
Lincoln 98, 205
Lisle Letters 18, 224
Little Sodbury Manor 203
Lombard Street, London 75
London Bridge Station 36
Louis XII 141, 161
Ludlow Castle, Shropshire 93
Lyng, Thomas 68
Lyssons, Daniel 25

Magdalen College School, Oxford 142
Maiano, Giovanni di 101, 197
Maidstone 137, 166
Mall, The 63
Man for All Seasons, A vii, 225
Mantel, Hilary vii, 65, 142, 147, 203, 225
Margaret (Henry's sister) 7, 70, 142
Margaret of Austria 97, 215
Margaret of Savoy 94
Maria, Henrietta 149
Marillac, Charles de 56
Mary (Henry's sister) 8, 103, 141, 142, 161, 164, 165, 174, 212, 213
Mary (Henry's daughter, later Mary I) 12–13, 14–15, 22, 25, 51, 52, 66, 74, 104, 131, 163, 164, 166, 183, 187, 194, 196, 199, 203
Mary II 116, 118
Mary Rose 122, 149, 177, 181–183
Mary, Queen of Scots 152
Maximilian (Emperor) 40, 97, 207
Merton Priory 147, 155
Metropolitan Museum of Art, New York 34, 221
Michelangelo 130
Ministry of Defence Building, London 47, 48, 61–63, 73
Mireflore *see* Greenwich Castle

Index

Monox, Henry 104
Montfort, Simon de 79
Montreuil-sur-Mer 221
Moor Hall, Sutton Coldfield 202
More, Sir Thomas vii, 14, 30, 72, 74, 76, 84, 142, 190, 200
More, The 193, 206
Morice, Ralph 174
Morton, John 69, 174, 194

National Archives (Kew) 18
National Gallery, London 43
National Gallery of Art, Washington DC 51
Needham, James 111, 147, 199
Nelson, Admiral Lord 134
Neville, Edward 10, 13, 80, 95
New Bridge Street, London 44–45
New Hall Palace, Essex *see* Beaulieu Palace
Newhaven 182
Nichols, John Gough 55, 224
Nicholson, John (also known as John Lambert) 53–54
Nonsuch Mansion 151, 152, 155
Nonsuch Palace 122, 146–155
Norfolk, 3rd Duke of *see* Howard, Thomas
Norris, Sir Henry 17, 201
North Marston 191–192
Northwood Preparatory School 193

Oatlands Palace 57, 149 177–9, 181
Odo, Bishop of Bayeux 137
Old Royal Naval College, Greenwich 5, 25
Order of the Garter 15, 60, 129
Orley, Bernard von 111
Otford 173–174
Oursian, Nicolas 115
Oxford ix, 34, 93, 138, 142, 186, 188
Oxford, Earl of 30, 69

Pace, Richard 41, 187, 214
Pageants 10–13, 15, 48–50, 79–81, 94, 124, 144, 164, 183, 208, 214, 218
Paget, Sir William 57, 59
Painswick Lodge 203
Palace of the Bishops of London 40
Pall Mall 64
Parr, Catherine 58, 103, 104, 110, 120, 128, 151, 169, 177, 187, 194, 197, 203, 221
Pasqualigo, Piero 12
Paulet, Sir William 59
Penni, Bartholomew 148
Penshurst 173–174
Pepys, Samuel 149
Perpendicular (architectural style) x, 110, 111
Peyto, William 87
Philip of Burgundy 8, 123–124
Pickfords Wharf 34, 36
Pilgrimage of Grace 204, 205
Plantagenet, Arthur, Viscount Lisle *see* Lisle Letters
Pole, Cardinal Reginald 131
Pole, Edmund de la 189
Pommeraye, Giles de la 32
Ponet, John 116
Pontefract 205
Portinari, Giovanni 131
Portsmouth viii, 122, 181
Prince and the Pauper, The vii, 225
Princes in the Tower 29
Private Life of Henry VIII vi
Puttenham, Frideswide 7
Pyrgo House 196

Richard II 19, 71, 74, 88, 113
Richard III 37, 189
Richard of Shrewsbury (the younger of the Princes in the Tower) 68

Richmond (district of London) 82, 91, 98, 100, 101
Richmond Green 89–91
Richmond Palace ix, xi, 8, 9, 30, 32, 82, 87–97, 100, 120, 142, 144, 146–147
Richmond Park 93
Ridge, Richard 16, 110, 111
Rochester 19, 20, 121, 156–163, 173
Rome 2, 15, 40, 43, 215
Rovezzano, Benedetto da 130
Royal Armouries (Tower of London) 25
Royal Naval College, Greenwich *see* Old Royal Naval College, Greenwich
Royal Observatory, Greenwich *see* Greenwich Observatory
Roydon Hall 196
Royne, Martin van 33
Russell, Lord John 55, 158, 190
Ryalle Book 7

Sackville-West, Vita 173
Sagudino, Niccolo 11
Sandwich, Kent 161–162, 165
Sandys, Sir William 20, 69, 84
Sansovino, Jacopo 130
Schorne, Sir John 191
Seusenhofer, Conrad 34
Seymour, Sir Edward 16, 57, 58, 85
Seymour, Jane 3, 16–19, 52, 53, 56, 57, 103, 108, 109, 111, 129, 134, 135, 163, 166, 196, 203
Seymour, Sir Thomas, 58, 203
Shakespeare, William vii, 14, 34, 49, 225
Shard, The 36, 140
Sheen Palace 88, 113
Shurland House 174
Sidney, Sir William 174
Skelton, John 141–143
Sloane, Sir Hans 82

Smeaton, Mark 17
Smith, Lacy Baldwin vii
Somers, Will vii, 13–14, 42, 52, 171
Somerset, Charles (Lord Herbert) 221
Southsea Castle 122, 181–183
Southwark (district of London) 33–36
Southwark Cathedral 36
Spear, Francis 26
Speed, John 130
Spurs, Battle of the 207
St Alfege Church, Greenwich 24–27
St Catherine's Dock 28
St George's Chapel, Windsor 123, 127–130, 134–136, 191, 198
St James's Palace 3, 48, 63–66, 118, 199
St James's Park 47
St Margaret's Church, Westminster 74–78, 195
St Paul's Cathedral, London viii, 3, 37, 39–41, 67, 70, 93
St Stephen's Chapel, Westminster 69–71
Stafford, Edward, Duke of Buckingham 75
Starkey, David 189, 224
Stephen (King of England) 34
Strand, The 30, 50, 68
Strickland, Agnes 87
Strype, John 59, 127, 158, 224
Sudeley Castle 202–203
Suffolk, Duke of *see* Charles Brandon
Surrey Quays 28
Syon House and Abbey 59, 82, 84–87, 104, 127, 135

Tallis, Thomas 26–27, 66
Tapestries x, xii, 15, 16, 25, 51, 70, 75, 78, 79, 96, 97, 109–111, 149, 177, 204, 205, 212, 219

Index

Thames, River viii, 2–3, 6, 16, 19, 28, 37, 44, 47, 48, 50, 67, 78, 82, 84, 87, 89, 94, 98, 100, 113, 118, 121, 122, 128, 137, 138, 145, 164, 177, 188, 196
Thatcher, Margaret 71
Thérouanne 14, 207–208
Thorney Island 67, 74
Thyssen-Bornemisza Museum, Madrid 51
Torrigiano, Pietro 129–130
Toto, Antonio 109, 148
Tournai viii, 207–211
Tower Bridge 28
Tower Hill 36
Tower of London ix, 3, 28–34, 75, 94, 214
Trafalgar Square 47, 63
Tudor, Arthur 7, 38–39, 43, 70, 93, 124, 186
Twain, Mark vii, 225
Tyler, Wat 19
Tyttenhanger House 193–194

Unilever House, London 44
Uxbridge, Anne 7

Vanburgh, Sir John 187
Vergil, Polydore 102, 213
Versailles, Palace of 47, 118
Vesey, Sir John (Bishop of Exeter) 202
Vicary, Thomas 166
Victoria, Queen (and the Victorian era) 33, 57, 105, 116, 136, 155, 174
Victoria and Albert Museum, London 155
Villiers, Barbara 149
Volpe, Vincenzo 3
Vrelant, Paul van 33
Walsh, Sir John 203
Walsingham 121, 191, 203, 204

Waltham Abbey 77, 195, 197
Wapping 28
Warbeck, Perkin 30, 68, 204
Warham, Archbishop Thomas 75, 76, 79, 97, 173
Wars of the Roses vi
Watergate Street, London 44
Waterloo Station 47
Watling Street 157
Waynefleet, Willam (Bishop of Winchester) 181
Webbe, William 145
Westminster, Palace of viii–ix, 3, 34, 53, 67–75, 78–82, 84, 85, 88, 95, 97, 116, 142
Westminster Abbey viii, 30, 31, 52, 53, 65, 67, 73–76, 78, 86, 97, 125, 129–132, 134, 136, 145
Westminster Hall 53, 67, 69–74, 78, 80, 111, 113, 138
Weybridge 57
Weymouth 124
Whitehall, Palace of viii, ix, xii, 2–3, 17, 18, 47–63, 65, 66, 67, 78, 80, 85, 87, 88, 100, 101, 103, 104, 127, 149, 152, 153, 157, 181, 204, 206, 215
White Tower (in the Tower of London) 28–30, 32–33
William I, the Conqueror 28, 37, 67, 74, 123, 137, 161, 174
William II (William Rufus) 67
William III 51, 109
William IV 135
Winchester, Hampshire 163, 183–185
Winchester College 34
Winchester Palace, London 34–37
Windsor Castle; vii, ix, 57, 59, 60, 71, 75, 82, 85, 100, 120, 122–137, 161, 163, 191, 194, 206 *see also* St George's Chapel, Windsor

235

Woking Palace 179–180
Wolf Hall 203
Wolsey, Thomas 3, 9, 12–13, 15, 40–41, 48–50, 62, 73, 74, 98, 100–102, 108–110, 113–114, 117, 130, 134, 143–145, 161–163, 165, 173, 181, 187, 193, 201, 211, 212, 214–215
Woodstock Palace ix, 93, 186–189, 202
Woodville, Elizabeth 200
Woolf, Virginia 173
Woolwich 9
Wren, Sir Christopher 5, 22, 61, 98, 100, 109, 111, 118

Wright, Andrew (artist) 50
Wriothesley, Charles 18
Wriothesley, Thomas, First Earl of Southampton 59, 104
Wykeham, William of 34, 183
Wynesbury, Will 94
Wyngaerde, Anton van den x, 6, 21

York (city) 102, 121, 204–205
York (Royal House of) 7, 189
York Place 17, 48–49, 62, 73

Zelenskyy, Volodymyr 73